ADVANCE PRAISE FOR

TEACHING
British Women Writers
1750–1900

"An important, timely collection of essays that 'seizes this moment' to assess and point out new directions for the ongoing project of recovering and teaching British women writers. Of particular value is the volume's sustained focus on 'teachable moments' experienced through the student/teacher conversation in different institutional settings."
—*Greg Kucich, Professor of English, University of Notre Dame, and Coeditor of* Nineteenth-Century Contexts: An Interdisciplinary Journal

"This volume's emphasis on the dialectic between students and scholars makes for fresh and thoughtful approaches to pedagogy. Covering a wide range of material—from canonical to noncanonical texts and from single-author courses to surveys—the essays provide informative and useful models for scholars and teachers of eighteenth- and nineteenth-century British literature. Overall, *Teaching British Women Writers 1750–1900* is a valuable contribution to the fields of both literary and women's studies."
—*Sharon Harrow, Assistant Professor of English, Shippensburg University of Pennsylvania, and Author of* Adventures in Domesticity: Gender and Colonial Adulteration in Eighteenth-Century British Literature

TEACHING
British Women Writers
1750–1900

PETER LANG
New York • Washington, D.C./Baltimore • Bern
Frankfurt am Main • Berlin • Brussels • Vienna • Oxford

TEACHING
British Women Writers
1750–1900

JEANNE MOSKAL & SHANNON R. WOODEN,
EDITORS

PETER LANG
New York • Washington, D.C./Baltimore • Bern
Frankfurt am Main • Berlin • Brussels • Vienna • Oxford

Library of Congress Cataloging-in-Publication Data

Teaching British women writers, 1750–1900 /
edited by Jeanne Moskal, Shannon R. Wooden.
p. cm.
Includes bibliographical references and index.
1. English literature—Women authors—Study and teaching.
2. Women and literature—Great Britain—Study and teaching.
3. English literature—19th century—Study and teaching.
4. English literature—18th century—Study and teaching.
I. Moskal, Jeanne. II. Wooden, Shannon R.
PR111.T43   820.9'9287'071—dc22   2003025895
ISBN 0-8204-6927-0

Bibliographic information published by **Die Deutsche Bibliothek**.
Die Deutsche Bibliothek lists this publication in the "Deutsche
Nationalbibliografie"; detailed bibliographic data is available
on the Internet at http://dnb.ddb.de/.

Cover design by Lisa Barfield
Cover illustration, *A Study of a Maiden Seated in a Castle Courtyard*,
by Sir Edward Coley Burne-Jones

The paper in this book meets the guidelines for permanence and durability
of the Committee on Production Guidelines for Book Longevity
of the Council of Library Resources.

© 2005 Peter Lang Publishing, Inc., New York
275 Seventh Avenue, 28th Floor, New York, NY 10001
www.peterlangusa.com

All rights reserved.
Reprint or reproduction, even partially, in all forms such as microfilm,
xerography, microfiche, microcard, and offset strictly prohibited.

Printed in the United States of America

For Alice Moskal Zelenak
JM

For Ken, and for Oscar
SRW

Contents

Acknowledgments xi

Chapter One: Introduction: *Teaching British Women Writers, 1750–1900* 1
    Jeanne Moskal

PART ONE: READING TO TEACH:
CLASSROOM PRACTICES AND PEDAGOGIES

Chapter Two: We Can Do It! Putting Women's Texts to Work 11
    Shannon R. Wooden

Chapter Three: Teaching a "Highly Exceptional" Text:
    Krupabai Satthianadhan's *Saguna* and Narratives of Empire 20
    Kristine Swenson

Chapter Four: Teaching English Women's Conversionist Rhetoric 33
    Rebecca Shapiro

Chapter Five: Eliza Haywood: Mainstreaming Women Writers in the
    Undergraduate Survey 44
    Kathryn T. Flannery

Chapter Six: The Poetry of Friendship: Connecting the Histories
    of Women and Lesbian Sexuality in the Undergraduate Classroom 59
    Rick Incorvati

Chapter Seven: A Subversive Urn and a Suicidal Bride: Strategies for Reading
    Across Aesthetic Difference 74
    Elizabeth A. Dolan

Chapter Eight: Pedagogy and Oppositions: Teaching Non-Canonical
    British Women Writers at the Technical University 91
    James R. Simmons Jr.

Chapter Nine: Short Fiction by Women in the Victorian Literature Survey 101
  Elisabeth Rose Gruner

Chapter Ten: "This Particular Web": George Eliot, Emily Eden,
  and Locale in Multiplot Fiction 110
  Lawrence Zygmunt

PART TWO: TEACHING TO READ:
MAKING STUDENTS OF SCHOLARS (AND VICE VERSA)

Chapter Eleven: Making the Student a Scholar 121
  Jeanne Moskal

Chapter Twelve: Beyond "Great Crowds" and "Minor Triumphs":
  Teaching Students to Evaluate Critical Pronouncements 127
  Patricia L. Hamilton

Chapter Thirteen: Teaching Women Playwrights
  from the British Romantic Period (1790–1840) 140
  Catherine B. Burroughs

Chapter Fourteen: Working within a Community of Learners:
  Teaching Christina Rossetti at a Christian College 150
  Diane Chambers

Chapter Fifteen: Canon-Busting: Undergraduate Research into
  Romantic-Era Women's Writing in the Corvey Collection 160
  E. J. Clery

Chapter Sixteen: Teaching "Recovered" Victorian Female Intellectuals 165
  Peaches Henry

Chapter Seventeen: Everybody Learns and Everybody Teaches:
  Feminist Pedagogy and Co-editing Mary Ward's *Marcella* 181
  Nicole Meller Beck and Beth Sutton-Ramspeck

Chapter Eighteen: "Can Man Be Free/And Woman Be a Slave?" Teaching
  Eighteenth- and Nineteenth-Century Women Writers in Intersecting
  Communities 190
  Gina Luria Walker

Chapter Nineteen: Who Counts? Popularity, Modern Recovery,
    and the Early Nineteenth-Century Woman Poet..205
    David E. Latané Jr.

Chapter Twenty: Changing Course(s) At Mid- and Late Career: Teaching the
    Lives/Teaching the Works/Teaching the Teacher 224
    William B. Thesing

List of Contributors 233

Acknowledgments

We would like to express our gratitude to the organizers of the Seventh Annual Conference of the Eighteenth- and Nineteenth-Century British Women Writers Association, held at the University of North Carolina at Chapel Hill, especially the co-chairs of the organizing committee: Marya DeVoto, Michelle Mouton, Beth Dolan, and Julie Straight. Without them, the idea for this book would never have taken root in the conference and produced so many interesting and exciting conversations about teaching. We are also grateful to the conference attendees and plenary speakers—Isobel Armstrong, Nancy Armstrong, and Stuart Curran—who participated in those conversations.

Thanks also to Jane Danielewicz for her insights into pedagogical theory.

Grateful acknowledgment is hereby made to copyright holders for permission to use the following material:

Edward Burne-Jones, "A Study of a Maiden Seated in a Castle Courtyard," 1890s. Reprinted by permission of London Borough of Hammersmith and Fulham.

E. J. Clery, "Canon-Busting: Undergraduate Research into Romantic-Era Women's Writing in the Corvey Collection." *CCUE News* 9 (1998): 10–11. Reprinted by permission of the publisher. All rights reserved.

Finally, the editors and contributors would also like to thank the students who have shaped the work described in this volume for their curious, ornery, and surprising questions and for their passionate devotion to literature and to women writers.

Chapter One
Introduction: *Teaching British Women Writers, 1750–1900*

Jeanne Moskal

Liminality is the great moment of teachability.
—Barbara Meyerhoff and Deena Metzger

Every few months in the last several years, I have received in the mail a new teaching anthology from a publisher who hopes I will adopt it for my literature courses. The promotional material uniformly notes the number of women authors included and stresses that their inclusion brings the anthology up-to-date and makes it imperative for me to abandon the scribble-ridden anthology I currently use. This appearance of women writers as *de rigueur* in a new anthology marks a transition from one stage of the literary study of women writers, a stage in which decades of the scholarly work of recovery fought the relative absence of women authors from the classroom. Now we have numerous editions of individual authors, a few anthologies of eighteenth- and nineteenth-century women writers loosely modeled after Sandra Gilbert and Susan Gubar's *Norton Anthology of Literature by Women,* and the inclusion of substantial offerings by women writers in mixed-sex anthologies. Among publishers, Pickering and Chatto and the Broadview Literary Texts series have led the way in fostering editions of individual women authors. Important collections of women's writing include anthologies by Paula Feldman, Andrew Ashfield, Harriet Devine Jump, Moira Ferguson, Angela Leighton and Margaret Reynolds, and Roger Lonsdale. Furthermore, the outpouring of revised mixed-sex anthologies include the revision of the long-standard *Norton Anthology of English Literature,* the comparable Longman anthology, and new volumes such as Anne K. Mellor and Richard Matlak's *British Literature 1780–1830*; Duncan Wu's *Romanticism: An Anthology; The New Penguin Book of Romantic Poetry,* edited by Jonathan and Jessica Wordsworth; Dorothy Mermin and Herbert Tucker's *Victorian Literature 1830–1900*.[1] Of course, we have also the robust venue of the Internet, which has Websites for numerous women writers.[2] It appears that the days are past when we had to bring photocopies of pages from the Rare Book Room to class in order to show our students what women wrote. It is less clear whether the days of the culture wars, so hotly debated in the 1990s, are past as well.[3]

However, while anthologies celebrate the end of women writers' absence, they continue to bracket them as a specific group, as the major component that makes these anthologies "current," rather than being wordlessly assimilated into the list of "must-reads" of a survey course. Thus, anthologies have replaced the outdated assumption that women writers should be absent, or represented only by token selections, with the new assumption that women writers constitute a group that belongs but that must be continually marked as Other. That is, the usual term remains "women authors," while male authors are most commonly referred to simply as "authors." At this moment, then, women writers are no longer absent from teaching canons, but have been given a place of liminality.

Anthropologist Victor Turner gave the name "liminality" to the threshold stages of rituals, a "no-man's land betwixt and between...the subjunctive mood of culture, a mood of maybe, might be, as if, hypothesis, fantasy, conjecture, desire." Educational theorists Barbara Myerhoff and Deena Metzger, authors of the epigraph above, apply Turner's concept to pedagogy, and Donna Qualley, elaborating on their work, argues that in liminality, "an opportunity is provided not only for psychic and emotional reorganization but for theoretical and philosophical enlightenment as well."[4]

This new availability of women's texts—not absent, but liminal—has disrupted our sense of what literary canons might be. It is no longer clear what Matthew Arnold so confidently asserted, that we know what is "the best that is known and thought in the world." During the Culture Wars of the 1990s, that disruption was everywhere in the academy and in public discourse, reaching a flashpoint when the National Endowment for the Arts denied funding to feminist projects. Social conservatives such as Allan Bloom advocated a single canon for all students in the name of social coherence and "cultural literacy," while challengers argued for the inclusion of more writers of color and more women. The ferment of this public disruption has now largely passed, and the upshot is two versions of women writers' liminality, as articulated in the types of anthology mentioned above, the women-only and the mixed-sex anthologies, representing what John Guillory terms the "integrationist" and "separatist" versions of curricular revision. While Guillory is less interested in how many women authors are taught than in the historical factors affecting access to literacy,[5] for the teacher the theoretical choice between integrationism and separatism takes the practical form of which textbooks to order and which poems and novels can be fitted into the syllabus. In our view, the quieting of the cultural debate provides an opportunity to implement both integrationist and separatist teaching strategies and their ways of constructing the liminality of women writers. Both integrationist and separatist liminalities invite teachability.

More intimately, this fluidity of the canon creates the possibility of a different kind of teacherly self. No longer is it possible for the more senior scholars among us to pass on lore largely as we ourselves received it in graduate school; now we are often learning the material only months or weeks ahead of our students. Hence it is fresher and edgier than much of our other course matter. No longer is the junior scholar a mere apprentice, learning the ropes of a long-established guild; she is often as likely to be the first to publish on an author as her dissertation adviser. This new intellectual contemporaneousness of teacher and student shakes up our practical patterns of lecturing, testing, grading, and writing, of credentialing and being credentialed into the profession of literary studies. In this practical shake-up, too, there is a chance for teachability.

Our volume addresses two of the liminalities in this taxonomy. We reflect on how the relative newness of the subject matter—its liminality from the traditional canon—has shuffled the definition of our teacherly selves by explicitly thematizing our relation to our students. Like many teachers, the contributors to this volume define our endeavor in contrast to what Paulo Freire calls "the banking concept of education," in which a teacher deposits already known facts into the waiting vessels of generic, interchangeable students.[6] Though we have varied pedagogical styles, we share the underlying commitment of feminist epistemologies, which, as part of their critique of essentialism, seek to articulate our own situatedness and that of our students as part of understanding how we know. This commitment, called "standpoint theory," has been expounded by Sandra Harding, Nancy Hartsock, Evelyn Fox Keller, and others.[7] It dismantles the Cartesian, foundationalist model that the normative knower is the solitary, disinterested being in isolated contemplation; feminist epistemologies stress the place of the Other in our knowing. For example, Lorraine Code shakes loose traditional analyses that take as normative that kind of propositional knowledge that can be stated in the form "S knows that p." She contends that "epistemologists should pay just as much attention to the nature and situation—the location—of S as they commonly pay to the content of p."[8] By suggesting that knowing others, rather than propositional knowledge, be taken as a norm, Code breaks apart the traditional distinction between subjects who know and objects that are known, a pattern which, she observes, often pigeonholes women into the "objective" slot. Another feminist epistemologist foregrounding the Other is Lynn Hankinson Nelson, who challenges the Cartesian model of solitary knowing by arguing that communities, not individuals, are the agents of knowing. In contrast to Stanley Fish's emphasis on interpretive communities, to which already-formed individuals consent to belong, Nelson claims, "the knowing we do as individuals is derivative, that your knowing or mine depends on *our* knowing."[9] As Code concludes, "Knowers are always *somewhere*—and at once limited and enabled by the specificities of their locations," and that situatedness includes the other persons in the room. Moving from philosophy to pedagogical theory, we are intrigued by the work of Donna Qualley, who makes the case for teaching as a practice of "reflexivity." Qualley writes: "We need a method [of teaching] that will allow us to continually reflect on our own positions in light of our ongoing transactions with others. Reflexivity involves a commitment to both attending to what we believe and examining how we came to hold those beliefs *while* we *are engaged in trying to make sense of an other*" (original emphasis). [10]

Informed by such methodological considerations of the knower's situatedness and co-knowers, our contributors have paid more attention to institutional settings and to actual students than is usual in volumes devoted to teaching literature. The best regarded of such volumes, the "Approaches to Teaching" series published by the Modern Language Association, rigorously compile the teaching suggestions of teachers and scholars about a particular text or author. I contributed to the volume on S. T. Coleridge in 1991 and in that essay wrote almost nothing about the particularities of my students or of my own position as an untenured professor actively discouraged by the departmental administration from researching women writers. My essay is typical of the series as a whole. The MLA volume closest to the present volume is Stephen C. Behrendt's and Harriet Kramer Linkin's *Approaches to Teaching British Women Poets of the Romantic Period*.[11] Behrendt and Linkin surveyed instructors of college courses in British Romantic–period literature and found considerable wrestling with "the exciting but daunting project of catching up— of revisioning what we understand by Romanticism—in order to recover a vast number of heretofore largely invisible texts."[12] In 1997, when Behrendt and Linkin's volume was published, the new venture of teaching women writers required a substantial amount of exchange of historical information, for example, about the unexpected idioms and genres employed by women writers, and the essays accordingly are packed with the fruits of the contributors' researches. Now that more of the historical information has come into print, largely through the labors of Behrendt and Linkin's contributors, a volume on teaching women writers can address the situatedness of the venture in specific classrooms, in specific institutions, and with specific students. Our book differs from Behrendt and Linkin, then, in taking a longer historical period, in considering women writers in genres other than poetry, and, what we think is most important, in showing both halves of the student/teacher conversation.

To this end, our volume offers a version of the "thick description" pioneered by anthropologist Clifford Geertz, in which observers immerse themselves in the cultural context instead of assuming they can achieve a standpoint of objectivity. Taking a cue from this anthropological method, our volume stresses the embeddedness of teaching in specific institutions—

sectarian, state-supported, research university, liberal arts college, technical school—and seeks to understand how teaching women writers is variously inflected by, and embedded within, these differing academic subcultures. One important component of thick description is that the writer includes contradictory characteristics that previous historical and sociological analyses left out.[13] Our volume welcomes contradictions, real and apparent, between the experiences of teaching women writers by men and by women and in various institutions. We don't offer a totalized view; our point is that teaching is context-dependent. We achieve that articulation of context by writing about our students, what they say and what they don't say, and by reflecting on how that student feedback shapes our approach to this newly available material and, in consequence, how it shapes our teacherly selves.

Our volume's second focus is on small, local moments of liminality in the literary work. The actual presence of women authors would not itself be a threshold experience for our students—after all, they are used to Jane Austen and Emily Dickinson among the "greats" set up by Matthew Arnold and T. S. Eliot. Women "greats" can also seem unsurprising when we note that the majority of students in a college literature course are women. Instead, where the liminality of women's texts comes to bear on them—and on us—is in those disquieting moments of literary oddity, when the text falls outside our readerly expectations, many of them developed through years of reading canonical literature. Two classic works of second-wave feminism stake out the issues. Novelist Joanna Russ's essay, "How to Suppress Women's Writing," which deftly captures the ethos of the time before feminist recovery work began, argues that, when women were included in anthologies or courses, they were cast as anomalous, presented as solitary, without a tradition.[14] What is important for our purposes is Russ's catalogue of anomalies, literary moments that were aesthetically bothersome, embarrassing, or boring, that served as grounds for women's dismissal. She catalogues several kinds of anomalousness: something not quite right about the tone, such as "too much anger"; or about the characters, such as too much authorial identification with the heroine, or with the genre, such as the disreputable Gothic novel. In addition, Jane Tompkins's critical essay, "Sentimental Power: *Uncle Tom's Cabin* and Literary History," ascribes Harriet Beecher Stowe's fall from literary canonicity to readers' embarrassment over Stowe's forthright use of the conventions of sentimentality. The important implication of Tompkins's essay is that the practice of confronting our readerly embarrassment when texts fall outside our expectations is an integral part of learning to read women writers. Liminality again becomes the occasion of teachability.

Thankfully, most of us, as scholars of women authors, no longer need to justify our choices of whom to study to our colleagues or our deans. However, when we address our students, at least, the issue raised lucidly by Russ and Tompkins remains a live one. Many of the women writers seem to them anomalous, embarrassing, disquieting, aesthetically inferior. As a student said to one of our contributors, "Everybody knows that anything worth reading is in the *Norton Anthology*." We have, accordingly, used the concept of anomalousness as one of the organizing ideas of this collection, inviting our contributors to describe moments in which students confronted "oddities" of women's texts and to analyze how teachers might salvage or exploit or harvest them as "teachable moments." Our collection takes up the challenge of addressing students' discomfiture with anomalous subject-matters (scatological or homoerotic), anomalous genres (such as conversionist literature) and anomalous plotting (such as too-quick resolutions) and of harnessing such discomfiture for a teachable moment.

These essays analyze the shared enterprise of teaching some British women who wrote between 1750 and 1900, in literature departments and women's studies departments, in diverse institutions, at different stages of a career, as women and as men, with varied teacherly selves. They also share a desire to seize the moment between the old orthodoxies of the Romantic "Big Six Poets" and the male Victorian sages and whatever may be the new orthodoxies yet to be born—to seize this moment and to realize its teacherly potential.

Notes

[1] Among the numerous new editions of individual women writers, three series deserve particular mention: Broadview Literary Texts, Brown Women Writers Series, and Pickering and Chatto. Anthologies of eighteenth-century women writers include Moira Ferguson, *First Feminists: British Women Writers 1578–1799* (Bloomington: Indiana UP, 1985); Roger Lonsdale, *Eighteenth-Century Women Poets: An Oxford Anthology* (Oxford: Oxford UP, 1989); and Robert W. Uphaus and Gretchen M. Foster, *The Other Eighteenth Century: English Women of Letters, 1660–1800* (East Lansing: Colleagues Press, 1991). Anthologies of general nineteenth-century women writers include R. E. Pritchard, *Poetry by English Women: Elizabethan to Victorian* (New York: Continuum, 1990); Isobel Armstrong and Joseph Bristow, *Nineteenth-Century Women Poets: An Oxford Anthology* (New York: Oxford, 1996); Margaret Randolph Higonnet, *British Women Poets of the Nineteenth Century* (New York: Penguin 1996); Harriet Devine Jump, *Nineteenth-Century Short Stories by Women: A Routledge Anthology* (New York: Routledge, 1998); Adrienne Scullion, *Female Playwrights of the Nineteenth Century* (London: J. M. Dent, 1996); and Glennis Stephenson, *Nineteenth-Century Stories by Women* (Petersborough, ON: Broadview, 1993). Anthologies of Romantic-period women writers include Harriet Devine Jump, *Women's Writing of the Romantic Period, 1789–1836: An Anthology* (Edinburgh: Edinburgh UP, 1997); Paula R. Feldman, *British British Women Poets of the Romantic Era: An Anthology* (Baltimore: Johns Hopkins UP, 1997); and Andrew Ashfield, ed., *Romantic Women Poets, 1770–1838: An Anthology* (Manchester, U.K.:

Manchester UP, 1995). Anthologies of Victorian women writers include Jennifer Breen, *Victorian Women Poets, 1830–1901: An Anthology* (London: J.M. Dent, 1994); Harriet Devine Jump, *Women's Writing of the Victorian Period 1837–1901* (Edinburgh: Edinburgh UP, 1998); and Angela Leighton and Margaret Reynolds, *Victorian Women Poets: An Anthology* (Oxford: Blackwell, 1995). Mixed-sex anthologies include M. H. Abrams, General Editor, and Stephen Greenblatt, Associate General Editor, *The Norton Anthology of English Literature*, 7th ed. (New York: W. W. Norton, 2000); David Damrosch, General Editor, *The Longman Anthology of British Literature*, 2nd ed. (New York: Longman, 2003); Robert Demaria Jr., *British Literature 1640–1789: An Anthology* (Oxford: Blackwell, 1996); David Fairer and Christine Gerrard, *Eighteenth-Century Poetry: An Annotated Anthology* (Oxford: Blackwell, 1999); Roger Lonsdale, *The New Oxford Book of Eighteenth-Century Verse* (New York: Oxford UP, 1985); Anne K. Mellor and Richard E. Matlak, eds., *British Literature 1780–1830* (New York: Harcourt, 1996); Duncan Wu, *Romanticism: An Anthology*, 2nd ed. (Oxford: Blackwell, 1998); Jonathan and Jessica Wordsworth, *The New Penguin Book of Romantic Poetry* (New York: Penguin, 2001); *Victorian Literature 1830–1900;* Dorothy Mermin and Herbert Tucker (New York: Harcourt, 2002); Thomas Collins, *The Broadview Anthology of Victorian Poetry and Poetic Theory* (Peterborough, ON: Broadview, 1999); and Valentine Cunningham, *The Victorians: An Anthology of Poetry and Poetics* (Oxford: Blackwell, 2000). Harriet Kramer Linkin provides a judicious commentary on the Romantic-period anthologies in "Editions," in Behrendt and Linkin, 9.

2 Selected electronic resources on eighteen- and nineteenth-century women writers include these. For the eighteenth century:
- A Celebration of Women Writers, index of eighteenth-century women writers, http://digital.library.upenn.edu/women/_generate/1701-1800.html
- Women and Eighteenth-Century Literature, http://www.wright.edu/~martin.maner/18cwom99.html
- James May's Selected Bibliography http://www.personal.psu.edu/special/C18/women.htm
- Brown University's Women Writers Project http://www.wwp.brown.edu/

For the Romantic period:
- Elizabeth Fay's Bluestocking Archive http://www.faculty.umb.edu/elizabeth_fay/archive2.html
- British Romantic Women Poets Project http://www.lib.ucdavis.edu/English/BWRP/index.htm
- Women Romantic-Era Writers http://www.nottingham.ac.uk/~aezacweb/wrew.htm
- Women Playwrights around 1800 http://www-sul.stanford.edu/mirrors/romnet/wp1800/
- Corvey Women Writers on the Web http://www2.shu.ac.uk/corvey/CW3/
- *The Lady's Magazine, or Entertaining Companion for the Fair Sex, Appropriated Solely to Their Use and Amusement, 1770–1837* http://locutus.ucr.edu/~cathy/lm/ladm.html

For the Victorian period:
- Victorian Women Writers Project http://www.indiana.edu/~letrs/vwwp/
- VWW Letters Project http://delos.lib.sfu.ca/projects/VWWLP/VWWLP.htm

3 A sampling of the literature on canons and the culture wars would include: Allan Bloom, *The Closing of the American Mind: How Higher Education Has Failed Democracy and Impoverished the Souls of Today's Students* (New York: Simon and Schuster, 1987); The "Cheney Report" (*Humanities in America*, 1988); Barbara Herrnstein Smith, *Contingencies of Value: Alternative Perspectives for Critical Theory* (Cambridge, MA: Harvard UP, 1988); Charles Altieri, *Canons and Consequences: Reflections on the Ethical Force of Imaginative Ideals* (Evanston, IL: Northwestern UP, 1990); Dinesh D'Souza, *Illiberal Education: The Politics of Race and Sex on Campus* (New York: Free Press, 1991); Paul Lauter, *Canons and Contexts* (New York: Oxford UP, 1991); Paul Berman, ed., *Debating P.C.: The Controversy over Political Correctness on College Campuses* (New York: Dell, 1992); Gerald Graff, *Beyond the Culture Wars: How Teaching the Conflicts Can Revitalize American Education* (New York: W.

W. Norton, 1992); Henry Louis Gates Jr., *Loose Canons: Notes on the Culture Wars* (New York: Oxford UP, 1992); John Guillory, *Cultural Capital: The Problem of Literary Canon Formation* (Chicago: U of Chicago P, 1993); Avrom Fleishman *The Condition of English: Literary Studies in a Changing Culture* (Westport, CT: Greenwood Press, 1998); and Jan Gorak, ed., *Canon vs. Culture: Reflections on the Current Debate* (New York: Garland, 2001).

4   Barbara Myerhoff and Deena Metzger, using Victor Turner's idea of "liminality," and quoted in Donna Qualley, *Turns of Thought: Teaching Composition as Reflexive Inquiry* (Portsmouth, NH: Heinemann, 1997), 11.

5   Matthew Arnold, "The Function of Criticism at the Present Time" (1864), *The Norton Anthology of Theory and Criticism,* ed. Vincent Leitch (New York: W. W. Norton, 2001), 824.

6   Paulo Freire, *Pedagogy of the Oppressed*, trans. Myra Bergman Ramos (New York: Herder and Herder, 1970), 69–70.

7   Sandra Harding, "Rethinking Standpoint Epistemology: What Is 'Strong Objectivity'?" in Linda Alcoff and Elizabeth Potter, eds., *Feminist Epistemologies* (New York: Routledge, 1993), 49–82; Nancy Hartsock, *Money, Sex, and Power: Toward a Feminist Historical Materialism* (Boston: Northeastern UP, 1985); Mary Hawkesworth, "Knowers, Knowing, Known: Feminist Theory and Claims of Truth," *Signs* 14 (1989): 533–557; Evelyn Fox Keller, *Reflections on Gender and Science* (New Haven, CT: Yale UP, 1985).

8   Lorraine Code, "Taking Subjectivity into Account," in Alcoff and Potter, 20. See also Lorraine Code, *What Can She Know? Feminist Theory and the Construction of Knowledge* (Ithaca, NY: Cornell UP, 1991).

9   Lynn Hankinson Nelson, "Epistemological Communities," in Alcoff and Potter, 124. Among Stanley Fish's works, see particularly *Is There a Text in This Class? The Authority of Interpretive Communities* (Cambridge, MA: Harvard UP, 1980). The quotation in the next sentence is from Code, "Taking Subjectivity," 39.

10 Qualley, 5.

11 *Approaches to Teaching British Women Poets of the Romantic Period* (New York: MLA, 1997). See also Richard E. Matlak, ed., *Approaches to Teaching Coleridge's Poetry and Prose* (New York: MLA, 1991).

12 Stephen C. Behrendt, "Introduction: Overview of the Survey," in Behrendt and Linkin, 2.

13 Clifford Geertz, *The Interpretation of Cultures* (New York: Basic Books, 1973).

14 Joanna Russ, "Anonalousness" and "Aesthetics," excerpted from *How to Suppress Women's Writing* (1983) in *Feminisms: an Anthology of Literary Criticism and Theory*, ed. Robin R. Warhol and Diane Price Herndl (New Brunswick, NJ: Rutgers UP, 1991), 194–211. This anthology also reprints Jane Tompkins's essay on pages 20–39.

PART ONE
Reading to Teach: Classroom Practices and Pedagogies

CHAPTER TWO

We Can Do It!
Putting Women's Texts to Work

Shannon R. Wooden

Why do we teach women writers? In our most personal answers, we may confess that the practice is potentially "emancipatory," for students and teachers alike—especially women—who are thus invited into a new world of possible identification with authors and characters and encouraged to make connections with texts at least contemporary with the "classic," often male-authored ones that make up the canon. The reason I fell in love with nineteenth-century British literature, quite simply, is that I fell in love with Maggie Tulliver. However, as Jeanne Moskal rightly points out in the introduction to this volume, such a tendency toward emancipatory pedagogy, risking "too much identification with the heroine," is precisely one of the things that may alienate some readers, degrade the respect with which they treat women's writing, and, finally, inhibit our ability to effectively teach that which we strive to teach. This is particularly true as long as we persist in seeing women (and their texts) as constituting an outsider group, forever bridesmaids to canonical works, even as they increasingly appear in new and improved anthologies. By identifying with and exposing students to an inherently "outsider" group, teachers necessarily, even if unwittingly or unwillingly, politicize their material, and this practice, in a world of increasing fear of the academy's liberal proselytizing, may open our teaching up to criticism even more strident than that we are somehow too personally involved. Such is especially the case, as contributors to this volume explain, in institutions more conservative, more disciplinarily specialized, or more religious than the typical Research-I university. Our challenge is to professionalize the pedagogy behind our teaching of women writers by reconsidering our own pedagogical motivation and methodologies, our attitudes toward the formal elements of stylistic "anomalousness" in some women's texts, and the ideological problems (and possibilities) raised by canonicity and "liminality."

A more direct answer to the question of "why teach women writers?" is that teaching is a necessary next step in the long process of canon expansion and recovery work. As the introduction to this collection illustrates, a host of new texts has followed the last several years of scholarship. Even so, our work is far from finished. If not put to practical use, the recovery work of the past two decades may gather dust in a library until the scholarship itself needs recovering; even the most radical and exciting work, independent from the classroom, challenges the boundaries and paradigms of modern literary study for only the select few who seek it out from their own personal and professional interest. Each new generation of scholars and readers must pause to wonder where all the women were in the literary marketplaces of the eighteenth and nineteenth centuries; If teachers do not convey the names of Felicia Hemans and Mary Elizabeth Braddon alongside those of Wordsworth and Dickens, students (and the scholars they may become) must re-discover and re-present these writers' works in an endlessly new and rebellious, and inevitably impermanent act. As John Guillory's *Cultural Capital* explains, it is the syllabus, even more immediately than the ideological construct of the "canon," that constitutes "knowledge capital," or the information whose possession signifies education.[1] Our teaching, then, must be central to—not passively dependent on—reconsiderations of the canon.

An even more pressing question is why we pursue the recovery of women writers at all, particularly when their texts frequently depart from our learned aesthetic sensibilities. Often written by authors with less formal education and more overt "sentiment" than the writers of the canonized Great Books, with less "true wit" and more true feeling, women's texts may strike readers and students as aesthetically inferior to classic (male) texts, or less significant to their educations. The practice of teaching women writers is still often viewed through the lens of identity politics, partly because of the occasional difficulties in defending women's writing on aesthetic grounds. We teach women writers, students suspect, simply because they are women, or because *we* are (if, indeed, we are; see William Thesing's essay in this volume for the experiences of a male teacher trying to negotiate this feminist space). As Diana Price Herndl, citing Lillian S. Robinson, argues, "Feminist critics must examine their own politics, lest they make the exclusionary mistakes they criticize in others…to avoid a 'reverse discrimination' when putting together their own anthologies and syllabi."[2] The essays in this volume offer this sort of examination, alongside practical suggestions and real-world experiences of teaching women writers, challenging and guiding us all in a consideration of our own reasons and goals for such teaching endeavors.

Teaching as recovery work can indeed create an important political experience for female and male students alike, as it ungenders the quantity of literary "knowledge capital," and evens the score of literary production history and the selection process of decades of higher education, revealing not only new work but the very fact of literary foremothers' existence which Virginia Woolf famously sought in *A Room of One's Own*. It can decisively challenge students' beliefs that all great works of English literature were created by men, striking one more blow against gender stereotyping and societally inscribed but self-enforced limitations on the next generations of women. Moreover, as the essays in this section exemplify, women's absence from the canon has been a detriment to knowledge itself, limiting the content of the knowledge available through literary studies.

New texts alone increase the quantity of available information about literature—canon expansion in the classroom expanding or reconstructing what Guillory calls "symbolic" capital—and this dramatically altered pedagogical landscape offers teachers a brand-new set of difficult negotiations. Further, because the rhetorical structure of teaching literature is seldom entirely contained within the literary work itself in the post–New Critical environment of academia, "recovered" texts afford us the opportunity (or require of us the labor) to learn a fuller picture of social history. As Joanna Russ has said, "a mode of understanding literature which can ignore the private lives of half the human race is not 'incomplete'; it is distorted through and through."[3] To teach women writers with an eye to social history, as a great number of teachers and scholars of the eighteenth and nineteenth centuries do, we must expand the base of supplemental factual information and the rhetorical makeup of literary, social, and historical knowledge as we teach and learn it. We teach eighteenth- and nineteenth-century texts as cultural artifacts; to restrict our syllabus according to the (real or imagined) mandates of the canon or the curriculum, we limit also the richness and complexity of the culture we present.

In practical terms, the endeavor to teach women writers with a sociohistorical pedagogy has elements of both the chicken and the egg. In order to introduce women writers thoroughly and well, we must expand the information base we provide for students: It can become important, for example, that they know about historical events like the Parliamentary acts that abolished the slave trade, and then slavery itself (this topic commanding a section of its own in Anne Mellor and Richard Matlak's 1996 anthology *British Literature 1780–1830*), as well as the French Revolution, the more traditional historical focus of "Romantic" undergraduate surveys. At the same time, however, introducing the work of women writers may itself provide dramatic "new" information and perspectives to broaden and deepen our courses. As Mary Wollstonecraft has said about women themselves, it is time we saw that women's texts are objects of use as well as beauty. Many of the essayists in this collection use women's texts as prisms onto cultural histories, often (though not always) lovely when seen, but absolutely revelatory when seen through. Thus, the bright white light of literary historical pedagogy, shone onto women's texts by committed scholars and teachers, is refracted through these texts into different bars of color that collectively make up the whole.

When we put these texts to use, the effects can be profound. As our contributors demonstrate, ultimately we can complicate not only the content of literary history but the very nature of literary production; moreover, we can offer students the opportunity to interrogate the historical construction of gendered identity, and their present-day assumptions of gender itself. Further, teaching women writers can profoundly challenge the structural and institutional foundations of the canon. As these essays show, scholars' individual spotlights on recovered texts are gradually lighting up the entire framework of literary studies: Each new discovery reveals an obstacle that has previously inhibited such illumination. Recovery work in the classroom, then, interrogates the structures of our assumptions about literary history, using the inclusion of women writers to provoke a reexamination of the canon and of canonicity in general. Students are taught to think about what they are being taught, producing a new generation of scholars who will not unquestioningly accept the notion of a canon, who will see a syllabus as representative rather than reified.

The first eight essays in the volume examine constructions of gender itself, exploring the relationships between gender and other major identity-shaping concepts as they can be presented by eighteenth- and nineteenth-century literature and literary historical pedagogy. With an imperialist era novel by a woman and featuring a woman, Kristine Swenson uses students' notions of Victorian gender politics, developed from the few canonical women's novels to which they have been exposed, to elicit a new understanding of coloniality. The relatively familiar gender conflicts in Krupabai Satthianadhan's novel, *Saguna*, Swenson argues—conflicts that facilitate a parallel between the eponymous heroine and the likes of Maggie Tulliver—can never be wholly separated from their historical moment, so students' efforts to read gender quickly complicate the mythologies of empire they have constructed and can see reinforced by the imperialist adventure stories Swenson teaches alongside *Saguna*. Finally, Saguna's struggle can be seen as a way of resisting the very type of imperialism drawn by the yarns of H. Rider Haggard, Rudyard Kipling, or Joseph Conrad, an imperialism for which the western world has maintained (or continually re-manufactured) nostalgia even to this today. Moreover, Swenson provides both an example and a model: Saguna's struggle, through gender and against the totalizing forces of imperialism, actually mirrors students' deconstruction of the nostalgic post-imperialist "knowledge" they have garnered from texts like *Kim* and from the markers of what Swenson calls the "'Out of Africa' nostalgia" of late twentieth-century material culture. As such, this endeavor to teach women writers has many positive effects on students' knowledge bases and critical reading skills: They see imperialism as multifaceted, while they consider the construction of "imperialism" as itself imperialistic; they witness a realistic character's struggle against imperialism, and they perform the struggle, at one remove, themselves.

Like Swenson, Rebecca Shapiro introduces women's writing as a means of broadening students' understanding of the social and political climate of the period covered in the course. Her introduction of early nineteenth-century tracts and novels by women writers with a common aim of converting the Jews to Christianity not only interestingly textures her class generically and offers new historical and political viewpoints, but also highlights the narrow classicistic, religious, and racial assumptions of "Englishness" that have generally informed the canon itself. Ultimately, Shapiro's course challenges idealized notions of Romantic politics. She encourages her students to see women's participation in politics as multivocal and complex, rather than unequivocal and unproblematized by bias, blindness, and negotiations of political power. Moreover, the political tracts she brings to the syllabus allow her to model the deconstruction of literary political rhetoric by rigorously interrogating it within its historical context, paving the way for students to do the same work with even canonical texts.

Essays by Kathryn T. Flannery and Rick Incorvati demonstrate how women's writing can invite us to reconsider elements of identity as apparently unproblematic as material existence, sexuality, and friendship, drawing on students' own ideas and experiences to demonstrate the ways in which these things are historically situated. In so doing, teachers can prompt students to question not only the overt gendered limitations on literary production then and now, but the societal makeup of gender itself, even into the modern day. To maximize the potential of introducing women writers into our curricula, then, we must note the ways such an endeavor changes the framework of our curricula: As Flannery says, we must not introduce women as "disembodied names" but "to consider what difference different bodies have made in literary history." Flannery's project, which pairs Eliza Haywood with Alexander Pope, uses women's writing and notions of gender difference (then and now) to examine how sexuality, intimacy, and the material self are constructed by and influential in the construction of literature.

Flannery uses this pairing, prompted by the brutal parody of Haywood that Pope wrote in *The Dunciad*, to inspire students to "achieve thicker, richer understandings of the texts themselves, of the culture more broadly, and of historical inquiry as an interpretive strategy." In her essay, she offers an extensive methodological framework, arguing that having students engage with women's writing, rather than just lecturing on material culture and gender politics in canonical eighteenth-century texts, effectively responds to and works around their already constructed notions of gender. Finally, like many of the other essays in this section, her project also practices what it preaches, encouraging students to see the pervasive functioning of gender in literary production and pedagogy throughout history and continuing into the present day.

Incorvati's essay similarly sets ambitious goals for teaching and perhaps most explicitly reminds teachers of the potential political power inherent in their pedagogical decisions. Demonstrating the ways in which eighteenth-century women's writing requires us to rethink women's sexuality and intimate communication—seeing such basic human facets as sexuality and love through the prism of women's experiences—Incorvati also empowers us to begin this formidable intellectual project with even undergraduates. His essay instructs teachers methodologically, providing effective techniques for eliciting critical conversations about language, social convention, sexuality, and gender, while always considering our students' sensitivities and experiential limitations. This contribution, however, is not methodological alone; rather, in contextualizing his project amidst the political aims of recovery work, Incorvati reminds us of the ethical imperative behind teaching literature in the first place. Women's "poetry of friendship," he explains, necessitates a critical discussion of lesbian identity, which is itself necessary for critical conversations about women's identity in historical moments other than our own. Such conversations, of course, illuminate students' present-day assumptions about sexuality and its politics. The assumptions of the canon are revealed to students as immediately relevant, the constructedness of knowledge no mere abstract, academic observation.

As these essays demonstrate, talking about women's writing can underscore the constructedness of knowledge that has historically contributed to the very exclusion of women from the canon. Elizabeth A. Dolan's essay insists that we see history itself as rhetorical and explores what uses can be made of historical and artifactual authorities. Positing that our investigations into "Romantic" literary uses of history are often gendered, she explains that "poetry by men and women require us to invoke history differently." With Keats's "Ode on a Grecian Urn" and Felicia Hemans's "The Bride of Greek Isle," Dolan offers both a practical pairing for any course on Romanticism and a useful model of how students can be encouraged to make those invocations. In so doing, she moves us from teaching approaches to an investigation of the rhetorical structure behind the project to teach women writers. The act of highlighting the rhetorical uses of historical authority and gender's influence on determining those uses serves as both example and model of canon expansion, illustrating how historical authority can be claimed, created, and privileged.

The relationship between the canonical and the non-canonical, as Guillory points out, is itself quite problematic: Perhaps even more than gender, this division allows women's writing to inspire critical thinking about literary studies. Guillory raises the significant question of whether non-canonical writing must, on some level, stay "non-canonical," whether it can achieve its pedagogical potential without a decidedly "othered" status. James R. Simmons notes that the perceived political imperative behind "non-canonicity" itself offers a considerable obstacle to the project of teaching women writers, but like the remaining essayists in this section he concludes that non-canonical works can offer great inroads into the canon.

Simmons's account of teaching at a university with a decidedly technical mission and student body frankly tackles common, urgent facts of institutional pressures on the project of teaching women writers. Simmons, like many teachers featured in this section, argues that in a survey where "the idea is to expose [students] to the full spectrum" of issues and viewpoints, women's texts can provide a richer and fuller understanding of the literary history they represent. The obstacles teachers may face in pursuit of this goal, however, are numerous and bring to the forefront issues of quality, editorial bias, and anthologies that still indoctrinate students to define "great works" circularly— that is, according to standards gleaned from the works (largely by male writers) already deemed "great." How do we avoid reductive, superficial notions of gender politics in our effort to teach this spectrum? How do we keep our students from hosting popularity contests between male and female writers? Moreover, how do we keep students' notions of a reified canon, presented by prior instruction or the assembly of widely used anthologies, from influencing their judgments about individual writers' quality, or their receptiveness to individual works' possible offerings?

Simmons posits one answer to canonical pressures by simply expanding the genre offerings in his survey: to the novels of George Eliot and Charlotte Brontë, he adds nonfiction prose by Harriet Martineau and Frances Power Cobbe, which fleshes out the thematic "spectrum" as well as the generic one by offering additional points of view on political and social issues. In his essay, for example, he describes the richness that Martineau's "The Factory Boy" can lend to a discussion of industrial England and human rights. The remaining essays in this section employ a comparative pedagogy like Dolan's pairing of Hemans with Keats, Swenson's of Satthianadhan with Kipling, and Flannery's of Haywood with Pope, and like Simmons, these authors challenge the canonical reification of particular generic conventions and refocus literary instruction onto the variety and function of genres themselves. Elisabeth Rose Gruner's and Lawrence Zygmunt's essays show how non-canonical women writers can help teachers to return to the canon to mine its rich historical and aesthetic value.

Gruner strives to present a "truly 'integrated' survey" to her undergraduate classes. Besides endorsing the use of non-canonical genres to introduce a broad range of points of view, her definition of "integration" depends on these genres to represent the wide variety of texts the Victorians read and wrote. Including short fiction by women, Gruner shows, makes possible a much wider range of voices than is available from (usually longer) canonical texts alone; moreover, these works can deepen students' engagement with all the course texts, canonical and non-canonical alike. Margaret Oliphant's "Story of a Wedding Tour" complicates the marriage-or-death plot ending students may expect from Victorian standbys like *Adam Bede* and "The Lady of Shalott." Oliphant's story and Mary Elizabeth Braddon's "Good Lady Ducayne" employ images of technology which dramatically enrich the students' readings of the more familiar *Hard Times* and *Sartor Resartus*, and images of Europe which contribute greatly to their appreciating the significance of setting in *Aurora Leigh*. As Gruner uses recovery work to mark a path into canonical texts, she also shows how studying non-canonical genres reminds students that genre conventions are both deliberate and various, not simply the prescriptions of the period which all authors had to follow.

Similarly, Lawrence Zygmunt's study of teaching the Victorian multiplot novel uses a non-canonical text by Emily Eden both to map the variably frustrating and invisible intricacies of George Eliot's *Middlemarch* and also to study the structure and function of genre itself. Zygmunt's essay is founded on a marked sensitivity to students intimidated by the massive tomes of the Victorian canon. Such works of genius as *Middlemarch*, he argues, can be better taught by comparison to other works than in isolation, but, like Gruner, he acknowledges the logistical difficulty that any effort to substantially increase a survey's reading volume creates. The solution he presents here, found in Eden's *The Semi-Detached House*, brings with it other pedagogically significant elements. First, it invites examination of distinctions between types of Victorian realism. He reveals strong structural similarities between these Victorian women's texts, despite their considerable stylistic differences, and contrasts them particularly to the familiar work of male writers like Dickens. With several of the other essays in this section, then, it also brings gender to the forefront of literary study, raising questions of the complicated relationships between gender, art, and canonicity.

This section of *Teaching British Women Writers* moves recovery work forward in at least three ways. First, it provides useful methodological approaches to including writers from the eighteenth and nineteenth centuries: in these essays, teachers can see clear models for introducing many women writers into their courses. Second, it underscores a great imperative behind teaching women's writing, demonstrating ways in which gender can affect knowledge production both the past and the present. Finally, it affirms recovery projects' power to improve the quantity and depth of knowledge about literary historical periods. By shining traditional pedagogical "truths" through the prisms of women's work, we can see, and show our students, many more dimensions to the world that produced canonical works by men from Keats to Conrad. Such an endeavor ultimately models a necessary critique of the canon, not only teaching our students but training them—not only adding to their knowledge capital but showing them how to be creators and critics of that capital.

Notes

[1] John Guillory, *Cultural Capital: The Problem of Literary Canon Formation* (Chicago: U of Chicago P, 1993).
[2] Robyn Warhol and Diane Price Herndl, *Feminisms: An Anthology of Literary Theory and Criticism* (New Brunswick, NJ: Rutgers UP, 1991), 192.
[3] Warhol and Herndl, 204.

CHAPTER THREE
Teaching a "Highly Exceptional" Text: Krupabai Satthianadhan's *Saguna* and Narratives of Empire

Kristine Swenson

Every time I teach texts about empire to American undergraduates, a particular problem arises. Most of my students see and deplore the racism and, less clearly, the sexism of, for instance, Haggard and Kipling. However, they tend to classify these injustices as the inevitable attitudes of an older, less progressive time. Although I routinely teach recent postcolonial texts alongside nineteenth-century narratives, and although my students respond enthusiastically to the power of Jamaica Kincaid and Chinua Achebe, these late twentieth-century texts only seem to reinforce the idea in my students that Victorian imperialism is excusable, even charming somehow, because it is so hopelessly old-fashioned. Thus, even as the students catalogue the episodes of injustice in *King Solomon's Mines* or *Kim*, they indulge in the sort of "Out of Africa" nostalgia for empire that still sells products for Banana Republic, Pier One, and Ralph Lauren. I want my students to recognize imperialism as a culturally constructed ideology based on inequalities and injustices that, for one thing, deploys the pleasures of romance, nostalgia, and consumption in order to elicit consent from them as readers.

Because it simply does not allow for Banana Republic nostalgia, I now teach Krupabai Satthianadhan's autobiographical novel, *Saguna* (1890), alongside Kipling, Haggard, and other imperial narratives. In her introduction to the first edition of *Saguna. A Story of Native Christian Life* (1890), Mrs. R. S. Benson suggests that it may be "hard for ladies in England to realize the value of this...pioneer volume," but notes that because it is the first "work of fiction written by a Hindu lady in English," and because so few Indian women could read or even speak English, *Saguna* is "highly exceptional."[1] In fact, Satthianadhan was among the very first Indians, either male or female, to respond to British colonizers in their own language and in one of their most cherished genres, the realist novel. Furthermore, as reviews in British and Anglo-Indian periodicals attest, the colonizers responded warmly, if a bit confusedly, to Satthianadhan's representations of Indian life. Some reviewers called *Saguna* an Indian New Woman novel, others a Christian polemic, and one even compared Satthianadhan to Jane Austen.[2]

Just as its first British readers had trouble placing *Saguna*, instructors might find it difficult to know what to do with this "exceptional" novel. Since the 1970s, postcolonial women's writing, which had "represented something of a lost continent in…nationalist discourses," has gained increasing recognition and praise.[3] Krupabai Satthianadhan is the literary foremother of such novelists as Anita Desai, Bharati Mukherjee, and Arundhati Roy, who are assuming well-deserved places on literature syllabuses. At the same time, recent postcolonial and feminist scholarship has begun to ask critical questions about the relationship between gender and empire that a text such as *Saguna* is well placed to answer. When I have taught *Saguna* in upper-level undergraduate courses on British imperial narratives, my concern has been to help the (American) students understand some of the dominant narratives of nineteenth-century British imperialism, but also to help them read against those dominant strains with texts by "outsiders," subversives, and postcolonials. Technically, *Saguna* is among the latter, oppositional texts; and yet, like Mary Kingsley's *Travels in West Africa* (which has also been part of the course), its position in relation to British imperialism and Christian western culture is wonderfully complex. This complexity means that one might teach Satthianadhan's novel in relation to any number of texts on empire and/or the Victorian "Woman Question" with the goal of educating students about the interrelations of imperialism and gender discrimination.

Saguna has made a singularly strong impression upon my students and has acted as a corrective to Haggard and Kipling because, it seems to me, its treatment of empire is so *obviously* constructed. While *Saguna* is a fascinating cultural document, it is not what most literary critics would call aesthetically satisfying. Like Kipling, Satthianadhan borrows from a variety of genres in both western and eastern literary traditions. In *Saguna,* though, the seams show between the narrative pieces and the effect can be jarring to readers accustomed to the smooth sophistication of the late realism of Conrad or James or even Kipling. However, my students, like most American undergraduates, are not yet literary critics and are not yet accustomed to the prose of Conrad or James or Kipling. They frankly find *Kim* a difficult and confusing novel. Coming immediately after *Kim*, then, *Saguna* offers my students an enjoyable and manageable read. They can feel a bit demoralized by how difficult *Kim* is to *access* let alone interpret (they know they are *supposed* to read like budding critics). *Saguna*, in contrast, is simply awash in ideological tensions and contradictions that do not require special critical skills or a particular political stance to see. Perhaps because my students were able to "'ork" on *Saguna*, they found it a very satisfying novel; none noted or seemed bothered by its lack of aesthetic polish. Moreover, this new critical confidence enabled my students to take a second, more critical look at other texts in the course. Although they at first had read *King Solomon's Mines* and *Kim* as fairly unproblematic adventure stories, after reading *Saguna* they thought about them and the texts that followed with a new sophistication that, I hope, will help them avoid a romantic, consumerist stance toward nineteenth- (and twentieth-) century empire-building.

Saguna is the fictionalized autobiography of the daughter of Brahmin converts to Christianity. Though a girl, Saguna's interests are intellectual rather than domestic or religious. Encouraged by an intellectual older brother, she rebels against the traditional restrictions of Indian culture by insisting upon a western-style education. She works diligently at a western-run mission school and later, desiring an intellectual challenge and a life of public service, she attends medical school in Calcutta. However, after a difficult but very successful year of medical school, Saguna breaks down physically and mentally. During several months of recovery, she recants her desire for a career and an independent public life, recommits herself to her Christian faith, and marries an Indian missionary.

The principal tensions of the novel, then, concern religion and gender, though underlying both is the question of race. To maneuver among the evident textual and cultural tensions of such a narrative, Satthianadhan uses a variety of eastern and western literary models: Hindu and Christian religious parables, autobiography, the bildungsroman, narratives of early Indian nationalism, and the novels of George Eliot. In this sense, *Saguna* is an example of what Mary Louise Pratt has called an "autoethnographic" text, a concept that I introduced to my class to help them understand Satthianadhan's rhetorical position and strategies. As opposed to ethnographic texts in which colonizers represent the peoples they colonize, autoethnographic texts are those in which "colonized subjects undertake to represent themselves in ways that *engage with* the colonizer's own terms."[4] The result is often a sort of hybrid of metropolitan and colonized culture and language. In addition to this cultural hybridity, Pratt notes that autoethnographic texts are often a "group's point of entry into metropolitan literate culture."[5] Not surprisingly, the most successful autoethnographic texts tend to be "mediated" by prefaces which serve as recommendations of the author's character and which help a metropolitan audience to translate the colonized text "properly."[6] Because they lay out or at least point toward particular interpretations, such prefaces often expose quite blatantly the ideological assumptions of a colonized text, how it appropriates or resists the "idioms of the conqueror."[7]

To return to the first edition of *Saguna*, Mrs. Benson's preface prepares a specifically western female audience to read the novel by encouraging them to recognize themselves as the intended audience. Focusing on Benson's preface before we read *Saguna* tended to distance my students from the original western readers and to open up space for critical inquiry. "It is hoped," Benson writes, "that the story of 'Saguna' will rouse and sustain the interest and sympathy of English women in the women in India, and lead...to a wider interest in, and freer intercourse with, our Indian friends." Any faults in the text must be excused, implies Benson, by the fact that "English is almost entirely unknown among Native ladies throughout India"; with this in mind, "we can better understand that the work before us is highly exceptional."[8] Because of the striking ambiguity of Benson's phrase, "highly exceptional," my class and I took it as a key to interpreting the novel. We followed the connotations of "exceptional" in two different directions: toward the external, cultural conditions within which the text was produced (or, history) and toward the internal workings of the novel (or, its literariness).

First, of course, Mrs. Benson finds *Saguna* "exceptional" because, as a novel by a Hindu woman written in English, it is an anomaly. This is hardly a neutral issue. Teaching Indian *men* to speak English had long been seen as necessary to a united, smooth-running British India.[9] Toward the end of the nineteenth century, the British focused increasingly on "civilizing" Indian *women*, the cornerstone of which was teaching them to speak English. In fact, Mrs. Benson describes these language skills as particularly convenient for English ladies in India who cannot be bothered to learn the many native languages they will encounter.[10]

Mrs. Benson's remark about how few Indian women knew English helped my students to see Satthianadhan and her heroine as "exceptional" or "unrepresentative" Indian women in other important ways as well. Saguna's life is *not* typical of the lives of Indian women in the 1890s (any more than George Eliot's heroines or Mary Kingsley were typical English women). Saguna is separated from most of her countrywomen by her western-style education which not only enables her to speak English, but also trains her for a profession; she is separated from them by her western-style religion; and she is separated from them by her class or caste—for although Christian converts, her family remained proud of their Brahman blood.

This sort of exception that Saguna represents helped us to historicize the text and the issues it raises, such as the effects of empire. As a class, we asked questions such as: How did "typical" Indian women live in the 1890s and what allowed for Saguna's/Satthianadhan's difference? In what sense does Saguna share the position of educated, ambitious *western* women and how does her race separate her from them? What can this text tell us about the workings of imperialism upon the colonized mind and how does it foreshadow India's struggle for independence? Such questions prepared students to view the text as historically and culturally contingent, a piece of writing constructed in a particular moment for a particular audience and with a particular purpose. They could thus get beyond what I described earlier as their tendency to read racism and sexism as inevitable attitudes of an older, less progressive era.

The second, "literary" (and certainly more polite) interpretation of Mrs. Benson's description of *Saguna* as "exceptional" is that she thinks the novel a fine piece of writing. By what standards, though, I asked my class, is Mrs. Benson judging *Saguna's* literary merit? A careful reading of the preface makes it clear (and this is no surprise) that Mrs. Benson values the novel insofar as it conforms to western values and is indebted to western texts. For instance, Benson compares Satthianadhan (who wrote from her sickbed) to Harriet Martineau and Florence Nightingale; and she describes the novel in terms of western literary realism with its "objective" depiction of the details of daily life. However, these Victorian figures and conventions were nearly as alien to my students as those of nineteenth-century India. For this reason, Benson's need to represent East in terms of West—Satthianadhan as a lesser Nightingale or Martineau—helped my students to see the constructedness of this text—how it targets an intended audience for particular rhetorical and ideological purposes. In other words, what was a predictable, almost unconscious move for a Victorian imperialist, struck my students—who were unfamiliar with Martineau, for instance—as strange. Mrs. Benson's desire to read *Saguna* in western terms made my students want to unravel the western narrative strands that Satthianadhan had woven into her novel. As a result, we naturally spent much time drawing connections between *Saguna* and western texts we had read.

The western text that *Saguna* worked against most effectively was Kipling's *Kim*. Not coincidentally, it was at this point that the course really began to work. My students had struggled very diligently to grasp imperialist ideology and postcolonial criticism; and they'd applied it—rather mechanically—to Haggard's and Kipling's novels. It was when we read *Saguna* against *Kim,* though, that they first really *saw* the ideology working. We had read *Kim* primarily as a quest for cultural and spiritual identity. The orphaned son of an Irish officer, Kim grows up as an Indian, unaware of his lineage until his father's old unit identifies him. He is educated as a western boy but then is reinserted into the native life he prefers, now to act as a British spy. Kim spends much of the novel asking himself, "Who is Kim?" This question, though, is rendered much less desperate by his *essential* (racial) Western identity (albeit a marginalized, colonized Irish Western identity), which allows the novel to smooth over the very concerns about identity and cultural assimilation that it raises. Pretty quickly, in fact, *Kim* was assimilating my students—they got caught up in the spy plot, they repeated phrases from the book with Indian accents, and they kept suggesting that we hold class in the local Indian restaurant.

In *Saguna*, we also find a young Indian searching for identity within what she calls "the New Order" of the Raj, struggling to assimilate Christianity and western learning without losing her Indian heritage. However, the ease with which Kim moves between the cultures of East and West is not possible for Saguna, for two reasons: She is *essentially* (racially) Indian and she is *essentially* female. Because in the ideology of imperialism, Kim is of superior western stock, he shifts back and forth between a western and an eastern identity relatively easily. For Saguna, the assimilation of western values requires something more difficult. She must strike and maintain an uneasy balance between her eastern blood and her western ambition, between the old woman of traditional India and the New Woman of the progressive west.

My students read Saguna's struggle between east and west as "authentic" and, thus, Kim's trials began to seem less so. They began to see Kipling's novel as much less of an exotic travelogue or ethnography and much more of a game for the pleasure of western readers. They lost sympathy for the wily, shape-shifting western protagonist when they were confronted by the story of a simple Indian girl whose desires they could appreciate and identify with: pleasing her parents and siblings, education, meaningful work, love and marriage.

Similarly, both novels treat eastern and western religions, often valorizing a hybrid of the two. My students found Saguna's religious quest again more "authentic" than Kim's and therefore more worthy of sympathy. At the same time, though, my students registered the inconsistencies and religious agenda much more clearly in Satthianadhan's novel, which caused them to reevaluate how Kipling, too, might be using religion in the service of empire. They noted, for instance, how Saguna follows the religious paradoxes of her older brother, Bhasker, a staunch Christian convert, who explains to her how India had "superstition and bigotry lurking in every corner, before the light of Christianity" and in the next breath claims to be "a Brahman to the backbone" and "a real patriot...."[11] What, my students rightly wondered, does it mean to be a "patriot" in this context? Is Bhasker's first loyalty to India (and is that an English-speaking, Christian, British India or not?) or to the light of Christianity brought by westerners and maintained by western institutions—schools and hospitals as well as churches. Saguna does struggle with her faith at key points in the novel—particularly when it comes into conflict with her intellectual ambitions at the mission school. However, the victory of Christianity over Hinduism is inevitable from the beginning of this tale, first published as a serial in the *Christian College Magazine*, and so creates little suspense.[12] Again, then, religion in *Saguna* helped my students read the novel as a *rhetorical* document, a reading they then turned back upon *Kim*. During their first reading of *Kim*, most of my students lost patience with Kipling's catalogue of religious beliefs and practices in India. After reading *Saguna*, they grew suspicious of the ease with which *Kim* seems to reconcile Christianity, Buddhism, Hinduism, and Islam. Kipling, some thought, was not willing to "take a stand." Others suggested that maybe the particular religion was not as important as long as all were loyal subjects to the British crown.

The narrative tension created by religion in *Saguna* is closely linked to gender, an issue that my students, most of them women, tended to read as the central interpretive issue of the novel. Also, I suspect, gender is more interesting than religion in *Saguna* because it remains much more ambiguous. To be a good Christian woman, Saguna must reject what westerners viewed as the savage customs enforced upon Indian women—the most dramatic being child marriage, utter subjugation to the husband and his family, and suttee. Nevertheless, when Saguna does reject the traditional Indian role for women and chooses instead a western education and career, she comes perilously close to resembling the New Woman, an impious and frighteningly androgynous figure who threatened even *western* notions of man's superiority and woman's properly submissive role.

One of the most frustrating aspects of teaching American undergraduate women—at least the ones I have met in the Midwest between, say, 1990 and the present—is their refusal to identify with or even condone anything labeled "feminist" all the while insisting upon their rights to equal access, opportunity, pay, sexual experience, and so on…and often strongly identifying with feminist fictional creations. The nineteenth-century New Woman, whether here in *Saguna* or in any of a variety of western texts, helps them to historicize gender roles and to see the need for a feminist politics both in the past and the present. Saguna's struggle between old and new gender roles for Indian women was particularly effective in this regard, perhaps because of the ambiguity with which the narrative treats Saguna's struggle.

Satthianadhan dramatizes this gender struggle in a number of ways. The first third of *Saguna*'s narrative is given over to the story of her mother's girlhood and conversion to Christianity. It is through this story that Satthianadhan communicated to her western audience the horrors of women's lives in *traditional* Indian culture (a prejudice that the western audience was quite willing to believe). Young brides, often of ten or twelve years old, are virtually enslaved to their mothers-in-law and have nothing to fill their minds but the dread of "rough treatment" and dreams of jewelry and romance. "Poor girls!" exclaims the narrator, "what can we expect from such impoverished, stunted minds? …The refined, civilized mind shudders or looks down with pity on the exhibition [of their jewels] as a relic of savagery…."[13] Not surprisingly, despite her conversion to Christianity, Saguna's mother held onto many "savage" assumptions about the proper behavior of girls: "though her faith in her new religion was strong," comments the narrator, she "was still full of Hindu notions of things."[14] Among these notions, Saguna's mother discourages her daughter from playing and studying with her brothers: "'What is the use of learning for a girl? A girl's training school is near the *chool* (the fire over which everything is cooked).'"[15] Saguna rebels against her mother's traditionalism and, with the help of her older siblings, eventually enrolls in a western mission school where she will dream of studying in England. At this point, my female students were cheering on Saguna's rebelliousness; their experience at home and school is still, it seems, burdened by enough traditionally gendered expectation to allow them to identify with her.

Even so, the text hesitates to reject traditional (old) Indian customs altogether. In her introduction to the second, 1895, edition of *Saguna*, Mrs. Benson remarks that "In no way did [Satthianadhan] become denationalized, through her Western culture, in dress, or manner, or in her quiet style of living."[16] The novel's warning against women becoming too westernized and independent is dramatized through the cautionary tale of Saguna's friend, Prema, who had been educated in a western school, spoke "English as her mother tongue," and whose "*Ma*" gave her a novel to read.[17] With such decadent ways, Prema's head is easily turned by an adventurer, an "England-returned" young man who courts Prema but intends to "play with others also."[18] As a result of her broken heart, Prema falls ill and dies. "'Poor girl!'" Bhasker tells his sister, Saguna, "'If she had only kept to her old simple ways, and not gone in for fashion and false ideas....'"[19] Saguna, in other words, risks death when she flirts with western *ideas,* let alone westernized men.

As contradictory on the question of gender roles as these examples appear, the most striking example comes very early in the novel when the narrator tells a story about *suttee*. Here again, westernization brings with it the risks of humiliation and death for Indian women. Near Saguna's home there lived a rich and beautiful woman whose education is "the cause of all her after-misfortune," for "People in their mysterious dread of learning...had always held it unnatural for a woman to be clever or in any way learned."[20] When the woman's husband dies, the "long pent up rage of the Brahmans, to whom this woman was detestable on account of her learning, now found vent in the form of cursing on the unfortunate widow."[21] The town bullies the woman into becoming a *suttee*—into throwing herself on the burning corpse of her husband and dying with him. At the last moment, however, she escapes, "screaming into the hills" where legend has it she became a powerful witch doctress.[22]

With this story, Satthianadhan gives us a parable about gender in British

India: the traditional taboos against women's education, the "western" prejudices against suttee and child marriage, the stereotypes of unmarried native women as witch doctresses. Not surprisingly, my students sided strongly with the "witch doctress," suttee being a concept that they found utterly foreign and completely abhorrent. However, what is so fascinating about this story is that it is impossible to interpret Satthianadhan's attitude toward it. Structurally, it is treated as a mere ghost story. Thematically, the suttee story is highly suggestive, but the narrator refuses to make any direct connection between, say, the learning of the woman and Saguna's own education, or the ways in which both the suttee and Saguna rebel. When my students realized that the suttee's learning alienated her and nearly caused her death, they began to wonder if the text is not siding with Saguna's mother on the question of educating girls. Again, this ambiguity, this unresolvable tension between old and new gender roles, is what made the constructedness of gender clear to my students.

Of course, this struggle against traditional roles for women was a dominant concern in western fiction of the 1880s and 1890s as well. Saguna's desires for an education and a career explain why this was described as "a study of the 'New Woman' as she is in her Indian surroundings."[23] As in so much nineteenth-century British fiction, the female protagonist's desire to break the rules of her culture creates a dissonance in the text which culminates in and is resolved by illness. Saguna's struggle to balance the demands of East and West, old and new is dramatized in the novel by her mental and physical breakdown following a successful first year of medical school. She says: "I had not counted the cost of all of this. I had worked with all my might…and now when all was over, a feeling of complete prostration came over me. What was it? I was frightened, and I feared a breakdown."[24] Saguna's invalidism is not very well defined. (In this sense, the comparison to Nightingale seems telling.) What is clear is that her illness causes her to repent her selfish ambition and desire for independence and to dedicate her life to Christ and his servant, the missionary whom Saguna marries.

This ending might well have struck my students as "natural" because (as everyone knows) women "back then" were more religious and tended to get married rather than have careers. Formally, Saguna's embrace of Christ and husband together does create a neat sense of closure: "I felt an arm encircle me, and 'there we shall be, God helping, all our lives,' said a hoarse voice in my ears…. Christ was ours…and our lives were to be one full and joyous song…. Near the door he grasped my hand and pressed a kiss. It was a holy kiss that sealed forever the course of our lives."[25]

Accepting this ending, though, requires the reader to accept as well the transcendence of western romantic love and Christian faith over the material conditions of empire. In other words, my students and I would have to forget that this is a colonized text which has tried for 200 pages to address a western audience in its own terms. Perhaps this was no problem for the original Victorian reading audience. What shattered the illusion for us, what reminded us of the East and West of empire and the English ladies reading this novel, is that Saguna credits for her renunciation of education and independence not her deep faith or her deep love or even the dictates of Indian culture, but the novels of George Eliot. After her breakdown, she writes, she had been "devouring, with intense delight, George Eliot's books.... The lesson was on selfishness. Was I not selfish even in my dreams of work? ... Was it not selfishness to...dream of doing great things and leave the harder part of life's work to others? I had longed for independence and a life of intellectual ease. What does a selfish being, a savage, do less than this?"[26] Certainly, this is not an *impossible* reading for a devout Christian woman in 1890 to make of, say, *Middlemarch*, though early reviewers more commonly found Dorothea's ultimate "chastisement" puzzling.[27] But what is more immediately important about Satthianadhan's reference to Eliot than the specific interpretation is the way that it showed the seams of the ending to my students. Those students who didn't know Eliot asked, "Who's that guy?" and so at least were distracted away from the novel's neat closure. The reference that they couldn't understand reminded them of the rhetorical constructedness, the literariness, of the novel and that its original readers were quite different from themselves. A few of my students had read either *The Mill on the Floss* or *Middlemarch* and wanted to argue that Satthianadhan was misreading Eliot; they puzzled over the implications of Satthianadhan's reference until they had totally deconstructed *Saguna*'s ending: "But Dorothea isn't *wrong* and certainly isn't *selfish* in her desire to do great things!" "Eliot's critiquing the sexism of Victorian culture, isn't she?" "Why does Satthianadhan tie 'savage' to her dream of becoming a doctor of western medicine? It doesn't make sense." "Is it just selfish for women to want to do great work?"

As is no doubt clear by this point, *Saguna* is certainly a "uneven" novel in the formal and literary senses. Written at the height of western literary realism, it does not approach the seamless verisimilitude of the British texts, such as George Eliot's, which it evokes. Its first readers, not expecting that a Hindu text could reach such heights of perfection, appreciated Satthianadhan's attempt to write in the vein of western realism. From our postcolonial perspective, however, we can understand Satthianadhan's "failure" differently and in a way that is pedagogically productive. It is essential, first, to recognize that western realism is not a simple reflection of reality, but is a form that is value-laden and politically motivated. Scholars of colonial Indian fiction such as Mennakshi

Mukherjee have argued that "The conventions of realism...could not be transferred to the Indian situation, where the nature of social reality was substantially different."[28] Following Mukherjee, Priva Joshi finds a tension in *Saguna* "between the English books" Saguna reads (and Satthianadhan refers to) and Indian reality: "The imported English novel is neither about nor does it speak to the world Satthianadhan inhabits. Contrary to the Department of Public Instruction's insistence that English realism provides the best gloss to empire...at its most successful [realism] *glosses over* the disjunctions enforced between empire and its subjects."[29] In short, Joshi argues that the "failed" realism of *Saguna* actually exposes the failures of empire and the lies of "cultural unity and belonging propagated by English education."[30] In contrast to those who value only seamless literariness, critics such as Mary Poovey and Jane Tompkins have taught us the worth of the uneven and the non-canonical, how the seams of a "flawed" text expose its ideology and allow us to see the cultural work that it performs. *Saguna* is just such a text and is, I would argue, exceptional for a reason beyond Mrs. Benson's two: it is exceptionally effective pedagogically so that even if it had no "literariness" whatsoever (which it certainly does), it would nevertheless serve a high purpose as a foil and illuminator of more seamless imperial narratives and as the ancestor of powerful postcolonial fiction. *Saguna* can allow students to recognize the historicity of ideas such as empire, race, and gender so that they will not assume that injustice was (or is) inevitable or natural but was constructed, inscribed, and enacted.

Notes

[1] Krupabai Satthianadhan, *Saguna: A Story of Native Christian Life*, 2nd ed. (Madras, 1895), xi–xii. *Saguna* has been reissued recently and is now available through Oxford UP: Krupabai, *Saguna: The First Autobiographical Novel in English by an Indian Woman*, ed. Chandani Lokugé (Oxford: Oxford UP, 1998).

[2] In *The Daily Graphic* Miss Billington calls *Saguna* a "study of the 'New Woman' as she is in Indian surroundings"; the reviewer for *Harvest Field* (March 1890) comments on the "fervour and vividness" of Saguna's "strivings...after truer and fuller spiritual life" (quoted in Satthianadhan, "Opinions," (appendix to *Saguna*, 2nd ed.), v, iv). The comparison to Austen is made by Mrs. Fenwick Miller, "A Book of the Hour. Review of *Kamala* and *Saguna* by Krupabai Satthianadhan," *The Woman's Signal* (June 13, 1895): 379.

[3] Elleke Boehmer, *Colonial & Postcolonial Literature* (Oxford and New York: Oxford UP, 1995), 224.

[4] Mary Louis Pratt, *Imperial Eyes: Travel Writing and Transculturation* (London and New York: Routledge, 1992), 7.

[5] Pratt, 7–9.

[6] See, for instance, Harriet Jacobs's *Incidents in the Life of a Slave Girl* which was "edited," and introduced by L. Maria Child, a white northern abolitionist. In that introduction, Child gives

"credentials of [Jacobs's] character" and offers an explanation for the ex-slave's proficiency as a writer [quoted in "Incidents in the Life of a Slave Girl," *Ways of Reading: An Anthology for Writers*, 4th ed., eds. David Bartholomae and Anthony Petrosky (Boston: Bedford Books, 1996), 375.]

7 Pratt, 7.
8 Satthianadhan, xii.
9 See, for instance, Macaulay's *Minute on Indian Education* (1835) which took up the question before the British government's General Committee on Public Instruction of whether the British government should continue to sponsor instruction in Sanskrit and Arabic or whether it should sponsor instruction in English only. Macaulay argued on the "Anglicist" side of the question.
10 For a detailed analysis of the relationship between western feminist reformers and Indian women, see Antoinette Burton, *Burdens of History: British Feminists, Indian Women, and Imperial Cutlure, 1865–1915* (Chapel Hill: University of North Carolina Press, 1994).
11 Satthianadhan, 7, 11. Brahmans were not simply of a higher caste but were originally a caste of Hindu priests.
12 Noted in a review of the first edition, *Harvest Field* (March 1890), quoted in Satthianadhan, "Opinions," (appendix), iv.
13 Satthianadhan, 30–31.
14 Satthianadhan, 1.
15 Satthianadhan, 4.
16 Satthianadhan, viii.
17 Satthianadhan, 96.
18 Satthianadhan, 101, 115.
19 Satthianadhan, 118.
20 Satthianadhan, 9.
21 Satthianadhan, 9.
22 Satthianadhan, 10.
23 Noted by Miss Billington in a review of the first edition, *The Daily Graphic*, quoted in Satthianadhan, "Opinions," (appendix), v.
24 Satthianadhan, 216.
25 Satthianadhan, 230–31.
26 Satthianadhan, 223–24.
27 Gillian Beer, *George Eliot* (Bloomington: Indiana UP, 1986), 152.
28 Meenakshi Mukherjee, *Realism and Reality. The Novel and Society in India* (Delhi: Oxford UP, 1985), vii.
29 Joshi, 102–103.
30 Joshi, 103.

Studies in the English Novel II
Dr. Swenson

"More than any other literary form. . .the novel serves as the model by which society conceives of itself, the discourse in and through which it articulates the world."
—Jonathan Culler, *Structuralist Poetics*, 1975

Goals and Policies:

In this course we will read some of the major British novels from the Victorian period to the present. This is a formidable task, as you'll see when you stack the novels on top of one another, and I expect you to take it seriously—to read, think, discuss, and write in an open yet critical manner. At the same time, though, a major goal of this course is for you to enjoy yourselves. E.M. Forster, one of our novelists and an important critic of the genre wrote, "The final test of a novel will be our affection for it, as it is the test of our friends...."

You will be evaluated in several ways. Class discussion and informal assignments will allow you to work toward interpretations of texts that you'll be able to expand upon in papers and exams; class participation will also demonstrate "effort," and will be heavily rewarded. Exams will test how carefully you studied the assignments and how well you're able to synthesize what you read and discussed in class. Papers will allow you to articulate more carefully and formally your ideas about the readings for the course.

Required Texts:

- Jane Austen, *Mansfield Park* (Norton Critical)
- Jamaica Kincaid, *A Small Place* (Penguin)
- Charles Dickens, *Hard Times* (Norton Critical)
- David Lodge, *Nice Work* (Penguin)
- Rudyard Kipling, *Kim* (Oxford UP)
- Krupabai Satthianadhan, *Saguna* (Oxford UP)
- EM Forster, *A Passage to India* (Harcourt)
- Arandhati Roy, *The God of Small Things*
- Virginia Woolf, *Mrs. Dalloway* (Harcourt)
- Michael Cunningham, *The Hours* (Picadour)

Figure 1. Kristine Swenson, Sample Syllabus

CHAPTER FOUR
Teaching English Women's Conversionist Rhetoric

Rebecca Shapiro

This chapter examines the process by which early nineteenth-century English conversionist literature targeting Jewish women can be successfully taught in an undergraduate class. One of the goals of the course, entitled Eighteenth- and Nineteenth-Century British Women Writers and taught in 1998 at Westminster College in Fulton, Missouri, was to expose students to different kinds of writing during these centuries, and to complicate issues of feminism, ethnicity, class, even religion. The literature that I introduced in this section comprised some tracts or pamphlets of the Society for Promoting Christianity Amongst the Jews, Jewish responses to those polemics, as well as portions of a conversionist novel and an anti-conversionist novel. While I have been able to find only a few of these tracts and novels, the paucity of choice is not limiting in itself, for the content and style of this literature is uniform: It is didactic, strident, pushy, even obsequious, but it is never nuanced or deep and thus students do not need to experience a wide variety of texts to get the point. I did not, therefore, incorporate these minor texts into the syllabus in order to expand the canon, but to provide more cultural context for the students and give them the opportunity to interrogate the innocence or motives of the canon that already exists and to question the innocence or motives of the authors we instructors are trying to add to the canon.

I approach the topic of evangelizing and conversion of women by women by placing the literature surrounding it within a middle-class context; I introduce the ways that middle-class women could extend their influence outside the home by politicizing their cause and could become assertive by domesticating politics and religion and sentimentalizing empire as an extension of religion. (Our class discussed how, even today, women are often immunized against conservative criticism when their activism is religious.)[1] It is important for students to see that conversionist literature was instrumental to England's nationalist project of forging empire; in order for England to maintain its integrity as a colonizing body, it had to "teach" and enforce upon its subjects the mythos of religious, ethnic, and cultural homogeneity. Moreover, sexual submission operated by simultaneously asserting that women were essential to such nationalistic projects while their influence was really ancillary to that of men.

When I teach British literature, one of my early goals is to have students question and open the categories that generally define "Englishness," such as being white, Anglican, middle-class, heterosexual, native, virtuous, to name a few. Students examine why we read about some groups residing in England, assuming that they are "English," and ignore others because they do not fit the classification or are somehow otherwise marginalized. This is why it has become so difficult to disengage Ann Yearsley's poetry from her class status and from her relationship with Hannah More. Students are also introduced to the difficulty of defining and maintaining an English identity when I bring in such writers as Aphra Behn (Surinam), Charlotte Lennox (America), and Maria Edgeworth (Anglo-Ireland), all of whom would be taught in an English literature course, but none of whom could be labeled strictly "English." My attempt to promote skepticism is productive when examining any literary period or genre, but I find it most useful when I teach British Romanticism in particular, when concerns over the French Revolutions, the slave trade, the rise of the middle classes, the 1801 Act of Union, and concerns over women's rights, among other issues, all were raging. I suggest that Romanticism can be applied in less than noble or revolutionary ways when it is used to reinforce some view of England or Englishness that did not in fact exist and which promoted certain homogeneous and nationalistic ideals; indeed, I show how Romantic aesthetics can be moral, doctrinaire, and oppressive, particularly during the religion section of my course. The goal, then, is to have students question the revolutionary aspects of Romanticism and see how it can instead lead to very conservative and exclusionary projects. The way that I do this is to pair traditional texts with ones that are more propagandistic and explicitly hegemonic to show that sometimes the difference between them is merely subtle.

What is often most difficult to teach are polemics and political writing, such as the works of Thomas Paine and Mary Wollstonecraft; the conversionist tracts and literature written by evangelical Anglicans directed toward Jews were no different. By this time in the semester, though students could accept alternative paradigms about textual quality and authorial influence, they were not ultimately able to accept these texts as legitimate or valuable as literature and remained alienated from them, sometimes even hostile toward them. One reason in particular the students gave for not accepting those texts is that they felt that because certain conversionist literature was written by a group, not an individual; even if there was only one author he or she used the power that the group derived from the state religion to impose on a subordinated group with an attenuated social and legal relationship to England. Students believed that the conversionist group was "hiding" behind its authority and bullying another group, whereas the Jewish women who defended their religion wrote as individuals, which the students felt was more risky and bold. Here, of course, was the ideal opportunity for me to disable students' preconceptions of Romantic aesthetic concerns: I asked them to consider whether Romanticism really did grow out of a revolutionary drive for new and innovative literature when these same techniques and tropes were used both to valorize and to oppress.

The struggle for Jewish female conversion occurred in various ways, but the most common was for various groups, most notably the Society to Promote Christianity Amongst the Jews (Society), to engage in "good works" to "aid" Jewish women in material and in spiritual needs. The conversionist texts exhorted English women to help Jewish women and their families in the proper way to convert to Christianity and become more English, or rather, how to conform to the imagined homogeneous English society. While the texts were not conduct books for Jewish women, the written goals of the Society were to encourage Jewish women who sought to fit into English society to become more like their native sisters. A typical pamphlet published by the Ladies Auxiliary of the Society makes a pointed plea to English women to help Jewish women, asserting that it is:

> addressed to the hearts of British females. To the Jewish nation, let it be remembered, they are indebted for the difference which exists between the station they hold in society, and that of the women of those countries, where the inhabitants still groan under the slavery of Mahometan or Pagan superstition.... Will you hesitate to exert your utmost endeavors in order to the erection of a house for the reception of those children...?"[2]

These didactic conversionist works were written to attract Jewish wives and mothers responsible for the well-being of their families, and an important issue is that these writings focus on Jewish salvation in a context in which certain types of Christian identity are likewise questioned. For example, the struggle to convert the Jews similarly reveals a political contest between Catholics and Anglicans in which the "true" Christians in England, the Anglicans, prevail. For example, what if a Jewish mother converts her family to the wrong Christianity? Finally, these examples really show how the English conversionist project was meant to shut down religious difference, and to simultaneously other and subsume subordinate groups.

Because a unique feature of the conversionist texts in this section of the course is that they are written by women for women, I used them to problematize issues that students—especially those in a women writers course—had come to assume were rather clear: that women would work toward the emancipation of other women, and that they would naturally be interested in promoting the independence of other women. The features that would otherwise mark these texts as examples of incipient feminism, then, were nullified from the students' perspective by latent anti-Semitism, class distinctions, and Orientalism. For example, "Solemn and Affectionate Appeal to Jewish Females" highlights Judaism's alleged gender inequities by recalling the power the priest Miriam once held, in contrast to the powerless state of contemporary Jewish womanhood, and thus "recovering" a feminist history to serve assimilation in England. Moreover, it reminds Jewish women that as wives and mothers they control the sanctity of the family; they influence home life and they can change the family's religion. The tract even gives Jewish women a script to say to Christ requesting assistance from him:

> look upon the affliction of thy handmaids; we are outcasts in a strange land;…we have all gone astray like lost sheep, we have turned every one to her own way; we bring forth children in misery, and we are not able to teach them the fear of thee; we do not know the path of life ourselves, and how shall we show it to our infants…. Accept ourselves, our husbands, our children: save us from the wrath to come.[3]

The quote above shows how women can supplicate Christ directly without the intervention of men and allows them to become free from of the ignorance in which Jewish men supposedly keep their wives and daughters. At the same time that conversion to Christianity ostensibly gives Jewish women domestic authority, the implication is that it will lead wives to disobey their husbands if the men refuse to come along. In the wake of the conversion of Jewish women who follow the law of matrilineal descent, the unstated, though unavoidable, goal of the missionary societies is the dissolution of the Jewish family, and thus, of the religion itself. Issues of group identity and colonization are therefore particularly complex; in the context of religious and national identity, my students considered it unseemly and distasteful to consider the subjugation of one group by another when the group doing the oppression was already oppressed. That was the juncture at which we had some robust debates because initially, some students, mostly women, did not want to criticize women who wished to better themselves or assert an autonomous political identity. Furthermore, one reality students did recognize, though they were annoyed by it, was the fact that these Christian women really were concerned for the souls and well-being of Jewish women.

Students felt more comfortable challenging the Ladies Auxiliary after they read a selection from the anti-conversion novel *Caleb Asher* (1845) by Charlotte Montefiore in which Montefiore condemns conversions accomplished under duress or as a result of financial need, a common charge against the societies. She offers an alternate perspective to the zealous model of the Society and argues how, to the Society, converted Jews merely represented closer proximity to Heaven and salvation and that, once converted, they were neglected by their newfound "sistren."[4] The result was that students understood that once the evangelical English women were criticized by a Jew, it was acceptable for them to follow suit. Interestingly, then, the idea of permission to break ranks with a women's cause arose in this context; though none of the students were Jewish, reading Montefiore freed them from having much sympathy for the Society once they realized that Jewish women felt used.

Throughout this portion of the course the class members—myself included—discussed how we arrived at our conclusions and judgments about literary aesthetics; students often mentioned how their beliefs were acquired and influenced by their cultural experiences as well as the biases of past instructors and syllabus choices—such as my own—and were thus more plastic than they had imagined. What we tried to determine in this section, therefore, was what makes one work more acceptable and canonical than another. (Their responses to my questions I found were often more important than the discussions of the content of the readings as they were practicing the "critical thinking" that is pushed so hard at liberal arts colleges and which is not always achieved.) Why, for example, do we believe that Byron's *Don Juan* is more Romantic or less didactic or political than More's "On Slavery"? Both works are poetic and treat contemporary social issues, so what are the reasons we find *Don Juan* easier to read or more acceptable?—I moved students in the direction of thinking of the canon as set by taste and precedent rather than by some independent and Platonic idea. This is by no means a new idea for faculty, but it is to students, who, by learning to question traditional aesthetic models and by opening up categories of sex, class, and race, come to realize that their beliefs about literature and canonicity are as politicized as are non-canonical texts. That awareness was as freeing to them as it was frustrating because there seemed to be fewer ways of determining the set value or "goodness" of a work or an author. For example, an African American student was pleased by our discussions because I had brought up literature of the slave trade and mentioned that some works were written by either Africans or Anglo Africans, which provided agency and a perspective similar to the Jewish women who rejected calls to convert. At the same time, knowing that they were, as they termed it, "culturally determined products of their time and environment," did not, however, make understanding new ways of reading any easier. In fact, students were often frustrated when analyzing literature because they wished for absolutes and definitions of quality. Their negative attitudes changed once I asked them to examine their own literary aesthetics; they concluded that literary analysis is not completely relativistic and a free-for-all and not everything we read made it into their canon, including many readings on the syllabus.

It is furthermore productive for students to question what makes good literature when some of the women who subscribed to a conversionist novel or donated to the Mission were quite prominent and sometimes writers themselves. Subscription lists provide information about how women supported one cause or another, but students do not normally know how a writer's personal politics affects her public writing. Writing under the auspices of religious authority allowed women to express their views and, as Anne K. Mellor writes, "identify themselves as the voice of Christian virtue, answerable to no moral man, scores of female evangelical preachers…had by 1780 established the social practice and literary precedent of women's speaking publicly on both religious and political issues." Evangelical women invoked the higher authority of G-d and asserted a place for themselves and their positions through the biblical models of powerful leaders like Deborah and Judith. Mellor continues that "Christian women were traditionally responsible for the inculcation of virtue in the domestic sphere and for the moral and religious instruction of young children."[5] Similarly, the Ladies Auxiliary used this same argument to appeal to the supposedly unfulfilled needs and desires of Jewish women within their religion and family. This rhetorical move legitimizes the work of the domestic sphere while it also makes the work of women directly necessary to the work of G-d, and therefore indisputable by men.

Because didactic pamphlets and literature often have clearly, even aggressively, explicit agendas, the class needed to address issues of both form and content. Some of the conversionist works, either tracts by the Ladies Society or novels such as *Emma de Lissau* by Amelia Bristow, are not what can, or perhaps should, be called "great" literature, but do deserve a space for review and attention by students. When I introduced a selection from *Emma de Lissau* most of the students were repelled by the overt, sentimentalized, and recognizably negative depiction of stereotypes of Jews. Bristow's Jews are stiff-necked, rigid, greedy, close-minded, and abusive—possessing the full repertoire of ugly characteristics. The Anglicans in the novel are the binary opposite of Catholics, the first Christians Emma meets, who are well meaning but ignorant and potentially dangerous; misunderstanding the true words of Christ may lead converts from Judaism away from salvation.[6] Because the novel distinguishes between "good" and "bad" Christians in English society, I had an opportunity to illustrate nicely the centuries-old conflict between Catholics and Anglicans and how Jews functioned as both religious and cultural trophies. I must say that when I told students that Bristow may in fact have been a convert from Judaism, they were appalled, but they eventually understood a possible reason, for her fervor was the desire to be seen as a native or to avoid being othered herself. Moreover, at my college, where a fair number of students professed to be born-again Christians, many in the class had experiences with conversion, either through their friends or family, and the zeal and excitement that can accompany it.

Because students had already read from Delariviere Manley's and Eliza Haywood's thinly disguised political fictions,[7] students could debate the value of these texts as literature as well as the authors' political agendas, as one of the goals of the course was to determine where the boundary is between literary and polemical texts. Students read texts from the turn of the nineteenth century written by religious groups, and because students rejected some of these works as propaganda and not as literature, they were happy to criticize what they considered inferior. They were especially dismissive of the First Report by the Ladies Auxiliary (which did not even seem to be a report at all), which opens with a sympathetic vision of the once-great and now fallen Hebrew empire, and professes to be a response to centuries of Jewish oppression and appeals for assistance:

> "Behold, and see if there be any sorrow like unto my sorrow, which is done unto me, wherewith the Lord hath afflicted me in the day of his fierce anger." At length the pathetic appeal awakened a correspondent sensation in the breasts of British Christians. Compassion for the scattered bleeding branches of the once flourishing olive-tree was excited in those hearts, which were sensible that to the separation of those branches from the parent stock, was to be ascribed the present fruitful and lovely appearance of that heretofore wild shoot…gathered from the groves of Anglesea.[8]

For example, while students understood that feminism was not necessarily assertive in early nineteenth-century English society—and certainly not what we would consider feminism—and therefore not a given, they did question why a woman's group did not question religious intolerance as they did racial intolerance. One student concluded that she felt that the rights of the majority group, Anglicans, needed to be promoted at the expense of a minority group, and in the case of Bristow, the Jews and Catholics, in order to promote and maintain social homogeneity. It was often difficult for students to forget that the multiculturalism that they learned about in their public school days was a recent phenomenon, and difference was not always a good, or even an American, virtue. A major obstacle for my students was getting over their intolerance of the Christians and understanding that these works were written when English fears of difference and diminished authority were beginning to grow, while England was still at the height of its imperial power. As a result of exposure to these works that both accepted and denied tolerance, students learned that homogeneity in English society in the nineteenth century was largely a designed myth. Some of the changes in England during this time created tension by challenging established social structures; new technologies, industry, and class mobility, caused anxiety among the middle classes which then generated the kinds of conservative and dogmatic responses that provided the class with interesting and troubled social commentaries to analyze.

The result of adding these texts to a British women writers course is that students experienced a different kind of resistance to literature. It is common for students to have difficulty reading unfamiliar or non-canonical literature, and that did occur with works by authors such as Behn, Haywood, Manley, and Hemans, but it was most pronounced with the conversionist tracts and novels because they were seen as being dull, prescriptive, and sneaky. However, once the class placed the texts in other contexts—the Romantic period, the beginning of the end of Empire, Millenarianism, and the rise of the Industrial Revolution—some of the underlying issues were clarified and exposed. For example, once I supplemented literature with secondary sources and other primary texts students understood why during the late eighteenth and early nineteenth centuries the English became simultaneously intolerant of and interested in Jews. They learned that an unwillingness to accept religious difference in Jews coincided with a continuing conflict between Anglicans and Catholics as well as a reevaluation of Englishness in light of a troubled empire. All of these struggles represented an English social identity crisis in the early nineteenth century, and students saw with greater clarity that themes in conversionist literature were also manifest in other, more canonical works.

A result of a disunified definition of "Englishness" is that the Jews, and particularly Jewish women, became pawns in a power struggle between skirmishing Christian groups, and to gain converts, the English replaced the familiar anti-Semitism of the eighteenth century with nineteenth-century philo-Semitism, a spurious "love" of Jews. As a result of reading and discussing these texts in light of new understanding social or literary movements, my students began to question the literature they read afterwards. The point is that once students could decode the rather pointed agendas of political texts and place them in social and historical context, then other, canonical, more "literary" texts became suspect as well (for example, the End of Empire was explored similarly when students read Olive Schreiner). Once we gave up looking at texts purely for aesthetic beauty and instead focused on literary and social value, we—and here I say "we" because this was the first time I had introduced "bad" literature in a class and I also learned what to do with it as we went along—enjoyed questioning the integrity of all kinds of writing. Ultimately, this was a messy and sometimes unpleasant section, but I believe it was a useful one. I introduced students to some of the different ideas whirling around in society during the period of literature we studied, and rather than see literature as discrete students now understood a particular cultural context more fully. I must conclude by saying that while students were challenged by reading alienating texts in conjunction with familiar texts, I gained from the experience of learning how to teach material that is difficult and often not pleasurable. I had to take my own advice and think about reading these texts and teaching this section not as something likeable, but as something useful.

Notes

1. There are numerous texts that are very helpful in theorizing and working through some of these paradoxical concerns, selections from which I peppered and supplemented throughout the semester. As far as the idea of the Oriental and the racialized Other is concerned, I used Sander Gilman, *Inscribing the Other* (Lincoln: U of Nebraska P, 1991); Edward Said, *Orientalism* (New York: Vintage, 1979); and Anita Levy, *Other Women: The Writing of Class, Race, and 1832–1898* (New York: Princeton UP, 1991). For bringing together issues of feminism, religion, and Englishness, Michael Galchinsky, *The Origin of the Modern Jewish Woman Writer: Romance and Reform in Victorian England* (Detroit: Wayne State UP, 1996) and Moira Ferguson, *Subject to Others British Women Writers and Colonial Slavery, 1670–1834* (London: Routledge, 1992) were most appropriate, with Galchinsky's book being most appropriate to the course material. Though I did not ask students to read from the following texts because the material was largely covered in the others, Michael Ragussis, *Figures of Conversion: The Jewish Question and English National Identity* (New York: Duke UP, 1995) and Frank Felsenstein, *Anti-Semitic Stereotypes: A Paradigm of Otherness in English Popular Culture, 1660–1830* (Baltimore: Johns Hopkins UP, 1999) offered specific historical and political context for the class that the theorists did not. I also had students read the introduction to Eve Sedgwick, *Between Men: English Literature and Male Homosocial Desire* (New York: Columbia UP, 1986) because her theory of male homosocialism resonated when we examined the closed society of middle-class English women and its exclusion of women who were subordinated even more than they were.
2. *First Report of the London Ladies' Auxiliary Society in Aid of the London Society for Promoting Christianity Amongst the Jews* (London: A. M'Intosh, 1814), 9.
3. *Solemn and Affectionate Address: To Jewish Females* (London: A. M'Intosh, 1823), 7–8.
4. Charlotte Montefiore, *Caleb Asher* (Philadelphia: Jewish Publication Society, 1845).
5. Anne Mellor and Richard Matlak, eds. *British Literature 1780–1830* (Fort Worth: Harcourt Brace College Publishers, 1996), 65.
6. Amelia Bristow. *Emma de Lissau* (London: T. Gardiner, 1828).
7. Delarivier Manley, *The New Atalantis* and Eliza Haywood, *The Female Spectator,* both in Sandra M. Gilbert and Susan Gubar, eds., *Norton Anthology of Literature by Women,* 2nd ed. (New York: W. W. Norton & Co., 1996).
8. *First Report*, 2.

Eighteenth- and Nineteenth-Century British Women Writers
Dr. Shapiro

Course Overview:

Societies and cultures generate different and specific codes governing cultural behavior and beliefs, and it is often difficult to separate one from another, or rather, see where one begins and one ends. In addition, certain codes apply in some circumstances and not in others. Some scholars suggest that questions of sex and gender are constructed by relationships of authority and power and further argue that to maintain that authority, it is often necessary to perpetuate fixed roles for both women and men. Women, their roles, femininity, and other related concepts have been studied in great depth recently, and now we will relate those things to literature by British women during the eighteenth and nineteenth centuries.

Additionally, issues connected to several cultural codes can converge when one is examined. The particular codes that we will look at this semester will appear very differently when approached or examined from different perspectives, and when compared or contrasted with those of men. We will also examine how cultural discourses of sex and gender are related to other codes such as race, ethnicity, and class. Many of us are familiar with feminism or feminist studies, and this course is an opportunity to see these theories and ideas in a literary but also historical context. Therefore, I hope studying this topic will make for an interesting and enlightening semester.

Course Goals:

- Gain familiarity with Eighteenth- and Nineteenth-century literature, new ways to read
- Gain familiarity with literary criticism, applied to primary sources
- Situate texts in relation to contemporaneous cultural, historical, and political discourses (i.e., writing, class, race, religion, nationhood, the French)
- Learn close reading and apply critical literary research skills
- Draft and revise quality research papers
- Engage in stimulating discussions based on readings
- Workshop with peers on drafts, give and take positive criticism
- Visit the Writing Lab for more peer editing
- Conference with instructor

Required Texts:

- Uphaus, Robert and Gretchen Foster, eds. *The Other Eighteenth Century: English Women of Letters, 1660–1800* (East Lansing: Colleagues Press, 1991).
- Course packets.

Grading:

Assignments are given a letter grade during the semester and then translated to a numerical value at the end: 90-100=A, 80-89=B, and so on, for a total of 100 possible points.

Journals	10%
Article/book review	25%
Short research essay	25%
Long research essay	40%
Total	100%

Figure 1. Rebecca Shapiro, Sample Syllabus (continued on next page)

Eighteenth- and Nineteenth-Century British Women Writers
Dr. Shapiro

Reading Schedule:

	Introduction "Literature of the Seventeenth and Eighteenth Centuries"	Behn: *Oroonoko*
Behn: *Oroonoko* (continued)	Behn: *The Rover*, Act I	*The Rover*, Acts II and III
The Rover, Acts IV and V	Astell: "Serious Proposal to the Ladies"	Manley: *The New Atalantis*; Haywood: *The Female Spectator* (selections)
Montague: "To a Lady, from Her Former Husband"; "In a Paper Called the Nonsense of Common Sense"	Montague: "Account of the Court of King George the First at His Accession"; "A Letter from the Other World"	Leapor, "An Essay on Women"
Austen: *Lady Susan* and selections from juvenilia	Austen: *Lady Susan* (continued)	Wollstonecraft: selections from letters and *Rights of Woman*
Smith, selections	Hemans, selections	More, "On Slavery"; Yearsley, "To Indifference," "Addressed to Sensibility"
Hays, from *Appeal to the Men on Great Britain on Behalf of Women*	Edgeworth: *Harrington* 1–3	*Harrington* 4–8
Harrington 9–13	*Harrington* 14–16	*Harrington* 17–end
	Spring break	
Edgeworth: Letters to Literary Ladies	Shelley: *The Last Man*	*The Last Man*, continued
E. Bronte, selections	Browning, selections	Montefiore: *Caleb Asher* 1–3
Montefiore: *Caleb Asher* 4–end	conversionist pamphlets	Eliot: "Silly Novels by Lady Novelists"
Martineau, "Prison Discipline," "Society in America"	Rossetti, "Goblin Market," additional selections	Oliphant, from "The Autobiography and Letters"; Lamb, "The Taming of the Shrew"
Levy, "A Ballad of Religion and Marriage," additional selections	Lee, "Gospels of Anarchy"	Schreiner, "Eighteen Ninety-Nine," "The Buddhist Priest's Wife"
Schreiner, continued	Catch-up	Workshops
Workshops	Workshops	Conclusion, evaluation

Figure 1. Rebecca Shapiro, Sample Syllabus

CHAPTER FIVE

Eliza Haywood: Mainstreaming Women Writers in the Undergraduate Survey

Kathryn T. Flannery

The British literature survey is a common, if problematic, feature of many undergraduate English programs. Such courses challenge us to engage students in literary historical inquiry, and that requires creating some semblance of cultural depth despite the fact that surveys by definition promise a breadth of coverage (or as one of my students put it, "breathless coverage"). When I conducted a study of teaching practices in an English department at a large, state-supported university, I was troubled to find that the apparent demand for breadth served for some as an excuse to exclude women writers from the survey. With few exceptions, women writers were still treated as luxuries we could not afford to include for fear they would displace the literacy necessities. On the other hand, to bring women writers more fully into an undergraduate course is not simply to add more disembodied names to the assigned list of authors, but to invite students to read intertextually and recursively in order to reconstruct the cultural, material conversations out of which even familiar texts emerged, and thus to consider what difference different bodies have made in literary history. Eliza Haywood is a particularly interesting case in point. Although she was widely read in her day, Haywood is still best known today for her appearance in Alexander Pope's *Dunciad*, "where she has the dubious honour of being one of the few named women authors."[1]

Pope portrays Haywood as the prize in a pissing contest: two booksellers compete by seeing who can urinate the farthest as part of the goddess Dulness's "Olympic games." Haywood appears "with cow-like udders," sitting in a circle with two offspring—who are figured as her works, her writings—on either side of her as she awaits the outcome of the contest. One of Pope's footnotes makes clear the target of his satire:

> "In this game is expos'd in the most contemptuous manner, the profligate licentiousness of those shameless Scriblers (for the most part of That sex, which ought least to be capable of such malice or impudence) who in libellous Memoirs and Novels, reveal the faults and misfortunes of both sexes, to the ruin or disturbance, of publick fame or private happiness."[2]

As figured in the pissing contest, not only did Haywood (and women writers like her) have the temerity to write licentious fiction, but her work is identified with her body, as if female writing and female body were one and the same thing. To read the text is to read the female body and to read the female body is to read the text. Indeed, early on, the novel as a genre was associated with indecorous display of the body and it was a familiar move to see book and body as both "on offer."[3]

In the traditional survey course, Pope as canonical figure might get to speak without rebuttal, and the complicated relationship between genre and gender in the history of the novel would thus be elided. But by placing Haywood together with Pope within a longer literary trajectory, class members have the opportunity to develop a more complex, culturally situated reading of both. I regularly taught the second leg of a British Literature survey course intended to "cover" the period from 1600 (excluding Shakespeare) to 1800, a course required of all English majors. I included Haywood as part of a larger unit on what I called the "Literature of Intimacy."[4] This is one of the overlapping themes in the course that serve as broad inquiry topics inviting students to put texts together to achieve thicker, richer understandings of the texts themselves, of the culture more broadly, and of historical inquiry as an interpretive strategy (see syllabus). While students report that they expect the course to be a dry tromp across 200 years of unknown territory, I wanted the course to engage the students in the issues raised by literary historical inquiry. The pedagogy is not intended simply "to get students to *acquire* a body of information," but rather "to inquire into the issues raised."[5] The course thus poses a series of problems that students work at in recursive fashion. Each text is an additional dimension, an additional perspective through which to consider the problem.

The unit on the Literature of Intimacy invites students to consider a number of interconnecting questions: how is private life conceptualized, in what sense is there a newly emerging sense of the individual (the rise of "affective individualism" in Lawrence Stone's terms) and to what extent is this individuated self, this increasingly privatized self, embodied? Or put differently, to what extent does the body stand metonymically for the private (and whose bodies are so considered)? Throughout the course, students take responsibility for a selection of secondary readings. For any given class period, everyone reads a set of primary texts, and one or two students serve as consulting experts, having read an article or chapter that pertains to the primary reading. The success of the course really is a tribute to the students' willingness to work in recursive fashion with a complex series of interconnecting primary and secondary texts and to produce understanding through writing, reading, class conversation, and readers' theatre.[6]

We begin the unit by reading a set of early seventeenth-century, anti-Petrarchan love lyrics from Shakespeare, Donne, and Jonson. We generate working explications, and then class members compose their own "post-post-Petrarchan" poems in order to compass the span between the seventeenth-century poems and the present, and in some sense so that they have a stake in the debate, so that they have tried their hand at reconstructing contemporary gender relations in poetic form. Because students expect that they will be asked in survey courses to ingest a body of knowledge delivered to them and to "say back" that knowledge in test form, even those who find the very idea of writing poetry terrifying enter into the process with surprising goodwill, and more importantly, surprising astuteness. Having come to provisional understanding of the poems, and having explored the genre from the "inside" in composing their own poems, the class then draws on the expertise of class members who read about the Petrarchan tradition and family, sex, and marriage in the period.[7] My contribution is to suggest how the poems circulated in the culture, so that we can consider who was thought to be the audience and what work the poems can be said to do in their particular social context. We then move to a set of late seventeenth-century, early eighteenth-century poems from Aphra Behn, the Earl of Rochester, and Anne Finch, and again work closely with the poems in relation to a larger cultural context.

This range of poems registers a range of constructions of gender and sexuality leading to a rich set of responses, some students choosing to pursue questions of sexual orientation (prompted in part by Behn's "To the Fair Clarinda"), or to find out more about women's access to print production (prompted in part by Finch's "The Introduction"), and others considering further notions of "affective individualism" and the status of the family (reading diaries alongside poems by Katherine Philips). Because these short responses are not one-shot efforts, but workshopped and used to further the collective understanding of assigned readings, they generally require a higher level of intellectual investment from students than they expect. One of the poems—Rochester's "The Imperfect Enjoyment"—has proven to be a particularly important reading for students, and serves as a point of reference for them when they read Pope and Haywood.[8]

The explicitness and violence of Rochester's poem is jarring. If bodies are in some sense made metaphorical, veiled in the earlier post-Petrarchan poems, they are explicitly present in Rochester's poem—or perhaps more accurately, body parts are present. Through hyperbolic language verging on the mock heroic, the poet regrets the fact that his "Dart of Love" is left an "unmoving Lump" when he attempts intercourse with the object of his desire. He brags about his prowess in the brothels but when the stakes are raised, when he is with a woman he apparently loves, he is unable to perform. The first third of the poem describes the object of his desire as an enumeration of disconnected parts—arms, legs, lips, breast, hand, and foot. All these parts, however, are reduced to the woman's sexual function in its most limited—and vulgar—sense. However, this woman—who has been reduced to an empty space to be filled by the man's desire—is at least figured as desirous too. She even has a voice—or at least she makes a "kind of murm'ring Noise" to tell him what she wants (even though he cannot deliver and even though her desires seem to be little more than a projection of his carnal needs).

What little humanity is attributed to this woman, however, disappears when the poet turns to his earlier conquests—male and female. In the latter two-thirds of the poem, the poet himself becomes nothing more than his male member and the whores become mere receptacles. The sex is violent, disembodied, and crude. In a remarkably mature conversation, class members discussed what they took to be the language of rape that characterized the latter part of the poem. I had prepared for class discussion by owning up to my own discomfort with the language of the poem, and by asking the class to respect different sensibilities, different values among class members as we worked our way through a poem that could be offensive to some if not all of us in the class. One of the men in the class took the lead by offering a set of decorous contemporary euphemisms to replace the less than decorous language in Rochester's poem. The euphemisms were both amusing (not so unlike the effect Rochester's language had on his coterie readers) and at the same time provided a kind of necessary cover for all of us to enter into the conversation. I had been worried about how students would deal with Rochester and had prefaced the reading with a discussion of my own discomfort as a reader. The move to euphemism was, as I see it, a rather courteous way for the students to deal with their—and my—discomfort. As several students said, they thought that Rochester was more explicit than anything they had read in contemporary popular culture, and they found it both shocking and surprising. They had all engaged the "canon question" in one class or another, but they had no idea how much canonization sanitized literary history. If anything, they objected more to what they saw as prior censorship than to the level of explicitness that they found in Rochester.

Class members read Rochester's poem in relation to two prose selections: the proposal for an Academy for Women from Daniel Defoe's *An Essay upon Projects*, and Mary Astell's *A Serious Proposal to the Ladies*. In a sense these texts "authorized" students to read Rochester (and later, Pope) more critically. If students fear that their critique of Rochester is "unfair" because it comes from an early twenty-first-century sensibility, they find in Defoe and to some extent Astell the seeds of that modern sensibility. Defoe argues that "God has given to all Mankind equal Gifts and Capacities, in that he has given them all Souls equally capable…the whole difference in Mankind proceeds either from Accidental Difference in the Make of their Bodies, or from the foolish Difference of Education."[9] It is therefore, according to Defoe, a barbarous custom to deny the advantages of learning to women. Coming from a rather different political and religious orientation, Mary Astell's *A Serious Proposal to the Ladies* also makes the case for women's education. Astell, the monarchist who believes in God-ordained gender hierarchies, proposes a design that will improve women's charms and heighten their value "by suffering them no longer to be cheap and contemptible." Her aim is to "fix that Beauty, and to place it out of the reach of Sickness and Old Age, by transferring it from a corruptible Body to an immortal Mind."[10] These texts, read in relation to the amorous verse, are important for students in showing that there were competing and conflicting discourses about women circulating together and that apparently similar arguments could come from rather different ends of the religio-political spectrum.

Having read a range of poems in which women—or women's body parts—function primarily as objects of male desire, and two prose pieces that suggest that women could be conceptualized—by both men and women—as whole beings, students are prepared to be critically astute readers of Pope's *Rape of the Lock* and selections from *The Dunciad*.

I had not planned it this way, but I found that having Rochester's explicit poem precede our reading of Pope's *Rape of the Lock* (with its "mock rape") made it far less likely for students to read Pope's poem as "just a joke" as students have been inclined to do in the past. Class members read in Pope's poem, for example, how the Baron admires Belinda's bright locks: "He saw, he wished, he meditates the way,/By Force to ravish, or by Fraud betray:/For when Success a Lover's Toil attends,/Few ask, if Fraud or Force attained his ends."[11] The space between these lines and Rochester's thus appears rather narrow—and we had to contend with the violence that can be achieved through humor and decorousness. I should say that I am neither interested in setting up Pope's texts simply to have students dismiss them as misogynist,[12] nor am I interested in erasing the appeal of wit. These are not treatises after all, but works of satire. However, just as students can manage to understand—and respond with sympathy to—Rochester's self-lacerating humor at the same time they register the sexual violence of his poem, so too the course is designed to invite students to work with Pope's *Rape of the Lock* on multiple levels. They can see that his critique of vanity, for example, is not so far removed from Mary Astell's position when Pope expounds "How vain are all these Glories…/Unless good Sense preserve what Beauty gains;/That Men may say…Behold the first in Virtue, as in Face!"[13] At the same time, class members have a greater vantage from which to understand how the culture sets up the conditions for such vanity—in Defoe's terms through the barbarity of withholding education from women.

Students also begin to see the ways in which notions of poetic decorum were entangled with notions of personal conduct. As April London has argued, "Political satire, as a highly serious art, demands the decorum of a public persona to foster the illusion of objectivity." In these terms, Haywood's writing is indecorous because it requires a personal response of "vicarious sexuality." Pope sees Haywood's writing, as London argues, as public text that is a "reflection of private lubricity."[14] In reading *The Rape of the Lock* and the selections from *The Dunciad*, students thus find a tangle of motives, no one motive canceling out the others. They take seriously Pope's concern for decorum, perhaps in part because they had wrestled with what they took as Rochester's indecorous language. At the same time, they find disturbing how much Pope seemed to "get away with" under the cover of decorum, under the cover of the generic expectations of "mock heroic."

Class members thus come to Haywood's writing—*Fantomina: Or, Love in a Maze* (1724) published some four years before the first version of *The Dunciad*—with a complex set of expectations.[15] In the survey course, it is difficult to make room for extensive consideration of the novel as a genre, and if one were looking for a representative sample, one might think first of one of the more familiar male writers such as Defoe, Richardson, or Fielding. However, Eliza Haywood played a pivotal role in the development of a specifically English novel,[16] and *Fantomina* as a brief novel can provide the occasion for students to learn not only about the development of the genre—the "rise of the novel"—but also how genre considerations figure in larger cultural debates. In particular, class members can explore the extent to which genre is not only a formal or aesthetic category but a site for ideological negotiations.

Haywood's novels of the 1720s "mark the beginnings of the autonomous [native English] tradition in romantic fiction primarily addressed to and authored by women."[17] Haywood was remarkably prolific. She produced some sixty-seven novels, romances, and secret histories; she attempted to write—though less successfully—for the stage; and she created an essay-periodical, *The Female Spectator*, the first of its kind written for women by a woman.[18] Having left her husband sometime in the early part of the century, Haywood was successful enough as a writer to support herself and her children until her death in 1756. Her remarkable popularity combined with her financial independence thus made her a ready target for Pope's critique. Not only was she supported by Grub Street enemies of Pope, but the "matter" of her novels quite clearly threatened Pope's aesthetic and cultural principles. Put simply, for Pope, Haywood embodied Dulness.

Having read Pope's attack on Haywood, the class as a whole poses questions that they want to answer through their reading of Haywood's novel, questions that take Rochester's poem as a comparison point. Given Pope's scatological criticism of Haywood, in what sense would Haywood's writing compare in licentiousness to Rochester? Was she held to a separate standard of decorousness? If so, was this separate standard entirely a matter of gender—that is, was it considered unnatural for her to write in such a way? Alternatively, might it be that gender is here compounded by the public nature of the discourse? If Rochester's poems circulated within a much more restricted circle—he authorized the publication of few of his works—and thus kept more private the private body—does that somehow excuse his language? Conversely, the much wider circulation—indeed the remarkable popularity of Haywood's novel—might have accentuated the indecorousness of her story. To what extent is Pope free from the taint of commercialism of which he was so critical? The students' responses to Haywood's novel have in many ways paralleled Catherine Ingrassia's conclusion that Haywood provided her audience with "a reading experience that was at once instructive and erotic, normative and transgressive, realistic and escapist."[19] They begin to understand why Haywood was so threatening, and at the same time, why she was commercially successful.

Haywood labels *Fantomina* a "Masquerade Novel." Not only is the novel about disguise (a theme the class returns to at the end of the unit with readers' theatre performances of Restoration/eighteenth-century drama), specifically about the heroine, a "young lady of distinguished Birth, Beauty, Wit, and Spirit" who takes on a series of disguises in order to first win and subsequently retain the interest of the "accomplished Beauplaisir," it also plays with the disguises of fiction itself. Just as Beauplaisir is deceived by the multiple disguises, so too are we as readers caught in the deceptions of a "fictitious Tale."[20] The reader never learns the heroine's "real" name. Instead she takes on a number of pseudonyms—Fantomina, Celia, Incognita—and through her various disguises she believes that she has been able to "triumph over her Lover's Inconstancy." Even though he is sleeping with literally the same physical body, Beauplaisir never seems to recognize this fact. While the heroine takes his blindness as triumph, the reader can see that Beauplaisir cannot be said to love the heroine for "herself," but loves at best a variety of masks. While early twenty-first-century readers might be inclined to celebrate the self as always already a variety of masks, the novel refuses such a postmodern reading. In the end, biology triumphs. Behind the mask there is a female body. The heroine becomes pregnant, and when forced to reveal the father of her child, she finds that Beauplaisir refuses to recognize her. Indeed, he cannot recognize her because he has only known a series of disguises even as he has enjoyed the pleasures of the "same" body.

Students find that the language of the novel is never as explicit as Rochester's and is at times more indirect (one might say more decorous) than

Pope's *Rape of the Lock*. The heroine does not set out to have a sexual relationship with Beauplaisir, but once "Undone," she makes clear the pleasure she takes in the "luxurious Gratification of wild desires." We are never given any details about either the gratification or the wild desires.[21] However, we are given the sense of pleasure, the sense of triumph, and at times a bit of deadpan wit. At one point, for example, the narrator comments on the peculiarity of Beauplaisir's failure to recognize the woman behind the mask, given his apparent familiarity with the "same" body: "It may seem strange that Beauplaisir should in such near Intimacies continue still deceived: I know there are Men who will swear it is an Impossibility." She attributes the heroine's success to her admirable skill in the "Art of feigning."[22] We are left then to our imaginations to think about what parts of the body are masked and what parts are unmasked.

For some students, *Fantomina* is a tale of a woman's triumph over the inconstant male lover on the order of "turn about is fair play." Having read quite a bit about women's presumed inconstancy in earlier poems, some students find a certain justice in Haywood's novel. However, such a reading does not seem to take adequate account of the ending, as other class members point out. What sort of triumph is this when the "afflicted Lady" finds it impossible to conceal from her mother the fact that she is "with Child"? While she has the means to screen this knowledge from the rest of the world, "all her Invention was at a Loss for a Strategem to impose on a Woman of her [mother's] Penetration."[23] When the undone Lady confesses to what lengths she has gone to continue her dalliance with Beauplaisir, acknowledging that he is the "innocent Cause of [her] undoing," the mother assigns all blame to her daughter. To prevent the "Renewing of the Crime," the mother sends her daughter to a monastery (not a nunnery, oddly enough) in France. Such an ending might signal a morality tale. Instead of "turn about is fair play," we have the just punishment of immorality, but the novel resists this reading as well.

There is no sign that the Lady has learned a lesson. She experiences shame, but this feeling seems as likely to be caused by the "crime" of having been discovered as any reformation of morals. In addition, the tale does not conclude with the Rake Reformed. Rather Beauplaisir, who offers to take charge of the newborn daughter (and is refused), is left "full of Cogitations, more confused than ever he had known in his whole Life." Indeed the novel ends without "proper" resolution, registering in the last line the voyeuristic pleasure to be found in such a tale of sexual "Intrigue, which, considering the Time it lasted, was as full of Variety as any, perhaps, that many Ages has produced."[24] The reader is not offered some tidy lesson about how one should avoid the fate of the undone Lady. Rather, the reader is given at least three alternatives. We may be positioned with Beauplaisir, "full of cogitations" and confused, or we may be positioned with the mother, a person of "Penetration" but without much sympathy and more concerned about "the Injury...done...[to] Family" than about her daughter's (or the infant's) health and well-being. Another possible position is with the authorial voice at the end, seemingly titillated by this fictitious Tale full of Variety and Intrigue. My interest is not in settling the matter for the class. However disconcerting a text *Fantomina* appears to the students, refusing as it does any reading that reduces it to a stable or familiar generic pattern, students nonetheless find something more than titillation in this story about a young lady with a "Turn of Wit." If women's bodies had been made to serve as signs—the body itself as a kind of signifying text as in earlier works they had read—then Fantomina could be read as writing her own body, as claiming a kind of authorship. She cannot claim absolute control of this signifier—as the ending makes clear—but she can write the text of her body at least for a time. Such at least provisional control of the signifying body can be contrasted with Pope's manipulative use of woman to signal weakness of mind, triviality, and vanity.

If part of Pope's concern in *The Dunciad* is the extent to which novel reading displaces the "higher art" of poetry with a more equivocal art, an art whose "Truth" is difficult to come by, packed into that concern is his fear that the culture at large is weakened through the influence of the feminine. The very qualities that society traditionally assigns to women, when they exceed their proper bounds, threaten cultural foundations. As Catharine Ingrassia asserts, "these feminine characteristics, when kept in the proper context, can be controlled and even admired by men...Yet, these same tendencies, practiced by Dulness, become ominous signs of destruction in this world turned upside down."[25] Belinda's foibles in *Rape of the Lock* are treated with comparative gentleness, but Haywood exceeds the bounds of gender decorum and becomes the focus of more acid satire in the *Dunciad*. *Fantomina* puts on display—without sufficiently certain moralizing check—the very feminine inconstancy that characterizes Dulness. The heroine of the novel exhibits qualities, in Ingrassia's terms, which are precisely those most culturally destabilizing: a woman's desire for "pleasure" and "sway": "Sway suggests a type of subtle persuasion or influence, the kind of disguised force women, denied access to public tools of power, must use to achieve any sort of personal power."[26] Sway allows one to divert another person away from a proper conduct. The danger in a novel such as *Fantomina* is that it makes clear how ready Beauplaisir is to be swayed to satisfy his own and inadvertently his lover's pleasure, and it is pleasure for pleasure's sake, without regard for anything else. That such a novel would be popular suggests how easily the reading public could be swayed, diverted from what Pope would see as a more serious course, of the sort to be found ideally in poetry.

In the close of the unit on the Literature of Intimacy, the unsettled, variable gendered relationships between power and pleasure are explored further through reading and performing Restoration/Eighteenth-century comedy. Through readers' theatre, students have an opportunity to consolidate what they have learned thus far about the ways literary texts participate in the cultural process by which private life—and the privatized self—has been conceptualized and contained through gendering. As I have argued elsewhere, because performance necessarily involves the entire body, drama brings the figuration of the gendered body quite literally to the fore (see Flannery). In emphasizing the simultaneity of collective bodies in time and space, performance, even in the relatively low-key form of readers' theatre, also reinforces what I take to be the central intellectual orientation that has developed through the unit: the ability on the part of students to recognize the multiple and competing motives that drive any textual performance.

In groups of five or six, class members are responsible for developing a scene from one of six plays: Wycherley's *The Country Wife* (1672), Behn's *The City Heiress* (1682), Congreve's *Way of the World* (1700), Farquahar's *The Beaux Strategem* (1706), Gay's *The Beggar's Opera* (1728), and Goldsmith's *She Stoops to Conquer* (1773). Each group chooses a key portion of their play to perform, approximately twenty minutes' worth, and each plans how to stage the scene in order to engage the class as whole in further consideration of the gender dynamics they have thus far been studying. Each group researches the play in order to compose an informational handout for the rest of the class that includes a synopsis and performance history of the play, and background on the playwright. The performances of the scenes provide a powerful opportunity to interpret the plays through the complex historical frame the students have been constructing throughout the unit. The performances evidence historically grounded understanding in a variety of inventive, astute, and witty ways, from composing an alternative and remarkably authentic-sounding prologue that allowed one group to comment on the cultural role of masking; to creating a choral presence not provided by the play-as-written in order to offer historical commentary on the action (background on marriage contracts for the famous proviso scene in *Way of the World*, for example). Another variation was to play a scene first as a period piece and then as a contemporary production. In all cases, the actors have to bring to bear a critical understanding of the gender dynamics, including a sense of the body as itself operating as an already read signifier in time and space, even when or perhaps especially when students, not as a matter of design but as a matter of the happenstance of groupings, often have to play a part in drag.

In their post-performance discussions and written reflections, most students demonstrate a level of sophistication that I attribute to the recursive structure of the unit. They have to draw explicitly from their earlier readings, comparing texts, noting especially shifts in the range of behaviors constructed for male and female characters from the earliest play (Wycherly's) to the last play (Goldsmith's). In the shifting of gender options, they generally do not find "progress," in either a moralistic or a feminist sense, but something more like the ambiguity of possibility and constraint evident in Haywood's novel. It might seem preferable—given the time constraints of the survey—to economize by lecturing students about, for example, Pope's fear of cultural feminization (to borrow Catherine Ingrassia's useful phrase) rather than have them actually read Haywood. Alternatively, the better option might seem preferable to teach women writers as if they constituted a separate literary history. However, I have found undergraduates rather too accustomed to being *told* about misogyny or having writers preread for them as protofeminists, and thus anticipating that they are expected to regurgitate a "party line" or to reject the interpretation as feminist prejudice. For undergraduates to understand what is at stake in Pope's attack on Haywood, in complex literary and cultural terms, and to have some sense of Haywood's popularity—to understand why she could be perceived as such a threat to generate such a vulgar response—they need to have other than a lecture on Pope's psychosocial difficulties with women or an introduction to women writers as operating a separate cultural sphere. By reconstructing something like the cultural conversation out of which the attack emerges—a conversation that has to do with genre conventions, shifts in systems of patronage and the literary marketplace, as well as issues of literacy and access to the means of literate production—students are surprised and often disturbed to find gender figuring in matters where they least expected it. Their writing and their conversation become more nuanced because they come to find out that no single critical category can explain—or explain away—a textual performance. In this course, I do not hear in class discussion or read in student papers either feminist backlash or pat critiques of patriarchy or female victimhood. Even on the basis of a necessarily limited reading—limited by the very constraints of the survey—students find that neither Pope nor Haywood can be easily slotted into a single category. Such understandings of the instability of cultural constructions of gender are generalizable, I would argue, beyond the immediate case of Haywood and Pope and can enrich subsequent readings in this and other courses.

Notes

1. Ros Ballaster, *Seductive Forms: Women's Amatory Fiction from 1684 to 1740* (Oxford: Clarendon, 1992), 160.
2. Alexander Pope, *The Dunciad*, in *The Poetical Works*, ed. H.F. Cary (London: Routledge, 1850), 123–200. As Ballaster explains, it is "not so much the use of personalized satire itself to which [Pope] objects, since, after all, this is the dominant mode of his own poem, but rather the 'unnatural' use of it by women" (161). Pope's immediate complaint against Haywood has frequently been taken to be her satiric portrait of one of Pope's friends—in some versions, his neighbor, Lady Henrietta Howard; in other versions, Martha Blount—represented in scandalous terms. However, as Ballaster reads it, Pope's larger concern has to do with Haywood's shameful display of her works. Not only did Haywood write licentious fiction, but she published under her own name and included a portrait of herself as part of the introductory apparatus. In a sense Haywood "invites" the conjoining of author's body and author's work: as figured in *The Dunciad* Haywood exposes her cow-like udders to public view and sells her self to the highest bidder.
3. Catherine Gallagher has traced this equation in *Nobody's Story: The Vanishing Acts of Women Writers in the Marketplace, 1670–1820* (Berkeley: U of California P, 1994). See for example her discussion of Aphra Behn whose "sexual and poetic parts" were treated as the same, as both "contaminated by…sexual distemper" (26).
4. See also Madeleine Foisil, "The Literature of Intimacy," in *A History of Private Life*, ed. Roger Chartier (Cambridge: Belknap, 1989), 327–361.
5. Barry Kroll, *Teaching Hearts and Minds* (Carbondale: Southern Illinois University Press, 1992), 10–11.
6. See my "Performance and the Limits of Writing," *JTW* 16.1 (1998): 1–31.
7. Class members read about the Petrarchan tradition in William Kerrigan and Gordon Braden. "Milton's Coy Eve: Paradise Lost and Renaissance Love Poetry," *ELH* 53 (1986): 27–52. Others read about family, sex, and marriage in Lawrence Stone, *The Family, Sex and Marriage in England, 1500–1800* (New York: Harper, 1979).
8. John Wilmot, Earl of Rochester, "The Imperfect Enjoyment," *British Literature: 1640–1789*, ed. Robert Demaria (Cambridge: Blackwell, 1996), 462–64.
9. Daniel Defoe, "An Academy for Women," in Demaria, 496.
10. Mary Astell, "A Serious Proposal to the Ladies," in Demaria, 574.
11. Alexander Pope, *The Rape of the Lock*, in Demaria, 708, ll. 29–34.
12. See also Catherine Ingrassia, "Women Writing/Writing Women: Pope, Dulness, and 'Feminization' in the Dunciad," *Eighteenth-Century Life* 14 (1990): 55.
13. Pope, *Rape of the Lock*, 719, ll. 15–18.
14. April London, "Placing the Female: The Metonymic Garden in Amatory and Pious Narrative, 1700–1740," *Fetter'd or Free? British Women Novelists, 1670–1815*, eds. Mary Anne Schofield and Cecilia Macheski (Athens: Ohio UP, 1986): 121–22 n. 4.
15. Eliza Haywood, *Fantomina: or, Love in a Maze* in Demaria, 786–803.
16. See also Ingrassia.
17. Ballaster, 158; see also Ingrassia, 51.
18. Eliza Haywood, *The Female Spectator*. Vol. 1. (London: Gardner, 1771). See also Mary Anne Schofield, *Eliza Haywood*, (Boston: Twayne, 1985); Kathryn Shevelow, *Women and Print Culture: The Construction of Femininity in the Early Periodical* (New York: Routledge, 1989).
19. Ingrassia, 52.
20. Haywood, *Fantomina*, 802.

21 Janet Todd notes that "a kind of dream of equal sexuality" was made possible when writers such as Delarivier Manley, Aphra Behn and Haywood concentrated "not on the sexual act itself, but on its prelude and setting." Referring specifically to Manley, Todd notes that in her writing "there are details of the heat, flowers and gardens, opened windows...the atmospheric details emphasiz[ing] the inevitability and naturalness of sexual expression for male and female alike." *The Sign of Angellica: Women, Writing and Fiction, 1660–1800* (New York: Columbia UP, 1989), 89. Similarly, in *Fantomina*, Haywood concentrates on what leads to each sexual encounter, on the costuming, and the verbal repartee, rather than on the sexual act itself.
22 Haywood, *Fantomina*, 795.
23 Haywood, *Fantomina*, 801.
24 Haywood, *Fantomina*, 803.
25 Ingrassia, 45.
26 Ingrassia, 48.

British Literature, 1600–1800
Dr. Flannery

Literary works and aesthetic products...are always inscribed within the field of possibilities that make them thinkable, communicable, and comprehensible. (Chartier 20)

The work of art is the product of a negotiation between a creator or a class of creators and the institutions and practices of society. (Greenblatt 12)

Literary history is concerned with reconstructing how literature was made and how it was understood, enjoyed and used by readers. To begin the work of reconstruction requires not only that we read the literature, but that we consider under what circumstances it was produced, through what systems of thought and practice it was made readable, what readers did with the literature, and finally how the literature was itself taken up into the process of literary creation by later writers. Such questions are important for understanding another time and place allowing us to gain access to writings that range from the grand to the homely, from the devout to the bawdy, from the serious to the silly (and sometimes a mixture of elements we may find surprising). The greater access we have as readers to this rich body of work the more able we are to consider what such literature has to do with us, in what sense we continue to be shaped by the culture that produced and was produced by such writing.

One challenge we face in attempting to understand 200 years of literary history is the sheer volume of material. For much of this period from 1600–1800, "literature" had not yet narrowed to mean "imaginative writing" or "belletristic writing." It was not, in other words, confined to fiction, drama and poetry. Rather, literature included everything literate people wrote—history, prose essays, religious writings, diaries, as well as drama, poetry and the newly emerging novel. We won't even attempt to "survey" the whole realm of literature! Rather, we will consider a variety of texts through the frame of 3 interlocking themes: The Sense of Place, The Literature of Intimacy, and Religious Expression. These themes are rich enough to give us a sense of cultural constraints and possibilities that made writing in this period "thinkable, communicable, and comprehensible" (Chartier 20).

Works Cited

Chartier, Roger. *On the Edge of the Cliff: History, Language, and Practices*, trans. Lydia G. Cochrane. Baltimore: Johns Hopkins UP, 1997.

Greenblatt, Stephen. "Towards a Poetics of Culture." *The New Historicism*, ed. Aram Veeser, 1–14. New York: Routledge, 1989.

Required Texts
- DeMaria, Robert, ed. *British Literature 1640–1789: An Anthology*
- Wycherley, William. *The Country Wife* (on reserve)
- Behn, Aphra. *The City Heiress, or Sir Timothy Treat All in Works* (on reserve)
- Congreve, William. *The Way of the World* (on reserve)
- Farquhar, George. *The Beaux' Stratagem* (on reserve)
- Gay, John. *The Beggar's Opera* (on reserve)
- Goldsmith, Oliver. *She Stoops to Conquer* (on reserve)

Figure 1. Kathryn T. Flannery, Sample Syllabus (continued on next page)

British Literature, 1600–1800
Dr. Flannery
Reading Schedule:
Week One: A Sense of Place: This Garden England Bacon "Of Gardens"; Milton from *Paradise Lost*, Bk IV lines 131–159; Bk IV lines 205–263; Marvell "The Garden," "The Mower Against Gardens"
Week Two: A Sense of Place Jonson "To Penshurst"; Marvell from "Upon Appleton House"; Pope, from *The Guardian;* Gray "An Elegy Wrote in a Country Churchyard"; Goldsmith "The Deserted Village"; Crabbe "The Village"
Week Three: Literature of Intimacy Shakespeare Sonnet 130; Donne "The Good-Morrow," "Woman's Constancy," "The Indifferent," "Air and Angels," "The Bait," "The Relique"; Jonson "In the Person of Womankind"; Philips "Friendship's Mystery"; Behn "To the Fair Clarinda"; Rochester "The Imperfect Enjoyment"
Week Four: Literature of Intimacy Defoe *Academy for Women*; Astell *Serious Proposal to the Ladies*; Collier "To the Patroness" and "To the Wife"; Leapor "Essay on Woman"; Pope "The Rape of the Lock"
Week Five: Literature of Intimacy Continue with Pope; Finch "The Answer"; Selections for Pope's *Dunciad*
Week Six: Literature of Intimacy Haywood *Fantomina*
Weeks Seven and Eight: Readers' Theatre presentations
Week Nine: Religious Expression Donne Holy Sonnets I, V, IX, XIV, "Good Friday, 1613. Riding Westward"
Week Ten: Religious Expression Herbert, *Preface*, "The Altar," "Easter Wings," "Affliction," "Jordan," "Denial," "Man," "Jordan (II)," "The Collar," "The Pulley," "Love"
Week Eleven: Religious Expression Milton *Paradise Lost*
Week Twelve: Other Gardens/Outside the Garden Wall Shakespeare *The Tempest*
Week Thirteen: Other Gardens Marvell "Bermudas"; Behn, *Oroonoko*
Week Fourteen: Other Gardens Locke "Of Slavery"; Cowper "The Negro's Complaint"; More "The Slave Trade"; Equiano "Interesting Narrative"

Figure 1. Kathryn T. Flannery, Sample Syllabus

CHAPTER SIX

The Poetry of Friendship: Connecting the Histories of Women and Lesbian Sexuality in the Undergraduate Classroom

Rick Incorvati

Martha Vicinus spoke for a whole critical tradition when she asserted that "lesbian history should not be a marginal preoccupation of lesbians; rather it is pivotal to our understanding of women."[1] To be sure, the work done on romantic friendships—those intimate and ardent attachments between women that crop up with some frequency in eighteenth-century writing—has reinforced this notion that a history of women cannot be written exclusive of a history of sexuality.[2] The remarkable sea change over the years in the acceptable degree of amorousness in same-sex relationships has shown us that when we cordon off matters of same-sex desire from broader questions of gender identity, we miss important parts of the full picture. We also, I think, restrict the vitality of that picture, for when we do refashion our understanding of women so that it accommodates forms of same-sex desire, we put ourselves in a better position to challenge reified notions of gender, to think in more complex terms about gender identity, and to see more vividly its social contingency. Such an outcome certainly suits much important feminist criticism, which has taught us to be wary of long-held heteronormative notions of gender. However, quite aside from gender politics, I find a more immediate advantage when this vitality can be encouraged in the classroom: In unsettling such received notions of gender and sexuality, we encourage our students to approach these topics in terms that are more nuanced, complex, and challenging, and consequently we help them become more sophisticated critical thinkers in matters that are fundamental to their culture and to their own identities.

However, tell the average undergraduate that the history of women shares a pedigree with the lesbian past and you are inviting something akin to a revolt. Undergraduates, as I often need to remind myself, are not at a very far remove from the social world of high school, a world in which homosexuality supplies a wealth of useful slanders and which offers little opportunity for considering sexuality as an ethical issue involving the quality of life of real people. Far from offering such opportunities, in fact, the high school context more likely threatens social consequences for attempts at considering the topic with any degree of earnestness. So it is not terribly surprising that the topic of homosexuality—in particular the prospect of it having some bearing on broader matters of normative behavior—should elicit resistance, and that this resistance, in turn, should complicate the way the issue can be handled in a college classroom, particularly one centered around student discussion. The instructor who does decide to suggest an affiliation between women and lesbianism in an undergraduate course confronts a pedagogical dilemma: He or she must either devise a way of appropriating that all-too-predictable resistance for instructional ends or make plans to ease the notion of lesbian sexuality somewhat inconspicuously into the class.

I have tried both approaches. As a way of co-opting the revolt in an introductory fiction course, I have used Adrienne Rich's formulation of a lesbian continuum, the notion that women-centered activity and emotional bonds can be productively affiliated with a lesbian community. Once this prospect triggered an eruption, one bordering on disgust among some members of the class, I have used this reaction to illustrate that other key concept of Rich's, compulsory heterosexuality. Students did recognize, upon only brief reflection, how their responses (including the less egregious qualifications like "I'm not a lesbian, but...") effectively conveyed the message to any homosexual or potentially homosexual classmates that they will win only disdain by openly avowing such an orientation. This approach can be productive, but not without occasioning some troubling hazards and consequences. For one, some students need to be treated gingerly so that they do not feel too victimized or trapped when their own behavior is called into question; to be sure, homophobia itself may not warrant gentle handling, but at the same time there is a danger of rendering students defensive and consequently unable to examine their own thinking productively. At another level, it is also worth noting that this approach introduces notions of sexuality into the classroom in a way that fails to challenge the assumption of a radical difference separating hetero- and homosexualities. To the contrary, this method depends on eliciting a general disdain for heterosexuality's other—perhaps even reinforcing that disdain—in the process of pointing to the ideological or compulsory functions that rely on such sharp distinctions. In other words, students do learn to identify compulsory heterosexuality by catching it in the act, but they do not come to see lesbian identity as being in any way less alien, in spite of all that talk about a continuum.

So I have come to think that tempering the resistance is the pedagogically better way. What I propose in this chapter is a strategy I designed for an undergraduate survey of poetry in which eighteenth-century verse on women's friendships became the means of introducing sexuality into the classroom indirectly; through this poetry, students considered the less charged category of friendship and in the process discovered features that seemed to them patently homosexual. By framing the discussion of these features within the idea of friendship, this approach both rendered the prospect of primary affections between two women less stigmatized and demonstrated the relevance of such affections to an understanding of women's history in general.

The organizing idea and the instructional emphasis of such a session, then, is on defining the features of friendship, rather than making any claims about the dynamics of sexuality. Accordingly, when I selected the readings for this class, I looked not to the most passionate or erotic verse, but rather to the poems that, taken together, would represent something of the range of possibilities that could fall under the rubric of friendship.[3] The aim was to inspire curiosity about such relationships by hinting at the diversity of possibilities that could fall within that category in eighteenth-century verse. By assembling a group of poems that treat friendship between women in a variety of different ways, within different contexts, to different ends, in contrasting terms, and with different conventions, students readily take up the broader questions of the cultural historians: Just exactly what types of relationships qualified as friendship? What appears to be the function of friendship? What is friendship now? What happened to it? Why did it change? What aspects of these friendships seem culturally specific? To elicit questions such as these, I gave the students a fairly short reading assignment of four or five poems, each of which described or embodied friendship between women, and I asked them as part of their homework to jot down a few sentences for each poem, characterizing the attributes of friendship as they saw it expressed in that verse. Such responses can be wide-ranging—reflecting the diversity of the poems themselves—but even when the poems assigned were not the most passionate ones, students perceived many of the expressions of affections as, at the very least, peculiar and were often tempted, for want of different terminology, to categorize such moments as lesbian in nature. Moments like Mary Savage's profession (in "Letter to Miss E. B. at Bath") that she loves her friend "with all my heart" and writes to "prove/I still am yours,"[4] or Anna Seward's confession to the absent Honora Sneyd that "I could not learn my struggling heart to tear/From thy loved form, that through my memory strays,"[5] or Ardelia's pronouncement in Anne Finch's dialogue "Friendship between Ephelia and Ardelia" that friendship "*'tis to love, as I love you*" (original emphasis),[6] all these moments strike students as somewhat too heated and as marking a cultural difference in matters of friendship.[7]

Actually, such moments probably do not seem that peculiar to most long-time readers of seventeenth- and eighteenth-century texts. Many of us have grown accustomed to contextualizing such expressions as being conventional for their time and as having, in the intervening centuries, fallen out of literary fashion and favor. In fact, much recommends the notion that this language is to some extent conventional; after all, it is often the more public expressions of affection that tune the strings of emotive language to their highest pitches while those poems originally intended as private correspondence (and presumably less self-consciously "literary" in their approaches) often seem tempered by comparison. Nonetheless, whenever we invoke the category of convention, it behooves us to be aware of a couple of interpretive pitfalls. First, when we designate some feature as a convention, we risk implying that the peculiarities that confront us in a text verge on being meaningless, that they found their way on the page out of some manner of almost mindless repetition. We should be particularly wary of this tendency when we approach newly recovered texts by women, texts that frequently confront us with oddities that at once demand and elude explanation. To avoid rendering such works less rich and complex than they might otherwise be, we need periodically to remind ourselves and our students that the interpretive work does not end when we decide to label peculiar turns of phrase "conventional." Expressions become conventional because they do communicate, and they do so, we may assume, in ways that are not entirely arbitrary. Consequently, our task becomes one of understanding more fully the semiotic force of the conventions we identify. Along these lines, we should also be cautioned against assuming that conventional expressions are necessarily devoid of any denotative significance. One of my students aptly characterized this point by noting that a Hallmark card might be rife with conventional expressions, but it may nonetheless be used to express sincere affection. So if we decide that Ardelia's earlier quoted definition of friendship—"*'tis to love, as I love you*"—constitutes an instance of poetic convention, we still need to struggle with the question of what Anne Finch signified in having her speaker invoke such a convention. The answers to such questions do not come easily, but raising them certainly makes the poetry of women's friendship more dynamic and interesting.

Being cautious of what we designate as conventional and being aware of the way such a designation can impede our interpretive practices is of particular importance when reading and teaching the poetry of female friendship. In this instance, we risk not only foreclosing possible nuances of meaning that could enrich our appreciation of a poem, but we also may wind up effacing significant markers of cultural difference in the process. Such an effacement has the unfortunate consequence of reinforcing current norms by making contemporary standards appear perennial, even transcendental. When we explain any ardent expression between two women as strictly conventional without inviting further scrutiny of such conventions (as I recall one or two of my own undergraduate professors doing), we add force to contemporary forms of heteronormativity by making the past a mirror image of our own cultural moment.[8] The approach that I am proposing here aims to impede this practice by treating more openly the question of what such expressions of same-sex affection might mean and by placing an evocative context around the student's impulse to account for such expressions in terms of the present-day language of sexual identity. Students are typically poised to raise questions of same-sex sexuality in discussion of this poetry; in fact, it is usually in response to students questioning the import of loving expressions between women that the "conventional" explanation gets aired. From a purely practical standpoint, a summary reference to convention can certainly be a useful response that allows the instructor to deal quickly with a complicated issue, one that, if gone into, could potentially derail the planned lecture or discussion for that day. However, if we make friendship and sexuality the focus of discussion and invite students to define for themselves the features of friendship in poetry between women, we encourage them to follow their curiosity in a way that potentially demonstrates the importance of lesbian sexuality to the history of women in general. I will briefly describe three poems suited to such an exercise about the varieties of interaction and levels of intimacy that could be denoted by the term friendship: Constantina Grierson's "To Miss Laetitia Van Lewen" (1723), Anne Finch's "Friendship between Ephelia and Ardelia" (1713), and Hester Mulso's "To Stella" (wr. 1751, pub. 1775).[9]

Grierson's charming verse is an epistle between two young girls; Grierson is eighteen when she writes the poem to the fifteen-year-old Laetitia (later Laetitia Pilkington, the memoirist). The poem responds to a letter from the vacationing Laetitia who presumably had written glowingly of her diversions and the "belles and beaux" that constitute her company in her new setting.[10] Grierson, eager for the return of her young companion, playfully reinterprets the letter, assuring Laetitia that she is actually bored with her insufferable company. Grierson suggests that Laetitia has merely adorned these young men with the creations of her own "romantic brain" and that in reality she can only be dissatisfied with such pretentious and vacuous young upstarts.[11] Taking her poetic reimagining of Laetitia's diversions a step further, Grierson conjures an ostensibly more accurate response for her friend to have for such company, a response of which she seems to be unaccountably unaware: "Methinks I see displeasure in your eyes."[12] The imagining of Laetitia's absent face serves two purposes in the poem: It serves to highlight Grierson's comic, self-aware jealousy, and it also represents the speaker as indulging in the imagined visage of a her friend, a friend whose absence has left the speaker yearning. The second reading becomes more evident at the poem's close which openly expresses the motive behind the poet's revision of Laetitia's account: "O haste to town! And bless the longing eyes/Of your Constantina."[13]

The friendship represented by the poem partakes of a familiar teasing, and the pose of jealousy lends the poem its lighthearted quality. However, the more direct expressions of affection with which the verse is threaded (commands like "O my Laetitia, stay no longer there," references to "all thy blooming charms," and the calls to "bless [Grierson's] longing eyes" don't entirely participate in the comic posturing[14]; rather, they express the sincere affections that render the jealous expressions charming but not laughable. Those affections find expression that not only pay tribute to Laetitia's physical beauty, but also to the sense of yearning that her absence has inspired in the young poet, emerging in the interjected "O"s that accompany the calls for Laetitia's return and the "longing eyes" that await her.

While Grierson gestures softly toward the language of love poetry to express the affections of a young girl, Anne Finch's "Friendship between Ephelia and Ardelia" indulges in romantic love conventions freely and emphatically. The poem takes the form of a dialogue in which the lighthearted and passionate qualities which Grierson's poem navigates get partitioned. Ephelia (whose name suggests lightness or ephemera) typically teases the extravagantly ardent Ardelia (Finch's own pen name) whose expressions of passion within friendship come off sincere yet unsupportable. The poem begins with Ephelia's inquiry about what constitutes friendship. To Ardelia's response that friendship "is to love as I love you," Ephelia offers a mischievously dismissive retort: "This account, so short (though kind)/Suits not my inquiring mind."[15] This, along with the mock haughtiness of her subsequent command "Therefore further now repeat," sets up the power differential that marks the dialogue.[16] Rather than relying on terms of camaraderie or mutuality, the women's friendship both defined by and enacted within this poem imbibes self-consciously from a tradition of love poetry. Ephelia's demands for further elaboration lead Ardelia to offer a litany of self-sacrifices that would be endured for the sake of a friend, concluding that "'Tis to die upon a grave,/If a friend therein do lie."[17] Ephelia seems to draw attention to the extravagance of such a response (it is "more than e'er was done/Underneath the rolling sun") and mockingly challenges that such protestations—like their own positions within this dialogue, we might add—owes much to literary convention.[18] Ardelia can only respond, in the apparent sincerity that marks all of her statements, that "Words indeed no more can show:/*But tis to love, as I love you*" (original emphasis).[19]

The very explicit mix of teasing and sincere affections perhaps on one level aligns the friendship portrayed in Finch's poem to that in Grierson's. However, here positions assumed by women—one remote and the other devoted—evoke not the camaraderie informing Grierson's verse but a relationship that shares more with the lover's devotion to the cruel but fair lady of a courtly love tradition or to the idealized object of Petrarchan verse. In fact, Ardelia's own claims echo the pleas found in seventeenth-century verse like Robert Herrick's "To Anthea, Who May Command Him in Anything." The students, of course, do not need to identify any of these literary tips of the hat in order to sense that such open inequity is more typically indicative of a pattern of consuming desire than of friendship. Finch's poem is interesting on a number of grounds, but the ease with which the conventions of romantic love become appropriate for a poetic expression of friendship between women is certainly one of its more conspicuous features.

Hester Mulso's "To Stella," like Finch's poem, makes a claim for the ardency of attachments between women, but in establishing the primacy of women's friendships, Mulso decidedly eschews the tropes of romantic love in an effort to depict a rewarding alternative to love for the coarser sex. In the context of Mulso's poem, women's friendship embodies virtue and propriety, even religious righteousness ("holy Friendship"), and offers enduring pleasures that more than compensate for the emotional jostling that attends love relationships with men.[20] The poem serves at once as a celebration of this stable and enduring form of friendship and as an invitation to Stella, a woman recently disappointed in love (who "Of blasted and luckless love complain[s]"), to partake of this woman-centered community, to "join the sports of Dian's careless maids/And laughing Liberty's triumphant train"; together, these women can "fill the vacant heart with calm delight."[21]

Considering the dramatic context of an addressee recently let down in love, one might consider the championing of women's friendships to offer a timely salve, a support on which Stella could lean while she recovers from her loss. However, the metaphysical scope of Mulso's poem strongly suggests that women's friendships function as much more than a consolation for the moment. The poem depicts a prelapsarian condition in which the personified figures of Love, Innocence, and Friendship walked "hand in hand" until Sin's presence scattered the happy triumvirate.[22] Without his original companions, Love not only lacks resolve and stability but becomes implicated with Sin's own designs. Under these conditions, women's friendships offer the closest available approximation of that bliss that once obtained in Paradise. The poem closes by exhorting,

> Fly then, dear Stella, fly th' unequal strife,
> Since Fate forbids Peace should dwel with Love!
> Friendship's calm joys shall glad thy future live,
> And Virtue lead to endless bliss above.[23]

Though it would be stretching matters to call this poem separatist in its intent (and, for what it's worth, the historical Stella did eventually marry), at the very least, Mulso's poem professes that women find the path to happiness when they establish primary relationships with other women. The dynamics of such friendships avoid the inequities that come to mark the condition of romantic love in a fallen world. Indeed, Mulso trumps the conventions of romantic love by resting her version of friendship on more hallowed grounds. Women's friendship intersects with a spiritual form of bliss, a more enduring—even eternal—form of pleasure in one's emotional life.

These poems, by virtue of their marked differences, are useful in representing the breadth of friendship. Despite these differences, though, they also all partake of an ardency peculiar to the eighteenth century, a free imbibing of romantic convention or profession of the primacy of attachments between women; in each case, commitment could be indulged—and indulged in a very public way—without fear of reprisal. In my experience with these works in the classroom, students had no problem identifying and questioning the borrowing of love poetry conventions, the strong language of affection, and the general celebration of women's friendships as singularly valuable. In this context of literary convention, students raised important questions about the extent to which a poetic expression can be taken as unproblematically representational of the historical friendships that inspired these poems, and this concern invited further questions of what *is* being communicated by appropriating these conventions if their function is not representational. Many, if not most, of the questions I experienced as a result of assembling this reading assignment do not have definitive answers, and this feature in itself is useful. The students with little prompting created a climate of curiosity, one in which matters of friendship, homosexuality, conventions of representation, and matters of historical record circulated. It is within this climate that I delivered a short lecture based largely on the history of lesbian sexuality posed in Faderman's *Surpassing the Love of Men*.[24] I presented this material not as an answer to their questions so much as a theory that might address some of their concerns in a provisional way. The key features of this historical narrative can be expressed in the following three points.

1. The eighteenth century does seem to have admitted, even encouraged, strong attachments between women, perhaps marking the homosociality of a culture in which—as Mary Wollstonecraft's *Vindication* pointedly notes—men and women received disparate educations which consequently hindered relations of companionship across lines of gender. Strong friendships, it has been argued, could best be found in one's own sex. The example of the Ladies of Llangollen, two Irish women with an independence who shared a fifty-year "marriage" in Wales, provides a particularly vivid of image of the possibilities of romantic friendships within this homosocial climate.[25]
2. Foucault famously posits 1870 as the birth of the homosexual as a "species"—that is, a category defined not by sexual practices *per se* but

by "a certain quality of sexual sensibility, a certain way of inverting the masculine and feminine in oneself."[26] Faderman similarly, but more generally, charts the pathologizing of this species by means of the very psychological discourse that constituted the terms of its identity. In short, the homosexual, once merely the perpetrator of an abominable crime, takes on a newly visible form as a type of aberrant person, one with symptoms that can be identified and tendencies that require treatment.

3. With the rise in visibility of a lesbian type or species, once encouraged forms of affection begin to carry the taint of perversion. Lesbian behavior itself no longer need be present to suggest same-sex activity or to identify the likely perpetrators as the marks of a lesbian predisposition begin to be codified. From this codification sprung a sense of the ubiquity of the threat of this perversion, and this burgeoning anxiety occasioned a delimiting of forms of female friendship.

According to this historical scheme, the unself-conscious borrowing of love poetry conventions in eighteenth-century verse between women, then, marks the absence of the implication of perverse affections, and, conversely, the peculiarity with which students within our cultural time and place are struck at seeing such expressions in a same-sex context similarly marks the presence of that threat of perversity in our culture.

As with the explanation that such expressions are purely conventional, this historical narrative has its own set of limitations, and I think it is worth introducing those problems into class discussion to promote debate. As Martha Vicinus has noted, Faderman's narrative assumes a considerable degree of power on the part of psychological discourse—perhaps much more than those not steeped in structuralist and poststructuralist theory will allow. One also wonders if this narrative undervalues the coercive force that severe penalties for same-sex behavior could have—species distinctions notwithstanding. To be sure, the Foucaultian timetable has its share of disputants, among them Emma Donoghue, who provides an account of cross-dressing women assuming the roles of men in the workplace, in the military, and in matrimony through the eighteenth century.[27] Nonetheless, I have found that Faderman's historical narrative makes sense to many students who know all too well (from one point of view or the other) the compulsory force behind words such as "homosexual," "gay," and "lesbian." In fact, one of the big advantages of this pedagogical technique is that it enables students to make connections between the way anti-lesbian or anti-gay rhetoric can function in their own lives and the peculiar forms that friendship could assume in something as seemingly remote as eighteenth-century poetry. Underlying that connection is the proposition that the history of women and the history of sexuality are productively intertwined, and, happily, that point gets across implicitly, without inspiring the more emotional and unproductive rejection incurred by direct assertions of this connection. When introduced in the right climate—a climate that can be created especially well with women's poetry—lesbian history as tied to women in general becomes less an unwelcome houseguest than a plausible resource for satisfying the students' own intellectual curiosity over the peculiar shape friendship apparently could assume in a centuries-old British culture.

The ability to create a hospitable climate for matters of lesbian sexuality notwithstanding, perhaps the most beneficial outcome of this approach is that it can generate curiosity in the condition of eighteenth-century women. When cultural history of this order becomes vivid for students, some of them will take up the challenge of thinking critically about their own time and place as they begin placing their own assumptions in dialogue with the assumptions of another historical moment. Reaching this level of engagement on any aspect of cultural history makes for valuable pedagogy, but achieving such critical thinking in matters of gender is a particular virtue because, in my experience, students all too often hold the assumption that little can be learned from women of past generations, women ostensibly limited by the oppressive conditions of times gone by. Almost everything about women in the hazy centuries that came before the civil rights movement gets disparagingly associated with passivity, incapacity, and submission to stifling constraints, a submission for which the corset seems to stand as ample metaphorical proof. Unfortunately, not even reading Mary Wollstonecraft can remedy matters. To students, the *Vindication of the Rights of Women* only makes their own "having arrived" all the more obvious. After all, those privileges that Wollstonecraft argues for so strenuously and at such length are largely entitlements that our students see as their birthright, such things as equal education and a marriage based on companionship rather than servitude. Reading a text that argues for all those rights that one perceives as well within one's grasp has the unfortunate effect of fostering more of a sense of self-justification than of an imperative to engage matters critically. Approaching the history of women through the range of friendships apparently available at a different cultural moment, on the other hand, draws attention not to historical limitations but to an unforeseen capacity, and in the process students can recognize the possibility that women's friendships have undergone constriction over the last couple centuries. That recognition, important in itself, raises the prospect that some women in the eighteenth century may have had access to types of fulfilling experiences which may be largely unavailable in our own time, and viewing historical women as uniquely enabled in some way can, on the best days, initiate a more self-critical view of gender history.

Treating same-sex affections as once-valued and celebrated dimensions of experience also encourages the students to conceive of potentially lesbian qualities as constituting a capacity rather than a sickness or an aberration; similarly, giving the students the conceptual category of romantic friendships provides them with a less emotionally charged way of conceiving same-sex affections, a way that perhaps renders the more familiar category of lesbian—or at least important features of that category—less alien. It is this initial step toward breaking down the otherness of homosexuality—a step that often seems very hard won—that I see as a second key advantage of approaching the issue of sexuality through a consideration of friendship. In broad terms, the poetry of romantic friendship provides a way of complicating the pervasive binary quality that characterizes the way we articulate and even the way we may experience sexuality at this cultural juncture. Sexual orientation partakes deeply of a threshold logic that requires one to sit on one side of the fence or the other, and assuming a marginal sexuality in particular requires a decisive moment, a crossing the bar as it were. Bonnie Zimmerman, in defining a lesbian perspective, emphasizes the determining quality of such a moment:

> At a certain point some women act upon their feelings, choose a different life path, and claim a personal and sometimes public self-definition as a lesbian. It seems to me, then, that *choice* is essential to our understanding of a lesbian perspectivity, even if biological or developmental factors push some women toward making that choice (original emphasis).[28]

We could add that the significance of this choice and the ardency with which this position often gets assumed owes much to this marginal position being such an embattled one. A way of managing some comfort within an identity indelibly associated with perversity, abnormality, and pathology is to take it up loudly, to fend off charges of deviancy with sheer assertiveness. Under such conditions where so much rests on a decisive moment, it is not surprising that the sexuality has adhered closely to the oppositional tensions and security afforded by binary opposition. To be sure, the homo/hetero binary has served the gay and lesbian community in terms of personal and political needs, but, as queer theorists have amply pointed out, that binary lacks something when it comes to understanding the diversity of ways people negotiate their desires, experience affections, or sense emotional devotion. Our binary paradigm, to which we are unavoidably devoted at this juncture and which presents sexuality as a choice between ubiquitous pairs, obscures the fluidity of sexual possibility and the points of intersection that exist across diametrically opposed orientations.

Women's poetry presents an opportunity to address issues of women's sexuality and same-sex affection, a way that encourages an understanding of sexuality in more complex terms than the politicized binaries allow and that emphasizes the polymorphous character of human sexual and emotional experience. What I have suggested is a way of elucidating the forms that affection could take in a cultural moment before the *choice* that Zimmerman defines became the prerequisite for expressions of ardent same-sex affection and identification. Using poetry to raise questions about the contours of desire, affection, and devotion also demonstrates implicitly the way the histories of gender and of sexuality are closely intertwined.

Notes

For their typically invaluable suggestions, I wish to thank Jennifer Halloran, Kim Jastremski, Miranda Wilson, and Jeanne Moskal.

1. Martha Vicinus, "Lesbian History: All Theory and No Facts or All Facts and No Theory?" *Radical History Review* 60 (1994): 58.
2. For studies of romantic friendships, see Lillian Faderman, *Surpassing the Love of Men: Romantic Friendship and Love Between Women from the Renaissance to the Present* (New York: William Morrow, 1981) and Elizabeth Mavor, *The Ladies of Llangollen: A Study in Romantic Friendship* (Hammondsworth: Penguin, 1971). For studies that demonstrate the relevance of same-sex affections to the history of women, see Blanche Wiesen Cook, "Female Support Networks and Political Activism: Lillian Wald, Crystal Eastman, Emma Goldman," in *A Heritage of Her Own*, eds. Nancy F. Cott and Elizabeth H. Pleck (New York: Simon and Schuster, 1979), 412–44; and Carroll Smith-Rosenburg, "The Female World of Love and Ritual: Relations between Women in Nineteenth-Century America," *Signs: A Journal of Women in Culture and Society* 1 (1975): 1–29, on the emotional lives of nineteenth-century American women. On English boarding school relationships and the shaping of women's subjectivity, see Martha Vicinus, "Distance and Desire: English Boarding School Friendships, 1870–1920," *Hidden from History: Reclaiming the Gay and Lesbian Past*, eds. Martin Duberman, Martha Vicinus, and George Chauncey Jr. (New York: Penguin, 1989), 212–29. For a more general consideration of the constitutive part that lesbian sexuality has played in the shaping of normative gender roles, see Adrienne Rich, "Compulsory Heterosexuality and Lesbian Existence," *Signs: A Journal of Women in Culture and Society* 5 (1980): 631–60.
3. As sources for poems on friendship, the anthologies of lesbian poetry, of course, offer the most condensed and comprehensive collections. See in particular Lillian Faderman, ed. *Chloe Plus Olivia: An Anthology of Lesbian Literature from the Seventeenth Century to the Present* (New York: Viking, 1994) and Emma Donoghue, *Poems between Women: Four Centuries of Love, Romantic Friendship, and Desire* (New York: Columbia UP, 1997), each of which offers works too numerous to mention here. After those anthologies, the collections of women's verse of the period are the most helpful. Roger Lonsdale, ed., *Eighteenth-Century Women Poets* (New York: Oxford, 1989), includes the poems by Anna Seward, Anne Finch, Constantina Grierson,

Hester Mulso which I discuss in this chapter; also from this collection, see the anonymously authored "Chloe to Artimesa," Frances Seymour's "To the Countess of Pomfret," Esther Lewis's "A Letter to a Lady in London," Susanna Blamire's "Epistle to Her Friends at Gartmore," and Mary Savage's "Letter to Miss E. B. at Bath." Duncan Wu, *Romanticism: An Anthology*, 2nd ed. (Oxford: Blackwell, 1998) offers several useful works dealing with friendship, including Anna Seward's "To Time Past. Written Dec. 1772," Charlotte Smith's "To Friendship," and Ann Batten Cristall's "To a Lady on the Rise of Morn." The more expansive *Norton Anthology of Literature by Women*, ed. Sandra M. Gilbert and Susan Gubar, (New York: W. W. Norton & Co., 1996) is a bit scant on eighteenth-century verse; it does offer Finch's "Friendship between Ephelia and Ardelia" and the eighteenth century can be supplemented by earlier poems on friendship such as Katherine Philips's "Friendship's Mysteries, to My Dearest Lucasia" and "To My Excellent Lucasia on Our Friendship" as well as Aphra Behn's erotically charged "To the Fair Clarinda." *The Norton Anthology of Poetry*, ed. Margaret Ferguson, Mary Jo Salter, and Jon Stallworthy (New York W. W. Norton, 1996) includes the Philips, the Behn, and the Finch poems.

4   Mary Savage, "Letter to Miss E. B. at Bath," in Lonsdale, ll. 55, 57–8.
5   Anna Seward, "Sonnet. To Honora Sneyd," in Lonsdale, ll. 11–12.
6   Anne Finch, "Friendship between Ephelia and Ardelia," in Lonsdale, ll. 19–20.
7   For simplicity, I have relied solely on the texts reproduced in Lonsdale's anthology throughout this paper. The line numbers correspond to those in Lonsdale's collection.
8   Lillian Faderman addresses the heteronormative force of explaining all ardent expressions as purely conventional by pointing out that distinctions between conventional and sincere language were themselves common features of eighteenth-century writing. She writes,

> But even in a period of sentimentality, when feeling was often valued for its own sake and expressions of profound emotion were more common than genuine profundity of feeling, it is possible to make some distinction between superficial and artificial expressions of sentiment and the real thing. The eighteenth century made these distinctions as a matter of course…. fiction of the period contains numerous examples of forced and artificial expressions of love between women as well as those which were intended to be viewed as expressions of genuine feeling.

Faderman's observation suggests that the pertinent consideration in the classroom may not be whether all such expressions are conventional or sincere but rather where they appear to be conventional and where they seem sincere. Of course making such fine determinations in the undergraduate classroom may be an impractical effort because it would demand more experience with eighteenth-century stylistics than can be expected from all but the most atypical of students. Nonetheless, opening up these difficult questions at the very least communicates to students that the question of conventionality poses complications that should make us suspect of summary verdicts.

9   Besides being reproduced in Lonsdale's anthology, Grierson's poem is also available in various editions of Laetitia Pilkington's *Memoirs*, a number of which are no longer under copyright and so suitable for the photocopier.
10 Constantina Grierson, "To Miss Laetitia Van Lewen," in Lonsdale, l. 29.
11 Grierson, l. 34.
12 Grierson, l. 20.
13 Grierson, l. 46–7.
14 Grierson, ll. 21, 28.

15 Finch, ll. 2, 3–4.
16 Finch, l. 5.
17 Finch, ll. 12–13.
18 Finch, ll. 15–16.
19 Finch, 19–20.
20 Hester Mulso, "To Stella," in Lonsdale, l. 5.
21 Mulso, ll. 2, 3–4, 8.
22 Mulso, l. 50.
23 Mulso, ll. 61–4.
24 See in particular the chapters "Romantic Friendship in Eighteenth-Century Literature," "Romantic Friendship in Eighteenth-Century Life," and "The Contributions of the Sexologists." See also Bonnie Zimmerman, "'The Dark Eye Beaming': Female Friendship in George Eliot's Fictions," in *Lesbian Texts and Contexts: Radical Revisions*, eds. Karla Jay and Joanne Glasgow (New York: New York UP, 1990), 126–44 for useful formulation of this historical narrative.
25 The lives of the Ladies of Llangollen, Sarah Ponsonby and Eleanor Butler, have their fullest account in Mavor and receive more concise treatment in Faderman's *Surpassing the Love of Men*. See also selections from Eleanor Butler, *The Hamwood Papers of the Ladies of Llangollen and Caroline Hamilton*, ed. G. H. Bell (London: Macmillan, 1930) and *Life with the Ladies of Llangollen*, ed. Elizabeth Mavor (Hammondsworth: Viking, 1984). Ponsonby and Butler's journals and letters are also available on microfilm from Adam Matthew Publication (1997).
26 Michel Foucault, *The History of Sexuality, Volume One: An Introduction* (New York: Random House, 1978), 43.
27 Emma Donoghue, *Passions between Women: British Lesbian Culture, 1668–1801* (New York: Harper Collins, 1993).
28 Bonnie Zimmerman, "Perverse Reading: The Lesbian Appropriation of Literature," *Sexual Practice and Textual Theory*, ed. Susan J. Wolfe and Julia Penelope (Cambridge, MA: Blackwell P, 1993), 136.

The Poetry of Women's Friendship
Dr. Incorvati

Session description and objectives:
This single session brings together works by and about women, to encourage students to raise questions about the nature of friendship, the social contingency of gender roles, and the various shapes that same-sex desire might assume. Though this plan particularly suits courses on women's literature—where matters of gender and social context tend to occupy the foreground—it could also find a home in more general surveys. Accordingly, the following list offers some suggested readings from anthologies commonly used in a variety of classes.

Sample readings:
From Sandra Gilbert and Susan Gubar's *Norton Anthology of Literature by Women*. (NY: W. W. Norton, 1996.)
- Katherine Philips's "Friendship's Mysteries, to My Dearest Lucasia"
- Katherine Philips's "To My Excellent Lucasia on our Friendship"
- Aphra Behn's "To the Fair Clarinda"
- Anne Finch's "Friendship between Ephelia and Ardelia"

From Margaret Ferguson, Mary Jo Salter, and Jon Stalworthy's *Norton Anthology of Poetry*. (NY: W. W. Norton, 1996.)
- Katherine Philips's "To My Excellent Lucasia on our Friendship"
- Anne Finch's "Friendship between Ephelia and Ardelia"

From Roger Lonsdale's *Eighteenth-Century Women Poets*. (Oxford: Oxford UP, 1989.)
- Constantina Grierson's "To Miss Laetitia Van Lewen"
- Hester Mulso's "To Stella"
- The anonymously authored "Chloe to Artimesa"
- Frances Seymour's "To the Countess of Pomfret"
- Esther Lewis's "A Letter to a Lady in London"
- Susanna Blamire's "Epistle to Her Friends at Gartmore"
- Anna Seward's "Sonnet. To Honora Sneyd"
- Mary Savage's "Letter to Miss E. B. at Bath"

From Anne Mellor and Richard Matlak's *British Literature, 1780–1830*. (NY: Harcourt, 1996.)
- Ann Yearsley's "To the Same [Stella]"
- Joanna Baillie's "To Mrs. Siddons"
- Letitia Elizabeth Landon's "Felicia Hemans"

From Duncan Wu's *Romantic Women Poets: An Anthology* (2nd ed. Oxford: Blackwell, 1998)
- Anna Seward's "To Time Past. Written Dec. 1772"
- Charlotte Smith's "To Friendship"
- Ann Batten Cristall's "To a Lady on the Rise of Morn"

Unfortunately, *The Norton Anthology of English Literature* does not offer enough titles to constitute a good day's reading; volume one does reprint two very useful poems by Katherine Philips but not much else. To supplement any anthology, see Emma Donoghue's *Poems Between Women: Four Centuries of Love, Romantic Friendship, and Desire* and Lillian Faderman's lamentably out-of-print *Chloe Plus Olivia: An Anthology of Lesbian Literature from the Renaissance to the Present*, both of which offer suitable works too numerous to mention here.

Figure 1. Rick Incorvati, Sample Class Plan

CHAPTER SEVEN
A Subversive Urn and a Suicidal Bride: Strategies for Reading Across Aesthetic Difference

Elizabeth A. Dolan

> *In spite of my good intentions to respect Felicia Hemans, the best-selling poet of the nineteenth century, I am not sure I can do it. At least, the first poem I have read by her—"The Image in Lava"—has given me doubts. Sentimental? Is that the derogatory term that has been used against her? For me it is the rhyme scheme that is annoying. It reminds me of 'home-grown' poems found printed in small town newspapers. Am I being harsh? Do 'by' and 'agony' really rhyme in the first stanza? Did Hemans intend for them not to rhyme so the effect would be jarring? And the ending, with the emphatic plea, 'It must, it must be so!' is also bothersome. Bottom line is that I think the poem is bad.*
>
> —An English major

This excerpt from an English major's response paper for my upper-level Romanticism course illustrates a central and by now quite familiar challenge in teaching Felicia Hemans's poetry—how to respond to students' concerns about its aesthetic value.[1] Citing a colleague whose remarks about Hemans's poetry anticipate my student's, Paula Feldman framed a July 1997 discussion on the NASSR list with the following question: "What is the best way to respond to this sort of dismissal [of non-canonical poetry on aesthetic grounds] as we try to include writers such as Hemans, whose style and subject matter many in the profession have been taught to find unappealing?"[2] In online discussions like the one Feldman initiated, and in publications such as Jerome McGann's *The Poetics of Sensibility* (1996), and Nanora Sweet and Julie Melnyk's volume, *Felicia Hemans: Reimagining Poetry in the Nineteenth Century* (2001), Romanticists have begun to elaborate ways to understand Hemans's poetry on its own terms.[3] However, as my student's comment demonstrates, undergraduates continue to find "aesthetically bothersome" the stylistic differences between, for example, Hemans's *Records of Woman* (1828), and poetry that "load[s] every rift...with ore."[4] In this chapter, I describe a way of framing this stylistic disjunction that engages students in aesthetic and historical discourses of the Romantic era.

One can certainly sidestep the issue of aesthetic value by focusing class discussion on the significance of Hemans's poetry to the portrayal of women in literature, to the gift book tradition, or to the representation of non-British cultures at the dawn of the imperial age. While changing the terms of the conversation is productive, it leaves unanswered the question of how we determine aesthetic value, leaves standing the assertion that while some poems have cultural value, they are still "bad." I propose a strategy for reading across aesthetic difference that engages history but does not leave the question of aesthetics behind. In so doing, I join those teachers of British women writers who extol the pedagogical value of pairing women's and men's literature from the period.[5] I wish to add to this practice of pairing a consideration of how we as teachers bring history into the Romanticism classroom and of how literature by women poets such as Hemans requires us to invoke history differently from works by many male poets of the era.[6] It has been my experience that comparing male and female Romantic poets' rhetorical uses of history helps students appreciate the differences in these poets' aesthetic choices.

To demonstrate how a dialectic between poetics and history enlivens the Romanticism classroom, I describe in this essay a three-class-period lesson plan for teaching two pairs of poems: Hemans's "The Image in Lava" (1828) with Percy Bysshe Shelley's "Ozymandias" (1818) in the first class, and Hemans's "The Bride of the Greek Isle" (1828) with John Keats's "Ode on a Grecian Urn" (1819) in the second and third classes—all poems that refer to (apparently) historical artifacts. The first two short poems invoke the Burkean aesthetic of the sublime and the beautiful to describe quite different historical objects—the bodies of a mother and infant preserved in the ash of the volcanic eruption that killed them, and the disintegrating statue of Ramses II. Together, "The Image in Lava" and "Ozymandias" offer students a quick introduction to the rhetorical uses of history and aesthetics.[7] The second set of two poems, which I treat at greater length both in the classroom and in this essay, also have striking similarities and differences. Both respond to the early nineteenth-century fascination with Greek culture, yet the poets use Hellenic allusions to different ends. Keats centers his ode on what seems to be a Hellenic artifact but is in fact an imaginary piece of pottery. In contrast, Hemans grounds her dramatic narrative on an actual cultural artifact—a 1761 painting of the 1571 Turkish invasion of Cyprus. As students analyze how the poets represent their respective artifacts, they explore differences in the authors' aesthetic goals and subject positions.

Day One

What Lasts?
In preparing to discuss Shelley's "Ozymandias" and Hemans's "The Image in Lava," students also read the excerpts from Edmund Burke's *Philosophical Inquiry into the Nature of the Sublime and Beautiful* (1757) in Mellor and Matlak's anthology. We read the poems aloud in class, listening for differences in style and for references to the sublime and the beautiful.[8] Our discussion of

"Ozymandias" begins with a debate about what lasts, what is most sublime, what Shelley most values. Identifying references to the sublime in the poem, students immediately note that Shelley values nature ("the lone and level sands") more than political power.[9] Encouraged by questions—such as "How many storytellers are there in the poem? Why is it important for the speaker to tell us how he heard the story?"—students conclude that in Shelley's view narrative outlasts even nature. When we turn to "The Image in Lava," students quickly discern that, like Shelley, Hemans does not admire political power, asserting that maternal love outlasts "Temple and tower" and "Empires."[10] Admiring Hemans's disruption of Burke's aesthetic binary, one of my students notes, "The poem begins with maternal love, which is beautiful, moves to the sublime eruption of the volcano, and ends with a beautiful object that endures." The stylistic differences between the poems stay in the background of the conversation as we focus on the poets' rhetorical uses of the aesthetic of the sublime and the beautiful.

Having discovered something about the poets' values in our discussion of Burke's aesthetics, we begin to consider their invocation of history. In response to the question "What do we know about the objects the poets describe in their poems?" students observe that Shelley gives us a description of the crumbling statue and its inscription, while Hemans offers readers a footnote that identifies the inspiration for her poem: "the impression of a woman's form, with an infant clasped to the bosom, found at the uncovering of Herculaneum."[11] By conveying historical information through a series of narrators—"I," "a traveller from an antique land," "its sculptor"—Shelley emphasizes the act of telling history, even as the irony of Ozymandias's engraved words ("Look on my works, ye Mighty, and despair!") complicates the relationship between narrative and history.[12] Rather than focus readers on her own construction of poetic narrative, Hemans refers readers to the artifacts themselves via the footnote, thus emphasizing the historical value of everyday moments in common lives. While Shelley invokes an artifact in order to explore the narration of history, Hemans describes an artifact to emphasize the materiality of history.

I end the class with a simple question: "Which poem is better and why?" The students who choose "Ozymandias" often speak first, citing Shelley's multilayered narrative, word choice, and references to the Bible as strengths. Inevitably some students express frustration with Hemans's effusively emotional style, while others make connections between her sentimental style and the maternal love that she honors in the poem. In a course evaluation, an anonymous student comments: "I started out assigning more importance to Shelley's poem, but as I started to think about it, I began to recognize the powerful aspects of Hemans's poetry." In class, some students confess they are moved by Hemans's poem, and suggest that affective power has aesthetic value. We discuss how each poem's style might be appropriate to each poet's invocation of history. Considering the authors' engagement with the aesthetics of the sublime and beautiful and their related stances on what counts as history deepens student's understanding of the relationship between style and meaning.

Day Two

A Subversive Urn
During the first class devoted to Keats's "Ode on a Grecian Urn" and Hemans's "The Bride of the Greek Isle," I introduce students to the ekphrastic tradition in Romantic poetry. Many Oxford and Cambridge Prize poems, for example, describe statues and friezes, and William Wordsworth, Shelley, and Leigh Hunt all wrote poems describing paintings.[13] In this discussion, I have found it useful to read an example of ekphrastic poetry and show a picture of the work of art being described. Keats's "On Seeing the Elgin Marbles" works well because pictures of the Parthenon Marbles are widely available. In some versions of this discussion, students reconsider "The Image in Lava" as an ekphrastic poem, a productive digression that I welcome.[14] Indeed, remembering Hemans's footnote to "The Image in Lava" offers a nice transition into the organizing questions for our discussion of the two longer poems: "What do we know about the artifacts the poems are based on?" and "What does this information tell us about the poems?" Finding that Keats left no trail of foot-notes to inform readers about the urn that inspired the ode, students sym-pathize with nineteenth- and early twentieth-century scholars' attempts to identify a specific urn as the inspiration for Keats's ode. I share with students the photograph of a prospective source urn that Arthur C. Downer includes in his 1897 collection of essays: "There is some reason for thinking that the particular urn which inspired this beautiful poem is a somewhat weather-beaten work in marble, still preserved in the garden of Holland House, and figured in Piranesi's *Vasi e candelabri*."[15] I contrast Downer's search for a real urn with David Simpson's articulation of the now widely agreed-upon opinion that "there was no specific 'urn' behind the poem…Keats's urn seems to have been a composite creation, made up out of a synthesis of various classical objects."[16] One could spend much more time on this review of the criticism; as Jack Stillinger points out, practitioners of almost every theoretical approach arising since 1970 have proposed readings of the ode.[17] My much simpler goal is to convey to students that for years Keats's ode convinced scholars that there was a real urn.

With this background, we return our attention to Keats's ode. I ask students how the poem itself reinforces the reader's sense that there was a single, material urn, with a real history. Students cite the detailed descriptions of the urn's scenes, including the "heifer lowing at the skies/...all her silken flanks with garlands drest," and the "marble men and maidens overwrought,/With forest branches and the trodden weed."[18] They also point to the questions that the speaker asks the urn: "What leaf-fring'd legend haunts about thy shape...? What men or gods are these? What maidens loth? What mad pursuit? What struggle to escape? What pipes and timbrels? What wild ecstasy?"[19] Finally, they note the speaker's "names" for the urn, "still unravish'd bride of quietness," "foster-child of silence and slow time," and "sylvan historian."[20] As one student puts it, "It sounds like Keats is interrogating an urn that sits in the room with him." We build on these observations by bringing into the discussion Susan Wolfson's provocative question, "How can something unspeaking...displaying a static, unchanging tableau, be hailed as a 'historian'?"[21] Her question inspires us to think about what a historian does and who the historian in the poem really is, the urn or the speaker. This discussion builds productively on our observations about the narration of history in "Ozymandias."

Returning to Keats's invocation of the ekphrastic tradition, I ask students, "Why does Keats invent an artifact in order to pay tribute to it?" The last time I taught this poem, several students veered off my intended trajectory at this point, discussing allusions they previously learned about, especially regarding the sacrifice depicted in stanza four ("I learned that it was the cult of Mithras"; "My teacher told me it referred to a real sacrifice"). We talk about these differing readings as part of the search for sources that Keats's ode inspires. Other classes begin talking about the relationship between the ode and the urn in the context of the sublime and the beautiful. Representative of this approach, a student writes in a response paper: "This small urn does not at first seem to be sublime. It is a beautiful object—small, smooth, and unthreatening. However, everything that is depicted on the urn lives on forever; the figures never grow old or tire. The urn takes on a different meaning when it is a representative of the scope of time...history's vastness is a rather sublime encounter." In discussion, students cite lines such as, "Heard melodies are sweet, but those unheard are sweeter" and "Ah, happy, happy boughs! That cannot shed/Your leaves, nor ever bid the Spring adieu," observing that what lasts in Keats's ode, what is sublime, is potential itself, rather than nature, empires, or maternal love.[22]

Eventually our discussion of the dynamic between the fictional urn and the ode leads to a focus on the significance that this creation of an "artifact" gives to Keats's imagination.[23] Because the original source of Keats's urn is Keats's ode, the questions the narrator poses to the urn are answerable only by the ode. However, the ode's final enigmatic two lines—"'Beauty is truth, truth beauty,'—that is all/Ye know on earth, and all ye need to know"—provide no answers, catapulting the reader back into the interior of the ode.[24] This circle catches the questions—like the melodies, the near kiss, the almost sacrifice—in a web of potential rather than resolving them into actual answers. Although the ode addresses the ceramic form that the Greeks used to record their own history and culture, the ode is actually insulated from the material reality of history.[25] Students conclude that the truth of the urn cannot be found in any actual beautiful object, then, but only in Keats's imagination and in the reader's.

A Suicidal Bride

As with our discussion of Keats's ode, I begin our analysis of "The Bride of the Greek Isle" by addressing the origin of the poem: "What do we know about the artifact upon which Hemans based her poem?" Hemans offers her readers a clue in a footnote that leads us through a series of references, a series of steps toward the original artifact that emphasize both Hemans's own distance from the artifact and competing interpretations of the sublime. Although Hemans's sources are too rare to ask students to locate, I try to involve them in the excitement of this type of research by re-creating the search for these sources in class. We start with the footnote: "Founded on a circumstance related in the Second Series of the Curiousities of Literature, and forming part of a picture in the 'Painted Biography,' there described." I distribute copies of Isaac Disraeli's brief entry in *Curiousities of Literature* entitled, "Of a Biography Painted."[26] Students read the entry in class and pursue the following topics in small groups:

1. Describe the physical characteristics and history of the book Disraeli presents.
2. What do we learn about Maguis's biography from Disraeli's description?
3. Which painting described by Disraeli seems to relate to Hemans's poem?

These small group discussions, at first a bit confusing as students become accustomed to the density of Disraeli's prose, ultimately interest students in the complexity of Hemans's sources.

In large class discussion, we put together the pieces of this analysis, working to describe Hemans's distance from the artifact she invokes. The painting Disraeli describes comes from a volume of paintings chronicling the adventures of a noble Venetian, Charles Magius, who was taken prisoner in the 1571 Turkish invasions of Cyprus. After he was released, Magius commissioned an artist to draw his experiences, which Disraeli characterizes as "romantic incidents." Hemans did not actually see the painting herself but read Disraeli's description of it: "In one of the pictures are seen two ships on fire; a young lady of Cyprus preferring death to the loss of her honor and the miseries of slavery, determined to set fire to the vessel in which she was carried; she succeeded, and the flames communicated to another."[27]

Based on student comments, I attempt to represent visually on the blackboard the layers of narrative that lie between Hemans and the artifact. Hemans is removed from the actual event first by Magius's narrative to his artist,[28] second by the artist's interpretation on canvas, and finally, by Disraeli's written description of the painting. To explore the meaning in the intertextual spaces that the class identifies, we discuss the ways in which Hemans modifies her source. Students observe that Hemans names the "young lady of Cyprus" Eudora and that Hemans saves the conflagration for the end of the poem—leading up to it with a presentation of Eudora's circumstances and state of mind. She rewrites Disraeli's "romantic incident," focusing not on the sublimity of the powerful fire and the dying maiden, but rather on questions surrounding the woman's motivation for sacrificing herself.

Students quickly notice that Hemans "paints" a wedding veil on Magius's and Disraeli's Greek slave woman in order to develop a psychological basis for Eudora's actions. As the wedding ceremony is about to begin, Turks attack the island of Cyprus. A collective voice reveals that Eudora has the option to flee from enslavement by the invading Turks, but chooses not to: "Eudora, Eudora! *thou* dost not fly!" (original emphasis).[29] Eudora decides not to flee when her fiancé Ianthis is killed by the Turks; she risks enslavement in order to stay beside his body. While this portrait of Eudora's loyalty certainly heightens the sentiment of the poem, it also serves to sharpen the reader's awareness of the changes that marriage brings to a woman; Hemans suggests that Eudora's ties to Ianthis make her vulnerable to enslavement. If Cyprus had been attacked before her engagement, Eudora might have fled to her family instead of mourning her fiancé. Single, she might have escaped and never burned the ship, never burned herself to death. Hemans complicates Disraeli's description of the event as a "romantic incident" in *Magius*'s life by emphasizing the material differences that a change of marital status makes in a woman's life. Some students resist the connection between slavery and marriage, but those who have read Mary Wollstonecraft's *Maria* (1798) or *Vindication of the Rights of Woman* (1792) are able to explore this connection in relation to eighteenth-century discussions of oppressive marriage laws in England.

Students are also taken by Eudora's decision to stay on the slave ship, which she sets on fire after being captured. Disraeli notes that the "young lady prefer[s] death to the loss of her honor and the miseries of slavery," implying that she commits suicide on the ship to avoid rape.[30] Hemans complicates the picture by painting in the "swimmers…plunging from stern and prow" as the ship burns.³¹ In other words, she adds the option of jumping ship to those Disraeli describes for the young woman—rape and slavery. I ask students, "How does Eudora distinguish her situation from these swimmers? Why does she stay?" Eudora's death becomes increasingly dramatic and enigmatic as we lose her voice in the fire. Some students point to lines describing the fire as a funeral pyre as evidence that her intention is to die with Ianthis: "Proudly she stands, like an Indian bride/On the pyre with the holy dead beside."³² However, other students are disturbed by lines that suggest that Eudora might have had a last-minute desire to save herself:

> But a shriek from her mother hath caught her ear,
> As the flames to her marriage-robe draw near,
> And starting, she spreads her pale arms in vain
> To the form they must never infold again.³³

Students debate whether "the form" refers to Eudora's mother or to Ianthis, and whether the word "starting" implies that when she hears her mother's voice she reconsiders her decision to commit suicide. Into this animated discussion, I suggest that by interesting readers in Eudora's motivation for suicide, Hemans transfers the sublime experience of death from Magius and Disraeli back to Eudora, divesting the romantic observer of the claim that he experiences the sublime by observing Eudora's (or the slave woman's) death.

We conclude this class discussion with a consideration of the effect of each author's invocation of Hellenism. Whereas Keats describes ideal forms, Hemans immerses the reader in specifics. Keats presents an ideal portrait of Greek culture in the form of an imaginary urn. In doing so, he emphasizes imagination over materiality and "universal" truths over historical facts. A narrative voice asks questions of the figures on the urn and leaves the answers to his and our imaginations. In Hemans's poem, a narrative voice recounts the action, but the "object" also speaks. In addition to offering a description of Eudora's specific circumstances and an indication of her motivations, Hemans includes Eudora's voice in a section entitled "The Bride's Farewell." Hemans's footnoted reference to the artifact on which the poem is based invites readers to discover in the spaces between Magius's painted experience, Disraeli's description, and her poem, a revision of the masculine sublime.

Homework

In preparation for our next class, I ask students to respond to the question of how Hemans's Eudora might fulfill any of Keats's three apostrophes to the urn: "still unravish'd bride of quietness," "foster-child of silence and slow time," "Sylvan historian, who canst thus express/A flowery tale more sweetly than our rhyme."[34] In our third day of discussion, I elaborate on students' posted ideas, connecting them to our previous classes. I summarize our collaborative readings of the first and third apostrophes here: Together we notice that Hemans identifies Eudora as the virgin "bride of the morn," not engaged *to* quietness like Keats's urn, but who, in her awareness of the solemnity of marriage is engaged *in* quietness: "Mute be the song and the choral strain,/Till her heart's deep well-spring is clear again!"[35] Keats invokes the "unravish'd bride of quietness" to describe the urn's silence through time; Hemans describes an inexperienced bride, momentarily quieted by sadness. Keats's invocation of an "unravished bride"—not merely a virgin bride—places beneath the silence of the urn the violence of potential rape. The sexual language equates the observer's search for aesthetic experience with the libido, thus making the observer a potential ravisher, a way of looking which Freud labeled "scopophilia." However, Keats's maiden urn is "unravished"; the silence of the urn resists reading, understanding, and thus ravishment. This comparison helps students realize that the unreadableness of the urn is important to Keats. In creating a scene of incipient, yet never realizable violence, Keats instills underneath his description of the beautiful—of art—a current of the sublime. This distanced violence is sublime—titillatingly reminiscent of death, but harmless. In the progression of her poem, Hemans releases the violence lying beneath Keats's words. She begins with an unravished bride and then destroys her in violence complicated by Eudora's own choices.

Those who write on Keats's third apostrophe to his urn note that Hemans identifies Eudora as a kind of "sylvan historian" or preserver of the garden in her familial address:

> Why do I weep?—to leave the vine
> Whose clusters o'er me bend,—
> The myrtle—yet, oh! call it mine!—
> The flowers I lov'd to tend.[36]

Eudora does "express/A flowery tale." Hemans describes Eudora's family home in terms of its floral decoration. After Eudora sings her goodbye, however, Hemans shifts from these comforting elements of the beautiful that Eudora tends at home to more ominous foliage at the newlywed residence, "the home that stood/In the flowering depths of a Grecian wood." Eudora's new home is set among threateningly phallic vegetation: "Stars of Jasmine its pillars crowned," "vine-stalks," "a fountain's play/flung showers," and "a cypress which rose in that flashing rain,/like one tall shaft."[37] Hemans, like Keats, instills an element of the sublime, the threat of sexual violence, into her aesthetic of the beautiful. However, while Keats infuses the sublime into his representation of beautiful art, containing both beauty and terror in the aesthetic object, Hemans impregnates the beauty of the wedding and of the bride with the dangers of marriage to women, the danger of invasion. The dangers Hemans invokes are not contained, but rather released into action as the pirates invade the island.

Day Three

Song and Silence, Motion and Stillness

After considering each poem's uses of history, and references to the sublime and the beautiful, we return to the question of style on our third day of discussion. I ask students to attend to the differences in the poems' sounds and senses of movement, as we read alternating stanzas of the two poems aloud. Students then work in small groups to brainstorm a list of the ways the poems correspond to each other outside of the references to Greek culture that we discussed in the previous class. Many correspondences that students generate are both observant and entertaining—each poem presents a series of scenes, the two poems include lots of flowers and plants, and both the bride and the cow are dressed up and are sacrificed. Other correspondences that students observe tend to inspire more extended discussion—both poems repeat the words "bride" and "still," refer to songs heard and unheard, and explore the nature of youth and love. Bringing the two works into conversation in this way helps students think about what is at stake in these differing approaches to representation. The goal of our discussion of the poems' details—including verse form, diction, and the repetition of words and images—is to explore the relationship between each poet's values and his or her aesthetic choices.

One of the most striking correspondences that students cite is the poets' use of silence and stillness. As I am sure many other teachers have discovered, students love the irony that Keats's silent artifact can "thus express/A flowery tale more sweetly than our rhyme."[38] The ode praises the urn's ability to "tell" a tale. However, in noting the urn's silence, Keats heightens our awareness of his own words. Ultimately, this denial of sound within the poem intensifies the sounding of the poem. Students observe that while Keats's Grecian world is still with quiet anticipation, Hemans's resounds with voices and music repeatedly hushed into silence then released again. Hemans not only endows Eudora with a voice, she also surrounds her with sound. Once someone notices this aspect of the poem, students discover many references to sound in the poem. The opening lines tell the "Maids of bright Scio" to bring "lyres for the festal hours."[39] Sad to leave her family, Eudora first wishes that all the music of the wedding celebration would be quiet and then sings her own farewell.[40] Soon after, the invaders bring the wedding music to an abrupt end. In the middle of the festivities, "there came by fits, thro' some wavy tree,/A sound and a gleam of the moaning sea."[41] A voice calls "Hush!" and "Silence!"[42] The death of the Greeks killed by Turkish invaders induces, "a hush of fear thro' the summer grove."[43] These extreme fluctuations in sound bring alive the extreme emotions felt by Eudora and the other Greeks being invaded.

This distinction in the poets' uses of sound echoes their uses of motion. The word "still" inhabits both poems—most famously, of course, "Ode on a Grecian Urn." Students enjoy discovering the double meaning of "still" in Keats's poem—duration and motionlessness. "[S]till unravished bride" intensifies the possibility of violence held back.[44] The lovers appear "Forever warm and still to be enjoyed,/Forever panting, and forever young."[45] Because they cannot move, they last. Behind their stillness lies a panting sexuality. They hang on the verge of intense life, yet Keats stills them from participation, saves them from the death of fulfillment.

Once we notice the word "still" in Keats's ode, students observe that Hemans also uses the word "still" to represent potential. The stillness of the house the newlyweds are to live in conveys a sense of quiet waiting for the activity of the family that is to some day fill the house: "Still and sweet was the home that stood/In the flowering depths of the Grecian wood."[46] Right before the invasion, a voice cries, "be still!" freezing the wedding party as if they were on Keats's urn—still at the edge of action and danger.[47] Hemans also freezes the ship into an ominous stillness before the fire breaks out: "There its broad pennon a shadow cast,/Moveless and black from the tall still mast."[48] Unlike Keats, Hemans builds potential, stills motion in order to release it into action.

I ask students to take a closer look at verse form. Because we have already discussed the sonnet in class, students recognize that each of Keats's five stanzas is a ten-line version of a hybrid Petrarchan and Shakespearean sonnet (ababcde, with the last three lines varying dce, ced, cde). Keats's stable, repetitive structure and his consistent use of the present tense reinforce the still present of the poem. As critics such as M. R. G. Spiller have pointed out, the movement from scene to scene in the poem re-creates the circular motion of a person "reading" the urn itself.[49] Students are often impressed with Keats's artistry and innovation—a reaction that reinforces our sense that the poem emphasizes Keats's own imagination. Students note that Hemans's style reflects her use of motion. Typographically, "The Bride of the Greek Isle" alternates long lines and short lines, long stanzas and short stanzas. The rhyme scheme pulses from AA BB in most of the poem to AB AB in the four stanzas spoken by Eudora. The numerous imperatives infuse the poem with urgency. Incredibly, Hemans modulates the tense of the poem at least 16 times. She compels the reader to pant, to participate in the action. Generally, where Keats asks, "What mad pursuit? What struggle to escape?/What pipes and timbrels? What wild ecstasy?", Hemans answers with a dramatic presentation. She releases Keats's questions into active portrayal. Keats's ode is as circular and contained as the urn, while Hemans's poem is as vulnerable to consumption as is Eudora. In short, Hemans's representation of history and her aesthetic choices parallel one another. She divests the male observer of his claim to experience the sublime in his observation of a woman dying by complicating the story on several levels. The complex, shifting, and uncontainable structure of her poem replicates this revision.

Each time I teach this lesson plan, the discussion opens out into new questions and into other literature on the syllabus, reminding me yet again that real pleasures of teaching even the most structured lesson plans are the students' responses and insights. The first time I taught these poems together, students were prompted by our discussion about Eudora's resistance to slavery to ask: Were there black people writing in the time period? What was Hemans's view of slavery? In this class, I answered these questions with the historical facts of abolition and with reference to Romantic literature that takes slavery as its theme. Since then I have added a unit to my syllabus on enslavement, which includes both abolitionist poetry and several of Hemans's poems from *Records of Woman*. Although Hemans portrays women's oppression rather than slavery, her stylistic techniques are similar those used by abolitionist poets. Indeed, even students who do not fall in love with Hemans's poetic style see value in her poetry after we read more of it alongside sentimental antislavery poems in this unit. In an anonymous course evaluation one student wrote: "After the enslavement unit, I sensed a real strength in Hemans's work that I hadn't before. I began to recognize the power issues behind her poetry." Reading Hemans's poems in the context of social activist poetry inspired one student to suggest that in future classes I pair "The Bride of the Greek Isle" with Coleridge's "Rime of the Ancient Mariner" because of the similar story-telling quality, the references to slavery, and the use of ships as prisons in both poems. Underlying this comment is a crucial perception about the connection between narrative poetry and literary opposition to slavery, a connection, that is, between poetic form and history. Taking seriously the problem of stylistic disjunction among poems in the Romantic era plunges us into history and aesthetics, and ultimately into unanticipated connections and collaborative discoveries.

Notes

1. For this and the other student perspectives in this essay, I am particularly grateful to the members of my current and former Romanticism classes at the University of Missouri-Kansas City and at Lehigh University. I would especially like to thank Margot Stafford, Caitlin Maloy, Robert Alunni, LaVerne Williams, and Krystal Hubble, all of whom have given me permission to quote their comments.
2. "Reading Hemans: Aesthetics, and the Canon: An Online Discussion," in *Romantic Circles*, NASSR-L [Discussion List] (16–19 July 1997); available from http://www.rc.umd.edu/reference/anthologies/hemans.htm.
3. Jerome McGann, *The Poetics of Sensibility* (Oxford: Clarendon Press, 1996); Nanora Sweet and Julie Melnyk, eds., *Felicia Hemans: Reimagining Poetry in the Nineteenth Century* (Houndmills: Palgrave, 2001).
4. John Keats, "Letter to Percy Bysshe Shelley, 16 August 1820," *British Literature 1780–1830*, eds. Anne K. Mellor and Richard E. Matlak (New York: Harcourt Brace, 1996), 1309–10. Unless otherwise noted, the literary texts I cite are from this anthology, which I use in my classes.
5. Deborah Kennedy, Nanora Sweet, and Susan Wolfson, for example, all recommend the pairing of poetry by Hemans and Keats in their respective essays in *Approaches to Teaching British Women Poets of the Romantic Period*, eds. Stephen C. Behrendt and Harriet Kramer Linkin (New York: MLA, 1997). See also Anne Mellor and Richard Matlak's "Anthologising the New Romanticism," *Romanticism on the Net* 7 [Website] (August 1997); available from http://users.ox.ac.uk/~scat0385/mellor.html.
6. Stuart Curran, Greg Kucich, and others observe that Romantic-period women writers use history differently from male writers. See Stuart Curran, "Women Readers, Women Writers," *The Cambridge Companion to British Romanticism*, ed. Stuart Curran (Cambridge UP, 1993), 177–95; Greg Kucich, "Staging History: Teaching Romantic Intersections of Drama, History, and Gender," in Behrendt and Linkin, *Approaches to Teaching British Women Poets of the Romantic Period*, 89–96.
7. See Deborah Kennedy, "Introducing Felicia Hemans in the First-Year Course," for a different approach to pairing these two poems, in Behrendt and Linkin, *Approaches to Teaching British Women Poets of the Romantic Period*, 153–56). For a detailed discussion of the interplay of history and aesthetics in the two poems, see Isobel Armstrong, "Natural and National Monuments—Felicia Hemans's 'The Image in Lava': A Note" in Sweet and Melnyk, 212–230.
8. Like many of the scholars posting in the second half of the July 1997 NASSR discussion, I am committed to reading poetry aloud in class both because much of it was written to be read aloud and because feeling the words of a poem in your mouth creates a physical memory that is, in my experience, more powerful than reading silently ("Reading Hemans").
9. Percy Bysshe Shelley, "Ozymandias," in Mellor and Matlak, 1066, l. 14. Isobel Armstrong suggests that the sand represents "the humanly made devastation resulting from mishandled power" rather than natural power. "Natural and National Monuments," 215.
10. Shelley, ll. 5–6.
11. Felicia Dorothea Browne Hemans, "The Image in Lava," in Mellor and Matlak, 1242, ll 1, 6.
12. Shelley, l. 11.
13. Grant F. Scott, *The Sculpted Word: Keats, Ekphrasis, and the Visual Arts* (Hanover, NH: UP of New England, 1994), 122–23.
14. In "The Fragile Image: Felicia Hemans and Romantic Ekphrasis," Grant Scott notes that "Felicia Hemans wrote more ekphrastic poems than the major Romantic poets combined, thirty-eight to be exact" (36). In Sweet and Melnik, 36–54.

15 Arthur C. Downer, *The Odes of Keats* (Oxford: Clarendon Press, 1897), 37–38.
16 David Simpson, *Irony and Authority in Romantic Poetry* (Totowa, NJ: Rowman and Littlefield, 1979),11.
17 Jack Stillinger, "Fifty-nine Ways of Reading 'Ode on a Grecian Urn,'" in "'Ode on a Grecian Urn': Hypercanonicity & Pedagogy," *Romantic Circles Paxis Series* [Website] ed. James O'Rourke. (October 2003); available from http:/www.rc.umd.edu/praxis/grecianurn.
18 John Keats, "Ode on a Grecian Urn," in Mellor and Matlak, 1297–98., ll. 33–34, 42–43.
19 Keats, ll. 5, 8–10.
20 (1, 2, 3).
21 Susan Wolfson, "The Know of Not to Know It: My Returns to Reading and Teaching Keats's 'Ode on a Grecian Urn," in O'Rourke, paragraph 8.
22 Keats ll. 11–12, 21–22.
23 At this point in the discussion this semester, my students were quite interested to learn about David Collings' suggestion that Colin Campbell's description of consumer desire as the cultivation of a "daydream that is not satisfied by the commodity itself," is a useful way to think about an urn that is all potential with no material referent ("Suspended Satisfaction: 'Ode on a Grecian Urn' and the Construction of Art" in O'Rourke).
24 Keats ll. 49–50.
25 In order not to oversimplify this point, I offer students a summary of the poem's publication history. As John Kandl points out, the ode first appeared in *The Annals of Fine Arts* alongside essays by William Hazlitt and Benjamin Robert Haydon, which praised the "versimilitude of the Elgin Marbles, their truth to nature, over…the conceptual and artificial aesthetic favored by the Royal Academy." ("The Timeless in Its Time: Engaging Students in a Close-reading and Discussion of the Historical Contexts of 'Ode on a Grecian Urn,'" in O'Rourke, paragraph 2.) Keats's preference for ideal forms over realistic depiction does then enter into a debate that might be historicized. Because Hemans shared Hazlitt and Haydon's enthusiasm for the Elgin marbles, this topic is a fruitful point of comparison.
26 Excerpt from Isaac Disraeli's "Of a Biography Painted." *Curiosities of Literature*, vol. 4. Boston: William Veazie, 1864. 4 vols. 13-19. The work to which Disraeli refers is Carlo Maggi, *Description historique d'un volume composé de tableaux peints en miniature, qui représentent les voyages et les aventures de Charles Maguis*, Paris: J. Debure, 1761. I have located a copy of the book in the special collection at University College Dublin, but it contains the text only, no plates.

> This extraordinary volume may be said to have contained the travels and adventures of Charles Magius, a noble Venetian; and this volume, so precious, consisted only of eighteen pages, composed of a series of highly-finished miniature paintings on vellum, some executed by the hand of Paul Veronese. Each page, however, may be said to contain many chapters; for, generally, it is composed of a large center-piece, surrounded by ten small ones, with many apt inscriptions, allegories, and allusions; the whole exhibiting romantic incidents in the life of this Venetian nobleman. But it is not merely as a beautiful production of art that we are to consider it; it becomes associated with a more elevated feeling in the occasion which produced it. The author, who himself is the hero, after having been long calumniated, resolved to set before the eyes of his accusers the sufferings and adventures he could perhaps have indifferently described: and instead of composing a tedious volume for his justification, invented this new species of pictorial biography. The author minutely described the remarkable situations in which fortune has placed him; and the artists, in embellishing the facts he furnished them with to record, emulated each other in giving life to their truth, and putting into

action, before the spectator, incidents which the pen had less impressively exhibited. This unique production may be considered as a model to represent the actions of those who may succeed more fortunately by this new mode of perpetuating their history; discovering, by the aid of their pencil, rather than by their pen, the forms and colours of an extraordinary life.

It was when the Ottomans (about 1571) attacked the Isle of Cyprus, that this Venetian nobleman was charged by his republic to review and repair the fortifications…Invested with the chief command, at the head of his troops, Magius threw himself into the island of Cyprus, and after a skillful defence, which could not prevent its fall, at Famagusta he was taken prisoner by the Turks, and made a slave. His age and infirmities induced his master, at length, to sell him to some Christian merchants; and after an absence of several years from his beloved Venice, he suddenly appeared, to the astonishment and mortification of a party who had never ceased to calumniate him; while his own noble family were compelled to preserve an indignant silence, having had no communications with their lost and enslaved relative. Magius now returned to vindicate his honour, to reinstate himself in the favour of the senate, and to be restored to a venerable parent amidst his family….

[27] Disraeli, 18.
[28] As a Venetian, Magius himself was a sort of invader of Cyprus at the time—actually more unwelcome than the Muslim Turks as a Roman Catholic during a time of schism with the Greek Orthodox Church. Magius was removed from the slave woman's experience by religion, gender and an interest in overpowering her culture.
[29] Felicia Dorothea Browne Hemans, "The Bride of the Greek Isle," in Mellor and Matlak, 1229–32. l. 139.
[30] Disraeli, 18.
[31] Hemans, "Bride," l. 199.
[32] Hemans, "Bride," ll. 215-16.
[33] Hemans, "Bride," ll. 217-20.
[34] Keats, ll. 1-4.
[35] Hemans "Bride," ll. 6, 31-32.
[36] Hemans "Bride," ll. 43-46.
[37] Hemans, "Bride," ll. 95-96, 105-10.
[38] Keats, ll. 3-4.
[39] Hemans, "Bride," ll. 3, 2.
[40] Hemans, "Bride," ll. 31-32.
[41] Hemans, "Bride," ll. 123-24.
[42] Hemans, "Bride," ll. 125, 127.
[43] Hemans, "Bride," ll. 153.
[44] Keats, l. 1.
[45] Keats, ll. 26-27.
[46] Hemans, "Bride," ll. 95-96.
[47] Hemans, "Bride," l. 125.
[48] Hemans, "Bride," ll. 175-176.
[49] M. R. G. Spiller, "Circularity and Silence on the Grecian Urn," *Durham University Journal* 80.1 (1987): 53-58.

The Romantic Period
Dr. Dolan

Course Description:

Living between the beginning of the French Revolution (1789) and the Reform Act (1832), the writers we call the British Romantics witnessed rapid social change and radical shifts in political power in Europe. As the British Empire began to take hold in the world, the British population passionately expressed a variety of opinions about pressing social problems including parliamentary reform, the slave trade, the problem of poverty, women's rights, and the ethics of scientific inquiry. In this course we will explore the ways in which writers in this period translated into art this sense of unrest, acknowledgement of loss, and concern with power. We will focus in particular on the different ways in which canonical male writers (Blake, Wordsworth, Coleridge, Keats, Shelley, Byron) and female writers who were popular in their own time (Anna Letitia Barbauld, Helen Maria Williams, Mary Wollstonecraft, Charlotte Smith, Mary Robinson, Felicia Hemans) represent political, emotional, artistic, and natural power in their work.

Required Texts:

- Anne K. Mellor and Richard E. Matlak, eds. *British Literature 1780–1830*. New York: Harcourt, 1996.
- Jane Austen, *Persuasion*. Petersborough, ON: Broadview P, 1998.
- Additional Texts on Blackboard

NOTE: *The unit called "The Aesthetics of Loss" is based on Kay K. Cook's "The Aesthetics of Loss: Charlotte Smith's* The Emigrants *and* Beachy Head*" in* Approaches to Teaching British Women Poets of the Romantic Period*, eds. Stephen C. Behrendt and Harriet Kramer Linkin (New York:*

Figure 1. Elizabeth A. Dolan, Sample Syllabus (continued on next page)

	The Romantic Period
	Dr. Dolan
Reading Schedule:	
	Political Revolution

Week One: Edmund Burke, *Reflections on the Revolution in France;* Mary Wollstonecraft, *A Vindication of the Rights of Men;* Thomas Paine, *The Rights of Man*; Helen Maria Williams, *Letters from France*

Week Two: William Blake, "The Marriage of Heaven and Hell"; William Wordsworth, "Composed Upon Westminster Bridge, Sept. 3, 1803," "'I Griev'd for Buonaparte,'" "London 1802"; Lord Byron, "Sonnet on Chillon," "Ode to Napoleon Buonaparte"

The Aesthetics of Loss

Week Three: Burke, from *A Philosophical Enquiry;* William Gilpin, from *Three Essays*; Wollstonecraft, *Letters from Norway* (excerpts)

Week Four: Wollstonecraft, *Letters to Imlay* (excerpts); Charlotte Smith, "Beachy Head"

Romantic Fiction

Weeks Five and Six: Jane Austen, *Persuasion*

The Rhetoric of History

Week Seven: Percy Bysshe Shelley, "Ozymandias"; Felicia Hemans, "The Image in Lava"; John Keats, "Ode on a Grecian Urn"; Hemans, "The Bride of the Greek Isle"

Week Eight: William Wilberforce, from "A Letter on the Abolition of the Slave Trade"

Enslavement

Week Nine: Thomas Clarkson, from *The History of the Rise, Progress and Accomplishment of the Abolition;* Shelley, *Prometheus Unbound*

Week Ten: Ottobah Cugoano, from "Thoughts and Sentiments..."; Mary Prince, from *The History of Mary Prince, a West Indian Slave;* Samuel Taylor Coleridge, "The Rime of the Ancient Mariner"

Week Eleven: William Cowper, "The Negro's Complaint," "Pity for Poor Africans"; Robert Southey, "The Sailor, Who Had Served in the Slave Trade"; Hemans, "The Indian Woman's Death Song," "Joan of Arc In Rheims," "The Indian City"; Amelia Opie, "Black Man's Lament."

Poetic Revolution: Nature, the Everyday, and the Uncanny

Week Twelve: Wordsworth, "Preface to *Lyrical Ballads*"; Shelley, *Defence of Poetry;* Wordsworth, "Tintern Abbey"; Coleridge, "Frost at Midnight," "This Lime-Tree Bower My Prison"

Week Thirteen: Shelley, "Mont Blanc"; Coleridge, "Kubla Khan"; Wordsworth, "Simon Lee," "We Are Seven," "Resolution and Independence"

Week Fourteen: Anna Letitia Barbauld, "Washing Day," "Inscription for an Ice-House"; Amelia Opie, "Consumption"; Mary Robinson, "All Alone," "The Alien Boy," "A London Summer Morning"; Letitia Elizabeth Landon "Calypso Watching the Ocean"

Week Fifteen: Keats, "The Eve of St. Agnes," *Letters;* Keats, "Ode to a Nightingale," "Ode on Melancholy"

Figure 1. Elizabeth A. Dolan, Sample Syllabus

CHAPTER EIGHT
Pedagogy and Oppositions: Teaching Non-Canonical British Women Writers at the Technical University

James R. Simmons Jr.

As many college professors have discovered, it can sometimes be difficult to introduce and justify teaching those British women writers commonly considered non-canonical, even in departments where the attitude about what constitutes a proper curriculum is open-minded and permissive. Imagine, however, trying to teach non-canonical British women writers at a research university where the majority of the students, though intelligent and studious, have little regard for the humanities in general. I am a professor at a university where Ph.D.s are granted in fields such as Biomedical Engineering, Behavioral Psychology, and Computational Analysis, and although we do have an M.A. program in English, I think it is safe to say that we draw most of our English majors because they are residents of nearby areas, rather than because our university has a high-profile English program. Though we have one of the largest departments on campus, I do not think I exaggerate when I say that most of the faculty in the other departments see us as a group here for service, our department's perhaps most important function being the teaching of technical writing to students in twenty-nine different majors, and our duty to ensure that every biomedical engineer, architect, and marketing analyst who leaves this university can write professionally.

We are expected to expose them to a smattering of culture as well, this in the form of the American and British sophomore survey courses. There are advantages and disadvantages to teaching these courses at a university such as this, and a positive is that most of the students are highly intelligent in their fields. The negative, of course, is that the majority of students who come to a university such as this are apathetic towards literature in general—it is for "Bohemians," "liberals," and "artsy types." I realize that this is a problem at many universities, and I think that I have always been able to come to terms with this attitude coming from the unmotivated student who rarely comes to class or is unprepared. When I encounter this type of student, I realize that he or she is going to pay for it with a poor grade at the end of the term, and so in a sense justice will be served. However, it is a bit different when you are working with extremely motivated students who are bright, come to class, and are near perfectionists. When a student tells me, as did one junior with a 4.0 , that he fails to see the use of learning the literature I teach in the British survey course that he is required to take for his chemical engineering degree,

I have to admit that the situation is a bit different. I come back with all of the pat answers about how it teaches analytical skills and that in order to be successful you must be a good communicator and so forth, but still, this student's attitude, echoed by so many others, is troublesome.

What does this have to do with teaching British women writers? First, because I was fortunate enough to be in a graduate program where expanding the canon seemed to be something that most of my professors were interested in doing, as a newly hired assistant professor I walked into the classroom ready to expand the canon a bit myself. Change is never easy, and in our profession broadening the literary parameters may be met by two factions who do not want change of any type, and by this I mean the either the faculty (my peers), or the students. Ironically, though, I have found that perhaps teaching non-canonical British women writers has been easier to do here than it might have been in a setting where the study of Liberal Arts is the focus. The challenge that presents itself is how to make broadening the canon palatable to the faculty and the students, and how to make it interesting and necessary as well.

Fortunately, I have encountered little opposition from the faculty as to what I choose to teach in my British survey courses. It is clear that the selection of authors studied in the survey courses here in the past may have been a bit reductive, but I suppose that may have been true at any university until just a few years ago. In fairness, many of my colleagues, who are much further along in their careers than I am at this point, were themselves taught few, if any, of the women poets I introduce in my courses and whom I was taught in graduate school almost as a matter of course. In fact, their attitude seems to be that since it appears that this type of literary radicalism is cutting edge, go ahead and do it, and perhaps we will all benefit in the long run.

The harder sell, as I saw it, would be the students, both the majors and non-majors. In northern Louisiana, from my experience the typical student is extremely conservative, polite, and respectful of authority, and as such, a person who will generally abide by the rules if those rules are in writing. But with this conservatism and adherence to the rules come questioning minds that are apt to be somewhat suspicious when an English professor introduces anything completely new, especially when it is not in the text. They may hate Shakespeare or Dickens or whomever, but they recognize the canonical authors as a necessary evil. After all, these guys are in the book and they have heard of them, so boring or not, they must be okay. Attempting, then, to pull in women writers who are not in the text or who are but whom they haven't heard of, is a real challenge.

The first trial was in my British survey course. Although we have carte blanche with the specific selections we chose to teach, we are required to use the one-volume *Norton Anthology of English Literature: The Major Authors* as the primary text, though we may supplement freely.[1] Because this is not a course for majors, I generally do not push the envelope too much, and I supplement just a few nontraditional items in this course. Typically, I begin supplementing when we study the Romantic period, and I tend to do this by balancing the male and female Romantics in a compare/contrast type of situation. For example, what follows is a section of several days' reading assignments that I have lifted directly from my syllabus:

- *Monday 17 September*: William Wordsworth, from *Preface to Lyrical Ballads*; Joanna Baillie, from *Introductory Discourse* (on *Blackboard*)
- *Wednesday 19 September:* William Blake, "London"; Mary Robinson, "London's Summer Morning"(on *Blackboard*); William Wordsworth's "London 1802"
- *Monday 24 September*: Mary Robinson, "To the Poet Coleridge"; Samuel Taylor Coleridge, "Kubla Khan"
- *Wednesday 26 September:* John Keats, "Ode to a Nightingale"; Samuel Taylor Coleridge, "The Nightingale"; Charlotte Smith, "To a Nightingale," "On the Departure of the Nightingale," and "Return of the Nightingale"(all on *Blackboard*)

Following the list above, you can see that when we did Coleridge's "Kubla Khan," as a collateral reading, I assigned Mary Robinson's "To The Poet Coleridge," which I posted as an electronic file they could download by going to *Blackboard*. In class I asked them to write for about ten minutes and give me their impressions of the two poems. Although I had several responses that echoed the sentiments of the writers who said "honestly, I don't really understand either poem," and "I did not like either one of these but I did enjoy 'The Cry of the Children'"(introduced non-chronologically in comparison to social concerns in Blake's poetry as a paper topic), some students were a bit more specific. "'To the Poet Coleridge' is a lot better than 'Kubla Khan,' a student wrote. ['To the Poet Coleridge'] seems more descriptive and clear. Although many of the same images [found in 'Kubla Khan'] are in Robinson's poem they seem different. Her images are a little more detailed." Another student said that "['To the Poet Coleridge'] gives the reader a sense of wonder and awe, but of the two I like 'Kubla Khan' the most simply because I am more familiar with it. 'To the Poet Coleridge' was, however, an enjoyable read."

    The issue here is not which poem is better, because I wasn't attempting to have a contest, but rather whether students benefit from being introduced to literature by women considered non-canonical. Since as a Dickens and Brontë specialist I tend to find myself teaching from a biographical, historical, and/or new historical perspective most of the time, for me context is important, and I enjoy introducing the elements which make up the "story behind the literature" anyway. Thus examining "To the Poet Coleridge" in conjunction with "Kubla Khan" seems to me to allow a better understanding of Coleridge's work and life. Another, and perhaps even better example of a "paired" work, is Joanna Baillie's "Introductory Discourse," which we examined in conjunction with Wordsworth's "Preface to

Lyrical Ballads." While teaching "To the Poet Coleridge" seems to me an optional exercise for purposes of contextualization, the reasons for teaching "Introductory Discourse" are not just to provide context, but to examine a work that is important in its own right. In short, I don't think—and clearly this is just my opinion—"To the Poet Coleridge" stands on it own without "Kubla Khan," but "Introductory Discourse," while more meaningful if paired with "Preface to Lyrical Ballads," can stand on its own. It is quite possible to look at "Introductory Discourse" without Wordsworth's work, talk about the suggestions Baillie makes for quality drama, and then verbally make the transitions to "what if this were applied to poetry?" When one can eliminate a dependency on the literature by males and teach a work for its own merits, without using a comparison/contrast method to argue legitimacy, then clearly the work in question has a place in the canon. "Introductory Discourse," it seems to me, is one such work. It is made stronger by comparison with "Preface to Lyrical Ballads" to be sure, but legitimate without external comparative validation as well.

Of course by using the comparative mode, students do see the two works juxtaposed, and consequently seem to enjoy learning that Wordsworth was not perhaps the God that their high school English teachers made him out to be. They also enjoy seeing that he may have been guilty in fact of doing the very thing I warn them against—borrowing work without crediting the proper source. I think this type of collateral reading is time well spent, as students seem to benefit from exposure to it. Conversely, it often works in the reverse, as in the case where I had students compare Mary Robinson's "London's Summer Morning" to William Blake's "London" and William Wordsworth's "London 1802." Robinson's poem seemed to be favored over Wordsworth's poem, principally because the mere mention of Milton induces nausea for most of them, but Robinson's poem was not preferred over Blake's. This may be because I spend so much time on the condition of England at the turn of the century that students feel that Robinson and Wordsworth alike need to pay attention, as Blake does, to the social problems around them, and not just, as one student wrote, "turn a blind eye to streets filled with horse dung and prostitutes." Blake has, however, been extremely popular, perhaps because he writes about what students refer to as "neat things," such prostitution, death, disease, consumptive chimney sweeps and the like, and to be truthful it is doubtful if anyone could have surpassed him in popularity. However, this illustrates an important point too, that, once again, this is not a contest. Not all poetry by the women is supposed to be nor is it better than that by the men, nor is the opposite true. The idea is to expose students to the full spectrum, and let them judge for themselves.

The danger of teaching with the comparison/contrast method is that it still means that the men, i.e., "the big six," are determining the canon, even if I am introducing poetry by women. I feel that this method is a necessary evil because it is an effective introduction to these little known women poets, as the thin line separating what is in the anthology and what is not is extremely clear when illustrated in this fashion. This is only a starting point though, and after easing into to this subject matter, I begin to introduce work that stands in no direct relation to the work by male poets. When I include the work of Anna Laetitia Barbauld or Felicia Hemans, who are now in the *Major Authors* anthology, or Mary Robinson or Joanna Baillie, who are not, it is ingrained in the students' literary awareness that work by women being supplemental does not mean that it is unworthy of analysis, and they approach it more open mindedly. It does not have to be compared to the work by men for validity, and they love it—or loathe it—based purely upon their own interaction with the work. This is the ultimate goal, in that by educating them and exposing them to a wider array of literature than what the anthology provides I can allow them to make their own decisions based on a variety of factors, rather than a decision based on exposure to a narrow and selective range of works. How can one decide what is personally appealing or unappealing if it seems that roughly six poets wrote nearly everything of any quality during a forty-year span, as some anthologies seem to suggest with their focus? Even though anthologies continue to improve regarding the inclusion of work by women, students need only to look in any standard sophomore survey anthology's section on the Romantic period, compare the number of pages devoted to work by men as opposed to the number devoted to work by women, and it isn't hard to interpret the disparity as being an indication that Romantic-era women poets are unimportant. However, at least by exposing my students to a wide variety of selections by men and women, their opinions can truly be the result of an educated and informed experience.

While English majors and graduate students are not apathetic about literature as their counterparts in the British survey courses are inclined to be, that does not mean that they have been exposed to significantly more non-canonical women writers than the nonmajor survey students. Being at a technical university, we do not attract a lot of majors to begin with (about 150 total English and English education majors out of 12,000 students), and those we do draw often have a reading background very similar to the students who are in the technical majors. The difference between the students majoring in English here and those in the technical majors is that the students majoring in English just liked the reading they got in high school better than their classmates did, or, as is often the case, they want to go to law school (English being the preferred major for those seeking the J.D.). Having taught the sophomore-level British survey before I was given my first senior-level Victorian survey, I was aware of the possible challenges I faced, but this time I looked forward to introducing students in the major to a broadening of the canon. Perhaps (a little too smugly), I even saw myself in a position to educate the Philistines, or something of that sort.

What I wasn't prepared for was the opposition, and by this I mean the textbook I used that first year. Having just spent five years in graduate school, where there were separate courses not only for Victorian prose fiction, prose nonfiction, and poetry, but also subcategories where there were courses on Victorian realism and Victorian women writers and so on, I was a bit out of touch with the demands of the Victorian undergraduate survey as it related to the texts available. First I should point out that in my first year, 1997, there was basically only one Victorian anthology on the market, the Oxford *Victorian Prose and Poetry* edited by Lionel Trilling and Harold Bloom.[2] With only ten poems by women in nearly 800 pages of text—seven by Christina Rossetti, one by EBB, and two by Emily Brontë—clearly, without supplementing this text in some way, I could not give my students an opportunity to do a fair assessment of the work of these three canonical poets, much less allow them to examine the work of anyone traditionally considered a more "marginal" literary figure. Though I was a bit surprised by the lack of poetry by women, this was not nearly as shocking as the editorial comments in the text, which seemed geared towards undermining everything that I wanted to do in class.

I had learned in graduate school that some of the male professors of the "old school" have little use for "the scribbling women," and much to my disappointment, I first encountered this in my initial graduate Victorian novel course. There, the professor rather dismissively called *Jane Eyre* "the most overrated novel in English literature." This is not good to hear when you are an eager graduate student, a Victorian novel specialist, and *Jane Eyre* is one of your favorite novels. However, I quickly learned that this professor seemed to have no use for any of the women writers, and perhaps if I owe him anything it is that his dour attitude steeled me for the blatant misogynistic attitude towards women writers that we all, men and women alike, still occasionally encounter as we attempt to expand the canon. Nevertheless, I wasn't prepared for the comments in the Oxford anthology I used my first year here, negative comments right there in black ink for all the world to see.

Christina Rossetti was the only female included in the main body of the text (Brontë and EBB were in appendices), and even there Rossetti was clearly relegated to a marginal status. In the six-sentence introduction to her work, the editors mention "Goblin Market," though they did not include it, claiming it was "too long to include here" (apparently, though, this didn't apply to Tennyson's *In Memoriam*). Their way of evaluating Rossetti's work was to compare her, of course, to her male counterparts, and the editors claim that her poetry is "much simpler" than her brother's, and that "she lacks dramatic juxtaposition, in which Hopkins abounds."

If this is the feature that the only woman included in the main body of the text gets, you can imagine how those relegated to the back of the volume fared. Under "Other Victorian Poets," we find those poets the editors claim never achieved "major status," noting that "Mrs. Browning had an enormous contemporary reputation, and now survives in her husband's work and in a handful of lyrics…" Elizabeth Barrett Browning apparently isn't significant enough to warrant a first name, being "Mrs." only. However, the *coup de grâce* was the pronouncement on her work, as the editors note that *Aurora Leigh* "is very bad. Quite bad too are the famous *Sonnets from the Portuguese*…."[3] Emily Brontë fares only slightly better, simply because instead of derision, she is essentially dismissed as an oddball with a wave of the pen.

That first year I combated this text and its wretched editorial comments in a way that was really much simpler than I had anticipated—I let the poets' works be the standard. What student of literature can read EBB's Sonnet 43 ("How do I love thee? Let me count the ways."), and then agree that this wonderful poem about unconditional love is "quite bad" as the editors of the Oxford anthology indicated? "Goblin Market," as many of us know, can be one of the few poems that, even in a survey class of nonmajors, can open the eyes of even those students who have no interest in literature whatsoever. Indeed, can there be anything more traumatic than reading Emily Brontë's poems and knowing that the author of "Last Lines" will soon herself be a corpse, and that she knows it? Powerful poems all, and these are but a few. Are they somehow lesser than works by Tennyson, Matthew Arnold, and Robert Browning? I think that question answers itself with a decided negative.

Fortunately, since that first year, several fine Victorian anthologies have appeared, so I am no longer forced to supplement all of the work by women I need to do. However, even today, with more and more work by women appearing in the anthologies, to my English majors my selection of texts must often seem iconoclastic. They often know and have previously studied Emily Brontë, EBB, and sometimes even Christina Rossetti, but I have no doubt that they find the inclusion of Harriet Martineau, Elizabeth Gaskell, Mary Elizabeth Braddon, and Frances Powers Cobbe unusual, as they are not figures with whom they had become familiar in high school or in their British survey courses. If I were female, I know that there might be a tendency for some of my colleagues to say that I teach these selections in addition to the canonical authors simply to include more women, no matter what the quality of the literature, which simply isn't true. I teach these "other" women—just as I teach selections by Henry Mayhew, Wilkie Collins, Thomas Hood, and Henry Morley—to present a true picture of the Victorian literary spectrum. I added works that were significant and important, and I did not do a type of reverse discrimination just to provide gender balance. My contention is that many Victorians were exposed to a wide array of exciting and important literature by both men and women, and only through what we call canonization have we somehow decided that many of these works are now somehow of no significance. I disagree, again, not simply to balance the scales, but because I think that my students deserve a better and more comprehensive picture of the Victorian period than the anthology offered. This is hard to do in the sophomore survey course, as we study so many periods, but imperative in a focused course such as the Victorian survey.

Still, with each new Victorian survey I teach, I think my majors seem to wonder about the validity of the syllabus at first. If Martineau, Cobbe, and the others were so important, how come they had never heard of them? Remember, they are typically getting straight-line, no frills, no non-canonical writers in their sophomore surveys unless they had had me for that class, so the whole idea of there being anyone important outside of the authors listed or taught in the anthology is a new one. Consequently, the idea of introducing these "no-names" to the majors is a bit of a hard sell. If you think about it, perhaps the greatest Victorian novelists—and this is arguable—could be considered to be George Eliot, Charlotte and Emily Brontë, and Charles Dickens. Even if we slide Thomas Hardy in, in terms of numbers the women carry the day. Students recognize this, and even if we expand our numbers a bit and include William Makepeace Thackeray and Anthony Trollope, we'd probably also include Elizabeth Gaskell and Anne Brontë. The point is, students think the women in Victorian literature get a pretty fair shake, and to be honest I think that the novelists do, perhaps more so than in any area of literature. But that does not mean that all genres of Victorian literature are so inclusive, and therein lies the problem.

Harriet Martineau is the principal female essayist we work with who could be considered as being outside the normal parameters, though we do examine some selections by Frances Powers Cobbe too. In regard to the condition of England question, we not only examine Ruskin's *Unto This Last* and Carlyle's *Chartism* and *Past and Present*, but we also read parts of Martineau's *The Factory Controversy, A Warning Against Meddling Legislation*, as well as one of Martineau's didactic tales from *Sketches from Life* called "The Factory Boy." While most students seem to think that Martineau was bit sarcastic and hard-hearted (she could be—which is part of her appeal), and even completely unrealistic in "The Factory Boy," one student, a male, bravely chimed up in defense of Martineau's comments. Of Martineau's attempts to show that the blame for factory accidents did not all rest with owners, but that it was attributable to workers' neglect as well, he said "She's right. How could every accident that occurs in the factory be the fault of the owners, as Dickens and Henry Morley seem to indicate?" We thereafter had a very interesting discussion, and whether students agreed or disagreed with Martineau, to a person they felt that her point of view should be studied right alongside of Carlyle, Ruskin, and the others. After all, they said, in anthologies it sounds like all of the great thinkers are crying about the problems but are being ignored. Doing Martineau (and Malthus, whose pre-Victorian *An Essay on the Principle of Population* I also supplemented) showed them that there were opposing viewpoints which had validity. Did it matter that

Martineau was a woman? Not really, but her works were simply worthy of study, no matter whether a man or a woman wrote them.

Of course I have been lucky, in that I do have the freedom to choose my own texts in all courses except the British survey course, and I can supplement when I please in any class. However, some professors have university-mandated texts that are seldom (if ever) changed and that they are required to use, and I do have friends who apparently have little latitude in choosing the texts they must use, so supplementing is often the only answer. Perhaps even more common is the "I've been making these marginal notes for years and I'm not changing the text" attitude. Even with younger professors, it seems to become hard to change texts after it has served a purpose for even one or two classes, as the transferring of the ever-present marginalia is one of the most tedious of all processes. Supplementing is certainly easier than completely changing texts, and because I have never seen a text that has everything a professor wants, many of us supplement anyway, especially if our text at least covers the basics. However, above all, I realized that the old reviled Oxford text I had to use my first year actually served a purpose: It clearly illustrated exactly what many students question, in that it shows how some women's literature has been marginalized not because it was bad, but simply because some male editors and scholars felt it was not of a high enough quality to be studied. I tell students this, and we read literature by women that is superb, but still they seem to regard me with skepticism when I tell them that in some cases things as simple as personal preferences, selectivity, and perhaps even misogyny have kept the canon predominantly male. When they hear the comments in the Oxford text written before we had the variety of texts available now (I still trot the Oxford out from time to time, and read the comments after we've studied EBB or Christina Rossetti), the point is driven home better than it might be in any other way I can think of. As I tell them, if the respected and well-educated editors of that anthology can write these things, can't you see how it has been happening for centuries, certainly from far less enlightened minds? For young minds attuned to political correctness, I think this anthology provides a needed shock that illustrates the arbitrariness of inclusion in the canon and why women seem so poorly represented. That text has gone from being a first-year liability for me, to being one of my best teaching tools.

As a just tenured professor who has been eager to introduce more women into my courses than the anthologies offer or than the students are familiar with, I have been pleased with the results thus far. I think the idea behind providing one's students with a good education is that we teach them what is necessary for them to have an accurate and fairly comprehensive knowledge of the period they are studying. Although I am not, for example, as fond of Matthew Arnold as I am of John Stuart Mill, I know that I need to examine the work of both of them in order to give my students a true picture of the "spirit of the age." Consequently, just because at some indeterminate point in time someone decided that Harriet Martineau and other women were not an important part of the literature of the nineteenth century, I feel that omitting them is gross misrepresentation of the period. I have no axe to grind, and my objective is not to single-handedly try and make up for the century-plus of neglect that has caused the work of many of these women to be forgotten. I have no political agenda: I simply want give my students the first-rate education they or their parents are paying for, no matter what the student's major. That means, for me, teaching the non-canonical women, whether anyone else considers them marginal or not.

Notes

[1] M. H. Abrams, General Editor, and Stephen Greenblatt, Associate General Editor, *The Norton Anthology of English Literature: The Major Authors*, 7th ed. (New York: W. W. Norton, 2000).
[2] Lionel Trilling and Harold Bloom, eds. *Victorian Prose and Poetry* (New York: Oxford UP, 1973).
[3] Trilling and Bloom, 689.

CHAPTER NINE
Short Fiction by Women in the Victorian Literature Survey

Elisabeth Rose Gruner

The first time I taught a Victorian Literature survey, fresh out of a curriculum integration workshop in graduate school, I taught ten authors: five male and five female. One student evaluation after the course was over complained that despite the promise of "great" Victorian writers, half of those on the syllabus were women. While this did take place in the dark ages of the early nineties, I still find myself, as I design my syllabi, caught in the familiar conundrum as to what to teach, what to cut, and why. In my case, it seems simple: The Victorian period is characterized by great authors who are also women, so I try to teach them. Lest that seem flip, I hasten to add that one important element in the course is interrogating the notion of greatness, or of canonicity: Should we read what the Victorians actually read, or the texts that have become part of our intellectual history since the 1950s? Should we teach a story of the development of English, or, alternatively, the literary history of English engagement with its empire or, possibly, the rise of the professions? Faith and doubt, the Woman Question, Industrialization—the terms label sections of our anthologies and help to structure our courses. A truly integrated survey would cover all these issues and more, with authors representing the varied genders, sexualities, classes, and races of writers in Victorian England.

In that case, my course is not truly integrated. I do, however, value historical coverage, and attempt to acquaint students with at least some of the aesthetic, political, and social issues of the day. The course catalog description need not limit our design of a syllabus, of course, but at a time when the whole issue of "English studies" is on the table, when articles in *Profession* ask whether we really know what we are talking about when we talk about English,[1] the catalog description gives an indication of what we think we're talking about. In my Victorian literature survey course, I am asked to select "representative" works for my students. "Representing" a literary period in fourteen weeks, however—leaving aside the theoretical problems with the task—can be daunting. No longer can I blithely assume that whatever's in the anthology will simply do the trick; I've participated in too many graduate school discussions on canon formation and the exigencies of anthology-production, read too many works that were never included in an anthology, to do so. Even so, there are also the practicalities of the semester, and of student life, and of modern technology: there simply is not time to teach everything (could we even decide what "everything" is, or should be), students do not like to read off of photocopies, and the machines may break down anyway.

When considering the difficult question of what to teach, then, and what to cut, I have been assisted by the availability of short stories by women authors. Of course, Victorian short fiction may still seem like an oxymoron to many, who, like me, were not trained in short fiction in graduate school, and who associate the Victorian period with prolixity. Indeed, an MLA search when I began this project turned up only ten references when the terms "Victorian" and "short fiction" were paired. In fact, though, the short story throve in the period, and offered a publication outlet to a variety of writers, both canonical and not. Glennis Stephenson's recent anthology for Broadview, *Nineteenth-Century Stories by Women*, brings some of these to our attention; Harriet Devine Jump recently edited a similar anthology for Routledge, and other collections should be in the works.[2] In fact the major anthologists are not blind to these changes: For example, Norton's most recent edition of its classic anthology of English literature, as well as the newer Longman anthology of British Literature, both include more short fiction in their Victorian offerings than ever before.[3] In addition there are at least three major reasons for this growing interest in Victorian short fiction. One, the form itself is extremely teachable. Short stories, like shorter poems, can be read at one sitting and discussed, in depth, in one class period. Two, the form is vital to the period. Though we often focus on the longer works, most of the major novelists also wrote short stories, and many authors published exclusively or nearly so in this genre. In order to provide a full picture of the many genres of literature popular in the period, short stories are essential. Third, it is a form particularly congenial to women writers—as the examples of Elizabeth Gaskell, Margaret Oliphant, and Mary Elizabeth Braddon, to name only three, make clear.

I frequently teach stories by all three, and other writers, but in this essay I'll focus on only two, Mary Elizabeth Braddon's "Good Lady Ducayne" and Margaret Oliphant's "A Story of a Wedding Tour."[4] Both stories easily connect with the themes of the survey and with other works in this and similar courses, but can also function to comment on, enlarge, and revise those themes and to call into question our assumptions about those works and the period as a whole.

The course syllabus is a fairly traditional one, emphasizing historical coverage. We no longer require our students to take a traditional British literature survey, preferring to give them a slightly deeper acquaintance with fewer works in a selection of historical survey courses, thematically organized courses, and courses on genre. This course, then, does not fall into a sequence with other courses in British literature; it is in fact likely to be the only course that deals with British literature between 1660 and 1900 that some of our students take.

While I do not always teach from an anthology, I have found it useful as so many do, for the breadth of its coverage and the variety of its selections. I organize the course chronologically, not because I necessarily believe in "progress," but because I find it is a useful organizing category. My focus in the course is first formalist, next historical. I emphasize close reading skills, remembering that I am trying to build skills for English majors to transport to their other coursework. However, I try to put the works in historical context, both the purely literary-historical contexts of who read whom, and what allusions are you catching, to the more cultural and political history offered in the anthology headnotes, timelines, and other resources. The goal is to draw connections between the works, both thematic and formal; to give the students a sense that they are not simply reading a random assortment of works that happened to be published within a century or so of each other, but that they are seeing a variety of literary and social concerns expressed by a community of writers and thinkers. When we get to the Oliphant and Braddon stories it's rather late in the term, and we already have quite a wealth of allusions built up, as well as a clear sense of the varieties of Victorian writing styles.

As the syllabus demonstrates, students spend much of the early part of the term reading several longer works, usually including some or all of *Aurora Leigh*, a Dickens novel, perhaps an Eliot novel, and sometimes all of *Sartor Resartus* or *In Memoriam* as well. In this particular term, they had also read a Gaskell short story by this time, and I later taught both Stevenson's "Jekyll and Hyde" and Conrad's *Heart of Darkness*. Whereas Conrad has ended many a Victorian literature survey in the past, the implicit message has often been that it took until the end of the century for Victorian writers to learn compression or brevity. I have been guilty of the same easy dichotomizing; it is underscored, for example, by the presence of *In Memoriam* early in the semester, and Hopkins's sonnets to close it out. However, students no longer ask about being "paid by the word" or make other uninformed contrasts between Victorian prolixity and modernist compression when they read short stories throughout the period (and, I might add, when they encounter *Ulysses* rather than *Dubliners* as their "representative" Joyce).

The sensation story "Good Lady Ducayne," then, resonated for students with the mysteries of *Great Expectations* and the later sensationalism of *Jekyll and Hyde*. It is a tale of a young woman (Bella) who, engaged as a companion to the elderly woman of the title, finds herself mysteriously weakening in the lush and fecund atmosphere of the Italian Riviera. Befriended by a young English doctor and his sister, she is discovered to be the subject of a particularly unpleasant experiment: Lady Ducayne's vicious doctor, Dr. Parravicini, is transfusing her to keep his client/patient alive. Braddon's narrative is distanced and ironic: Bella neither recognizes the danger she has been in nor the specifics of what has happened to her. Much of the story is carried on through her happily naïve letters to her mother, and she ends the story engaged to the young doctor, for whom "the word 'mother-in-law' holds no terrors."[5]

Oliphant's "A Story of a Wedding Tour" has a similarly distanced narrative style, and also focuses on the fortunes of a single young woman—otherwise, though, it initially seems to have little in common with Braddon's story. Janey, Oliphant's heroine, is married off within paragraphs of the story's opening; an orphan, her guardians have accepted a proposal for her that would not suit one of their own daughters, that of the rather disgusting, but wealthy, Mr. Rosenman—a somewhat stock Jew whose appetites quickly disgust Janey. Fortuitously separated from him when he gets off the train at a short stop during their honeymoon journey, Janey goes on to live an unnarrated ten years without him in a tiny French village she has come to almost at random via a local train line. The mother of a son (she is carrying him, but unaware of the pregnancy, when she and Rosenman are separated), she has established herself in this village when her husband suddenly reappears. Seeing her out of the window of the train, he returns only to die of a heart attack brought on by years of dissolute living, anger, and, finally, the sight of her. The story ends leaving her in the village, reflecting on her responsibility: "she had not blamed herself before; but now seemed to herself no less than the murderer of her husband: and could not forgive herself, nor get out of her ears the dreadful sound of that labouring breath."[6] Far from celebrating her ultimate freedom, then, the story ends on a tragic note.

These brief summaries suggest only some of the richness of the tales. In class, students focused initially on the issue of the "independent woman" in the stories. Already familiar with the old dictum that the Victorian novel ends either in marriage or death, they were pleased to find an alternative future imagined for Janey, though they also noted the ways in which Oliphant qualifies that future with the lingering shadows of tragedy in the final paragraphs. Similarly, while they were romantically pleased by Bella's good fortune, they nonetheless recognized that she, despite her "independence" in seeking and finding work, finally ends her story as dependent and even ignorant as she has begun it; she is characterized by energy rather than wisdom. As one student claimed, Bella's stupidity is her strength. Another student, however, noted the generic differences between the two stories, and argued that, in the Braddon story, both Bella and Lady Ducayne are victims of a society that has no room for strong women; thus, Bella's life is compromised by Lady Ducayne, then Lady Ducayne herself is villainized for her independent-minded actions. The students astutely noticed the limitations of both genre and chronology as they wished for more modern heroines, while recognizing the achievements that are visible here. Their ability to compare these characters with those they had encountered earlier—from the Lady of Shalott to Dinah Morris—enriched their readings of all the texts in the course.

While the anti-Semitism of "The Story of a Wedding Tour" and the vampirism of "Good Lady Ducayne" may seem to be their most salient features, in the context of the course these were less significant to my students. Indeed, few registered the anti-Semitism of the Oliphant story, not recognizing "Rosenman" as a distinctly Jewish name, nor his features as stereotypically Jewish. Similarly, many of our students have not yet been "taught" that sensationalism is cheap or less aesthetically valuable than, say, the suspense of a Dickens novel or the tragedy of an Eliot novel. Thus, I encountered few if any objections to these texts on those grounds. Rather, as I noted, they were keen to connect these with other texts we would read during the semester—perhaps, indeed, flattening out the significant aesthetic differences they encountered.

Using short stories allows me to develop a variety of the themes of the course with more complexity than simply relying on the *Norton* had done. For example, both stories deal with the impact of technology on modern life. Students recalled the "vast steam engine" metaphor that haunts *Sartor Resartus* as they considered what Oliphant means in the final paragraphs of "A Story of a Wedding Tour": "the whole tragedy was one of the railway, the noisy carriages, the snorting locomotives."[7] The railway has of course brought freedom to Janey, and up until her husband's return we have been encouraged to think of her freedom as a positive good; the narrator says, for example, "she found a niche in the little place which she filled perfectly."[8] However, the ten unnarrated years of her freedom pale, in the story and in our imaginations, when placed against the drama of her flight and eventual discovery. Students were frustrated by what they see as Oliphant's ambivalence about Janey's plight; they, like me, preferred to see her as freed twice by the railway rather than trapped as she seems to be in the conclusion. These frustrations, however, are part of the experience of reading literature from earlier periods: Just as we fail to find Dinah Morris as "liberated" as even her creator was, so we may be frustrated with Janey. It seems to be a fruitful frustration, though, that reminds us of the differences between ourselves and our predecessors.

The fact that both stories are set in "old" Europe but deal with "new" technology was also central to our discussions. Our earlier reading of *Aurora Leigh* may have conditioned my students to read for representations of the continent as fertile, a refuge from the bustle of modern England. However, the luxurious overgrowth of the Italian Riviera tires Braddon's Bella: "southern" fecundity is too much for her, and she longs to return—with her English doctor/lover—to the tamer pleasures of Walworth. In this story technology is associated with the virulent overproduction of southern Europe—unlike the sterility it evokes in *Sartor*, but perhaps like the oddly naturalistic metaphors with which Dickens describes Coketown in *Hard Times* (the melancholy mad elephant, for example, which the steam engine's piston becomes, or the serpents of smoke that issue from the chimney).[9] The technology in Braddon's story, though less a part of her readership's everyday life, creates an even greater sense of anxiety than Oliphant's railway. Dr. Parravicini's blood transfusions are represented as an intrusion of a dangerous new technology into the natural course of life. Good Lady Ducayne ("born the day Louis XVI was guillotined") is associated throughout the story with bringing life out of death; young Bella, whose life she slowly drains for her own, is associated with youth, naïveté, and growth.[10] Bella is sexual, but it is a chaste sexuality she represents; significantly, she reads Scott and Dickens to her mistress, who prefers the racy French novels her maid provides.[11] Bella's young lover, Mr. Stafford, chastises Lady Ducayne in the final pages: "I think you have had your share of the sunshine and the pleasures of the earth, and that you should spend your few remaining days in repenting your sins and trying to make atonement for the young lives that have been sacrificed to your love of life."[12] Braddon offers an interesting twist on the vampire story; although Lady Ducayne, like so many other literary vampires, seems to represent the ancient world of continental Europe, she also—unlike them—embraces technology and uses it to further her own life rather than succumbing to it, as Stoker's vampires do. Technology is countered here by a natural love. Specifically, the mother-daughter bond that has motivated Bella throughout the story is retained to the end, as she returns first to her mother, second to a marriage—and a marriage, as we've noted, to a man who embraces his unknown mother-in-law as part of his wife.

Motherhood, then, that "natural" component of womanliness, seems to stand against technology in both stories, though in different ways. In a rare comment on Janey's interior life, the narrator notes that "sometimes, I think, she felt that if she had known the boy was coming she might have possessed her soul in patience, and borne even with Mr. Rosendale. But then at the time the decisive step was taken she did not know."[13] This rare honesty about the relationship between maternity and identity contrasts significantly with what students had already read in *Adam Bede* and offers a comparison to Gaskell's "Lizzie Leigh." More specifically, Janey, who becomes a single mother and raises her child—unlike the fallen women of the earlier tales—may be redeemed by her maternity. Furthermore, she also imagines it as offering the potential to redeem a loveless marriage. Her son figures prominently but ambiguously at the end of the story as well: "When she found herself and her son recognised, and that there could be no doubt that the boy was his father's heir, she was struck with a great horror which she never quite got over all her life."[14] What is it about this heirdom that generates horror? The thought that she is the murderer, not of her husband, but of her son's father? The thought that she will be indebted to him forever for the means to raise his son? The subtle but distinct possibility that the son will somehow inherit the father's temperament or, less subtly, his Jewish ethnicity, along with his property? Oliphant leaves this, as so much else in the story, merely suggested rather than fully developed, leaving us to work out the conclusion on our own. The openness of this conclusion disturbed some readers, who found themselves longing for a "longer" work—more like the novels we had read earlier in the semester.

However, that very openness allows us to discuss Victorian aesthetics in new ways. Undeveloped relationships, suggested connections, make the tales connect in ways that surprise me each semester with the longer texts I have always taught and continue to teach. Working both within and against formal constraints, the stories enact a critique both of longer novels and of the marriage plot that so dominated fiction by Victorian women. The stories are rich and suggestive, so mine is perforce a brief and rather partial demonstration of how they can work within the confines of the Victorian literature survey.

Incorporating short fiction by women into the survey course accomplishes several goals at once: it increases the number of texts by women, creating a greater sense of the actual publication rates of the period and the breadth of literature real Victorians were reading. It helps demonstrate the ways in which women writers engage both similar and different issues than male writers—in the cited stories, for example, technology and marriage are perhaps equally at issue, though one topic might be thought of as more stereotypically "masculine" than the other. In addition, it reveals another aspect of Victorian literary aesthetics, demonstrating that compression, brevity, and suggestiveness are all as available to the Victorian author as to the modern. At the same time, these are expansive short stories, often quite long short stories, and in many ways they demonstrate the pervasiveness of the more familiar aesthetic even as they demonstrate its flexibility. Like the heroines of these stories and their authors, we teachers have limited means and options; nonetheless, like them, we can make some tiny steps towards freedom, and these stories may offer one way to do so.

Notes

1. See, for example, Jonathan Culler, "Imagining the Coherence of the English Major," *Profession* (2003): 85–93.
2. The three anthologies I'm aware of are Harriet Devine Jump, ed., *Nineteenth-Century Stories by Women: A Routledge Anthology* (New York: Routledge, 1998); Glennis Stephenson, ed., *Nineteenth-Century Stories by Women: An Anthology*, (Peterborough, ON: Broadview, 1993); and David Stuart Davies, ed., *Short Stories from the Nineteenth Century* (Hertfordshire, UK: Wordsworth Editions, 2000).
3. Heather Henderson and William Sharpe, eds., *The Longman Anthology of British Literature*, 2nd ed. vol 2B: "The Victorian Age" (New York: Longman, 2003); Carol T. Christ and George H. Ford, eds., *The Norton Anthology of English Literature*, 7th ed. vol 2B: "The Victorian Age" (New York & London: Norton, 2000).
4. Mary Elizabeth Braddon, "Good Lady Ducayne," (1896), in Stephenson, 71–100; Margaret Oliphant, "A Story of a Wedding Tour" (1898), in Stephenson, 403–425.
5. Braddon, 99.
6. Oliphant, 424.
7. Oliphant, 424.
8. Oliphant, 420.
9. Charles Dickens, *Hard Times* (1854); (London: Penguin, 1988), 65.
10. Braddon, 95.
11. Braddon, 95, 79.
12. Braddon, 95–6.
13. Oliphant, 421.
14. Oliphant, 424.

Victorian Literature
Dr. Gruner

The period course in Victorian literature provides a survey of selected literature of the Victorian period. This course will proceed primarily by discussion; your presence and regular, informed participation are crucial to your success in the class and the success of the class itself as a shared scholarly endeavor.

The goals of the class are as follows:
- To acquaint students with the major literary genres and figures of the Victorian period, and to explore the process of canon formation in and after the period.
- To provide students with an understanding of some of the sociological factors and intellectual movements of the Victorian period, both as reflected and as constructed by the literature of the time.
- To develop more effective analytical skills in both discussion and writing, through class discussion and presentations, online "discussions," in-class exams, and papers.
- To explore some of the variety of online resources available for the scholar of Victorian literature, with an eye to developing a more thorough awareness of what the resources and their limitations are, and perhaps to developing our own.
- To identify some of the research "problems" in Victorian literature, and to begin to find approaches to those problems through research and writing.

Course schedule:

Introductory	Slide lecture—overview of the Victorian period. Read "The Victorian Age" (Norton)
Tennyson, "Mariana," "The Lady of Shalott," "Ulysses," "Tithonus"	Tennyson, selections from *In Memoriam*
Tennyson, selections from *In Memoriam*	In class: close reading exercise
Carlyle, biographical sketch & selections from *Sartor Resartus*	Browning, E., selections from *Aurora Leigh*
Browning, R., "My Last Duchess," "Fra Lippo Lippi," "Andrea del Sarto"	Dickens, *Great Expectations* (ch. 1–19)
Dickens, *Great Expectations* (ch. 20–39)	Dickens, *Great Expectations* (ch. 40–end)
Slide lecture: The Pre-Raphaelites Rossetti, D.G., "The Blessed Damozel"; Rossetti, C., "In an Artist's Studio"	Rossetti, D.G., "Jenny" (handout); Rossetti, C., "Goblin Market"
Fall Break	Gaskell, "Lizzie Leigh"
Eliot, *Adam Bede* (ch. 1–16)	Eliot, *Adam Bede* (ch. 17–35)
Eliot, *Adam Bede* (ch. 36–48)	Eliot, *Adam Bede* (ch. 49–end)
Arnold, "Dover Beach," "To Marguerite—Continued"	Oliphant, "A Story of a Wedding Tour"
Braddon, "Good Lady Ducayne"	Stevenson, *Dr. Jekyll & Mr. Hyde*
Pater, from *The Renaissance*	Hopkins, selections
Wilde, *The Importance of Being Earnest*	no class meeting (Thanksgiving)
Conrad, *Heart of Darkness*	Conrad, *Heart of Darkness*

Figure 1. Elisabeth Rose Gruner, Sample Syllabus

CHAPTER TEN

"This Particular Web": George Eliot, Emily Eden, and Locale in Multiplot Fiction

Lawrence Zygmunt

Although accustomed to students' hesitation, teachers of massive Victorian novels may assume that reluctant readers are simply daunted by the imposing distance between the books' covers. True, perhaps, for genuine novices facing page one, but a different reluctance arises from vexed experience. Harried and overcommitted students report demoralizing strain more on the memory than the wrist, and many despair less because the last chapters lie far beyond the right thumb, than because the present chapters—often read in snatches—twist and sashay through an undifferentiated tangle of people whom they fear they're supposed to recognize. An elaborate multiplot novel like *Middlemarch* (1871–72) compounds this threat of vertigo by launching readers into the midst of an extensive cast without the reassuring mooring of a single central character, a David Copperfield or Molly Gibson at the center of the imposing legion.

Ignoring this perplexity nourishes the suspicion that these novels are recommended only by deranged masochists. Actually focusing on such confusion, by contrast, allows teachers to stress that—panicked first impressions aside—the crowds in novels like *Middlemarch* do not actually mill about to no purpose, and that the interconnected arrangement of characters and events contributes to the novels' assessments of the places and lives described. One advantage of the multiplot form is its potential to range widely amidst a plausibly complete canvass of human endeavors, opinions, characters, and social classes; if the various threads of plot and character are woven with sufficient dexterity, a multiplot novel can contemplate the whole of the setting's social fabric, analyzing the nature of an entire community even as it minutely observes certain members. In addition to exposing students to one of the period's distinctive literary forms, multiplot novels may also offer an entree to social history, historiography, and other concerns for which literature serves as component or commentary.

However, the subtleties—indeed, the simple existence—of this expansive capacity can easily elude the notice of overwhelmed or hasty readers. Students' instinct to disregard "extra" details can produce readerly myopia; to focus on one thread or another blurs the effects of the multiplot novel as a whole. Even more careful readers may overlook telling intricacy as only a mechanical requirement. Since, in essence, great multiplot artistry simply (and usually silently) elevates and extends the skills of the literary artisan—the assembly and propulsion of a coherent story—cursory reading easily confuses social commentary or philosophical argument with mere competent construction, and thus obscures at least one purpose of the multiplotted multitude. Unless students are led to ponder the details of a specific multiplot arrangement and asked to consider how choices about juxtaposing and overlapping plots affect the thrust and timbre of a novel, they may, paradoxically, miss some of the ideas and assertions pervading it.

This concept, like so many, is more easily illustrated with comparison than defined with abstractions, but the sheer size of the nineteenth century's best multiplot novels often makes assigning several exemplars difficult to reconcile with the constraints of a plausible syllabus. Apportioned realistically, just one major novel can devour an appreciable swath of a term. Happily, Emily Eden, a Whig political hostess and occasional writer on India, made a conveniently brief foray into multiplot fiction in 1859 with *The Semi-Detached House*, an appealing comic novel that almost miraculously miniaturizes and concentrates the multiplot genre. Eden's novel begins with the pregnant Lady Blanche Chester's less-than-enthusiastic relocation to a London suburb, where she and her aristocratic circle soon find themselves variously entwined with her guileless middle-class neighbors, the Hopkinsons; romances, illnesses, charity work, sudden recognitions, nefarious financial dealings, and assorted other events soon produce an impressive sheaf of interlocking plots. Eden's ebullient prose speeds the reading of an already succinct novel, so *The Semi-Detached House* offers a useful complement to a larger multiplot novel with a relatively minor addition to students' labors.[1] Indeed, Eden's novel is much too short to divide into as many separate reading assignments as most other multiplot novels require, especially if a teacher is (wisely) attempting to re-create the experience of reading a serial novel (Eden did not publish in parts). The teaching opportunity of *The Semi-Detached House* depends upon students' watching multiplot operate on a scale readily grasped, where structure is easy to see as a whole, so the novel is best assigned entire, alongside a mid-to-late portion of a larger multiplot, in which students can try to discern structural choices and devices.

If Eden's novel is paired with *Middlemarch*, literary context proves especially compatible with pedagogical pragmatism. Like *Middlemarch*, Eden's novel limits itself to a single locale, but while both novelists use geography as an organizing principle, they do not simply unroll the backdrop of choice and send the company out to gambol before it. Both authors not only present a scene, but also convey a sensation of being surrounded and enmeshed by that place. The means used to tell the various stories encourage readers to ponder the character and atmosphere of the neighborhood as well as the activities of the individual inhabitants. Ironically, the very success of these local evocations obscures the novelists' common method—so much so that two novels with quite similar social and moral concerns initially seem as dissimilar as a provincial town and a London suburb. The pedagogical benefit of juxtaposing these novels arises largely from the subtle, almost surreptitious quality of this resemblance; eliciting and describing the parallel forces readers to connect ostensibly dissimilar examples of the shared technique and makes the excavated similarity more vivid.

Admittedly, formal issues on their own often fail to engage students thoroughly, but proposing a connection to a more obviously contentious topic may encourage readier discussion. Here, too, the pairing of Eliot and Eden proves apt. Teachers need only wonder aloud whether (or why) female Victorian novelists display a particular talent for geographically specific multiplot fiction to start debate on the interplay of literary technique, gender, and culture. Depending on students' previous reading, a teacher may have to deliver a quick primer on the manner of other (male) multiplot novelists, and on Victorian notions like the assignment of woman to a separate, spatially limited domestic sphere. Circumstances permitting, background on the development of multiplot fiction as a genre will also help shepherd discussion and prevent the literary element from disappearing behind the assertions about supposedly eternal verities with which students often meet culturally freighted subjects.

For these purposes, the brief history need reach no further back than the early Victorian era, when "thesis novels" like Benjamin Disraeli's *Sybil* (1845) or Geraldine Jewsbury's *The Half Sisters* (1848) use chance encounters or well-travelled characters to connect several essentially distinct stories. The links are baldly contrived, and the various plots, when stapled together, simply embody abstract ideas—like Disraeli's political philosophy—or strike obvious comparisons. Jewsbury manifestly makes the legitimate Alice and the illegitimate Bianca half sisters in order to comment on the gulfs between them; they pursue separate lives, and the relationship itself leads to nothing. Such novels have as much in common with fiction-draped treatises like Harriet Martineau's *Illustrations of Political Economy* (1832) as they do with later and more subtle novels like Eliot's, and their mechanical plots operate in similar fashion, no matter who jury-rigs and calibrates them.

As authors cultivate less transparently motivated multiplot novels, they relax the rigidities of the soapbox and combine variety and range with a more organic sense of internal coherence. Now, debate over gender preferences becomes more plausible. While many female novelists incline toward geography as a way to unite their characters, male writers often prefer less palpable catalysts. Consider, for instance, the role of financial law in *Bleak House* (1852–53), or the explicit comparison of dynamic vice and insipid virtue in *Vanity Fair* (1847–48). This latter approach can depart dramatically from the legacy of determined realism established in "condition of England" novels; as the convenient neatness of thesis novels becomes symbolically freighted Dickensian serendipity, elaborately geared and flywheeled plots do sometimes strain credulity. *Little Dorrit* (1855–57) elegantly orchestrates many versions of literal and metaphorical confinement, but appreciating its virtues does require accepting that a man could step off a boat from the Far East and almost immediately encounter a woman whom his mother (who is, naturally, not his mother) once robbed. In what other novel would a runaway maid seek refuge with the one person who possesses a crucial legal document, then repent and return with just that evidence as a peace offering?

While Dickens' narrative balancing act plainly demands attention, *Middlemarch* less flamboyantly examines the many elements of "provincial life" with a famous eye for the intricacies simmering beneath a seemingly mundane and parochial setting. This tightly focused, "local" technique animates a conspicuous number of novels written by women, creating places like Stoneborough and Cocksmoor in Charlotte Yonge's *The Daisy Chain* (1856), or Hollingford in Gaskell's *Wives and Daughters* (1866), or comparatively trifling Dulham, the London suburb where Emily Eden stages *The Semi-Detached House*. Complicated connections between characters and plots still require some suspension of disbelief, but this suspension depends upon a different sort of rigging. The knots seem more secure, largely because authors like Eliot and Eden assemble their plots (and our willingness to accept them) by arranging a few propitious initial circumstances and leaving them in place, rather than using various pulleys and cranks to manipulate circumstances as the story progresses—the difference between the stereotypical Dickensian coincidence and the Jamesian "donnee." Once we grant that the banker Nicholas Bulstrode has happened to settle in Middlemarch, where the Rev. Edward Casaubon also lives, and where Raffles' stepson will inherit property, the crises and discoveries that follow require only normal comings and goings. If we do not object to Lady Blanche Chester's inadvertently whiling away her pregnancy across a back garden from Mrs. Hopkinson, the wife of her husband's old friend, we have no call to protest the intimacies that develop between the two women's circles. While we must accept the capacious population that either author gathers, that initial consent permits the rest of the plot to unfold without placing any appreciable strain on the ropes.

However, concentration on a single locale does more than reduce ongoing reliance on chance; the realism of novels like Eden's or Eliot's involves tone and affect as well as credible incidents. Places like Middlemarch and Dulham also allow their creators to capture the experience of social life from the perspective of a participant instead of a detached, disembodied observer. Although the rationales behind the many links and contacts are all, upon inspection, quite lucid and sound, these novels do not encourage readers to treat plot elements as puzzle pieces, snapping each into the spot where it will help reveal a grand design. Secrets lurk beneath *Middlemarch* and misunderstandings prompt much of *The Semi-Detached House*, but the novels themselves are not mysteries to be solved; they do not emphasize the pleasure of looking down on a maze from above and enjoying its artifice. These novels deploy their many characters and shape their various plots to supply, not just facts or arguments, or even elaborately wrought chains of argument, but also a sense of immersion within a particular milieu. As Eliot remarks, "I at least have so much to do in unravelling certain human lots, and seeing how they were woven and interwoven, that all the light I can command must be concentrated on this particular web, and not dispersed over that tempting range of relevancies called the universe."[2]

These elaborate weavings quickly reveal the interdependence of the community's many layers and branches. Plenty of potential causes emerge from the profusion of characters and events, and because a single incident often influences several plot threads, the resulting effects can easily blaze separate routes into several different parts of the novel. When Fred Vincy trots off to sell his horse, for instance, he not only makes a bad bargain, leaving himself broke and compromising his security, Caleb Garth, but he also contracts a fever in the insalubrious alleys of the Houndsley horse-fair, and that illness introduces Dr. Lydgate into the Vincys' house and facilitates his romance with Fred's sister Rosamond. Eden's novel may not attempt quite the scope of Eliot's, but a whole catalogue of benefits can still follow from fortuitous attendance at a single party. Curious about the conniving financier Baron Sampson, Captain Hopkinson brings his family to Sampson's fete, and by the end of the affair not one, but both of his daughters have accepted proposals of marriage, and his wife has overcome her dislike for the Baroness' sardonic niece—fortunate indeed, for that niece, the only honest member of the family, will need an irreproachable protectress after all the swindlers decamp the very next day.

Next to such examples of polished plotting, however, *Middlemarch* and *The Semi-Detached House* both freely indulge in what any good modernist, or even any devotee of the Greek unities, would decry as abject sloppiness. The elegant compound consequences accompany a generous complement of, not quite loose ends, but superfluous details and extraneous interconnections. These novels do not offer narrative efficiency of the Horace Walpole sort. When Sir

James Chettam takes up Dorothea Brooke's schemes for cottage-building, for instance, Eliot informs us, apropos of nothing, that Caleb Garth is managing the enterprise. Because the philanthropic project plays no role in the novel except as an example of intellectual sympathy, clarity does not actually require any particular information about it. Similarly, Eden's Dr. Ayscough develops a professional interest in little Charlie Willis, Mrs. Hopkinson's grandchild, and Eden mentions several times that he looks in on the boy—a wholly unnecessary device, practically speaking because Charlie's illness leads to nothing and Eden needs no further excuse than Blanche's pregnancy to carry Ayscough to Dulham.

Both novels contain many such details, but these novelists are, of course, not clumsily slipping into irrelevant musings. These supernumerary links emphasize that the relationships among people are many and various, and the many trifling yet dovetailed particulars create a crucial sense of social intricacy. Instead of filing away a plot point, we realize that Ayscough can look beyond the pregnant aristocrat, and that Caleb Garth, who builds practically everything in Middlemarch, exists outside his own storyline. Because Eden's poor curate Greydon is someone's old friend and someone else's lodger and still someone else's ally in local charities, we could systematically catalogue his exact connections to all manner of roles and social classes, but a general impression debunking the supposed gulfs of rank matters more than several of the specific links. Middlemarch teems with ties that constrain, rescue, suffocate, delight, hinder, and cheer, but only a few readers will ever—or need ever—bother to work out that, by a tortuous series of removes, the stiff and sanctimonious Rev. Casaubon is distantly related to the drunken blackmailer John Raffles.[3] Rather than tracing a golden chain, we grasp the clutter and insuperable complexity of a living community. Indeed, *Middlemarch* refers constantly to a great battery of area residents who are sketched briefly if at all, and whose names—Hawley, Standish, Trumbull, Hackbutt, Mawmsey, and so on—repeatedly pop up in connection with chaplaincies, elections, sanitation, local amusements, medical practices, and all manner of assorted whatnot. The novel could function perfectly well without this basso continuo of the familiar and inconsequential, yet Eliot seldom allows it to flag, and with it conveys the sense of a setting with too much variety and depth to incorporate fully, even in a novel so lengthy that Blackwood had to publish it as a quadruple-decker.

Indeed, these geographically concentrated novels transform touches of blurriness into a unique virtue. To preserve the feeling of genuine immersion in a "particular web," Eliot and Eden qualify the sense of omniscience that third-person narration and precise accounts of characters' thoughts tend to create. Along with the abundant interconnections, both novelists orchestrate gaps in their readers' perceptions, as if to reproduce the impossibility of dwelling within these communities and looking everywhere at once. Significant events occur while our attention is directed elsewhere, and we must satisfy ourselves with secondhand comments from more fortunate witnesses when a concert, birth, scandal, or wedding comes off quite well without us. Eden draws us away from Willis' courtship of Rachel Monteneros and from Baron Sampson's swindles, although all their fates bear crucially on the novel's insistence that the deserving find happiness and the wicked are, if not struck down, at least shuffled off to the continent in disgrace. Similarly, Eliot never really follows Lydgate to the fever hospital, and never attends directly to the decline of Vincy's commercial concerns, though several lives are bound up in their careers. Amusingly, a novel that devotes so much consideration to marriage never invites us, even for the briefest moment, to anyone's wedding; we probably missed little at Celia Brooke and Sir James Chettam's, but we are also excluded from Dorothea's nuptials—not once, but twice. We can always interpolate sufficiently to orient ourselves, but this subtle compositional device places us distinctly within, and not above, the fictional setting.

With this ground-level position comes the risk of misapprehending what we *do* see and hear. While these novels forego virtuoso plot twists and figures in the carpet, they do take great care to portray more quotidian, although no less baffling, mysteries—those that face anyone moving through a crowded scene and trying to appraise it. Both Eliot and Eden arrange their narratives to emphasize this challenge, deferring introductions and lingering deceptively over ancillary characters. As so often happens with less fictional people, someone like Eliot's Rev. Farebrother may enter our awareness through statements of third parties well before we meet him personally. While Mary Garth's or Fred Vincy's remarks about him prove reliable, we must also cope with Bulstrode's bigoted comments—a more than modest task, especially when our first glimpse of Farebrother in person shows him en route to a whist-table. Eden's novel almost constantly occupies its characters with the dilemma of gauging people they do not yet know, and if we begin by accepting the voluble, charming, but "fastidious and imaginative."[4] Blanche Chester's opinion of virtually anyone from her semi-detached neighbors to her brother-in-law, we will end up in a decidedly false position. Similar contrivances even encourage us to misjudge who among the throng of characters will become a near acquaintance; both novels send us slightly astray by pausing pointedly over minor figures like the Cadwalladers or various of the Chesters' aristocratic acquaintance. Writers like Eliot and Eden force us to admit that life does not indulge all our curiosities, or designate any "main characters" to whom we should obviously attend. By disarranging our expectations and inveigling us into missteps, they compel us into the places they describe and limit us to an inhabitant's perspective.

At first glance, the blithe comedy of *The Semi-Detached House* might seem far removed from the measured discernment of *Middlemarch*, but examining the similar means used to convey their settings begs the realization that the two novels seem so dissimilar largely because Dulham and Middlemarch are such utterly different places. Actually, the two novels share a philosophical affinity, for beneath its diverting surface *The Semi-Detached House* persistently asserts that the trait that separates people into appropriate and comfortable circles is not wealth or station, but generosity. Every sympathetic character displays—or learns—an instinct for altruism; every distasteful action springs from selfishness. When Dorothea Brooke asks "What do we live for, if it is not to make life less difficult to each other?"[5] she expresses a concern as integral to Eden's lighthearted novel as to the vexed efforts and aspirations that fill *Middlemarch*.

However, the two novels present that shared concern in manners shaped by their very distinct environments. Eden's novel carries its point about benevolence and delicacy, but it also perfectly captures the character of a suburb. Abrupt lunges in focus from chapter to brief chapter echo the frantic comings and goings of people whose central interests lie elsewhere, and those leaps are wholly unlike the gentler, more fluid transitions possible with Eliot's frequent pauses for context or abstract reflection. Provincial life has a self-contained, bounded, somewhat slower quality that suburban flitting does not, and while only a few people—like Will Ladislaw—take up pursuits that involve contact with almost everyone in the district, *Middlemarch* acknowledges the possibility of an inhabitant's coming to know an area with a thoroughness that makes charting each tie exhaustingly futile. *The Semi-Detached House*, for its part, wisely remains a multiplot novel on a surprisingly small scale, and successfully implies that a patently artificial place is best regarded with a breeziness indicating that it has no depths to plumb; the social circle that does develop there has no intrinsic link to its very temporary headquarters. Unlike Middlemarch, Dulham has no mute inglorious grandeur, no capacity to encompass the sorrows and frustrations of people like Dorothea Brooke or Tertius Lydgate. Because no one stays very long—most of the characters arrange to move by the novel's end—and residents usually take perverse pride in not visiting their neighbors, calamities dependent on abiding local associations could find no purchase. At worst, Dulham tenants face a few months' annoyance by a noisy macaw of perpetually indeterminate ownership. Both novels capture the intricacies of deciphering any social setting from within, but the specific results could hardly differ more. Initially overlooking the several resemblances between these two novels only emphasizes the versatility with which the authors entwine readers in their "particular webs."

Notes

1. Speculating in print about the availability of less canonical texts courts inaccuracy, but in Eden's case the vagaries of publishers cause somewhat less trouble. Because two modern editions (Viking Penguin, 1992 and Virago Dial, 1982) do exist, locating a single copy of *The Semi-Detached House* is not particularly difficult, and its brevity makes it more than usually compatible with course packets or reserve rooms. Searchers should note that both these editions appear to be titled *The Semi-Attached Couple* & *The Semi-Detached House*, because both also include Eden's one other novel, which recounts the bumpy start of a high-society marriage. Though written much earlier, *The Semi-Attached Couple* was published only in 1860, following the success of *The Semi-Detached House*. All quotes in this essay come from the Virago Dial edition, 1982.
2. George Eliot, *Middlemarch: A Study of Provincial Life*. 1871. (New York: Modern Library, 1984), 137.
3. Still, now that I have mentioned the remote connection, I must sate any tormented curiosity. Raffles is Joshua Rigg's stepfather; Rigg is Peter Featherstone's natural son; one of Featherstone's wives was a Vincy; Harriet Bulstrode was also a Vincy; Nicholas Bulstrode, Harriet's husband, had previously married Will Ladislaw's grandmother; and Will is Casaubon's second cousin. Anyone tempted to assign a name to this attenuated relationship is advised to obtain a genealogical guide, Blackstone's *Commentaries*, a sextant, and a large bottle of aspirin.
4. Eden, 15.
5. Eliot, 698.

PART TWO
Teaching to Read: Making Students of Scholars (and Vice Versa)

Chapter Eleven
Making the Student a Scholar

Jeanne Moskal

In the beginner's mind, there are many possibilities;
in the expert's mind, there are few.
—Shunryu Suzuki, *Zen Mind, Beginner's Mind*

One semester while I was a graduate student, I used to walk every day to the class I taught with one of my colleagues, Jon Seal, a medievalist. Just as he ducked into his own classroom, Jon would give me a last theatrical look, place his right hand across his chest, and say histrionically, "Once more unto the breach, dear friends." I always found this gesture funny and moving at the same time, as Jon assumed both the character of the battle-weary Henry V and also that of a hammy Shakespearean actor playing him. For years I knew I liked the metaphor of teaching as repeatedly going into battle. Lately I have begun to realize how much I like the sense of theatricality, of comedy, of exaggerated self-dramatization. Jon's ritualistic gesture taught me, early on, that theatricality is an essential component of teaching.

Even more fundamentally, when we teach canonical authors, much of the pedagogical staging has already been done for us by the institutions of literary study and the received expertise of our predecessors and colleagues—what Matthew Arnold called "the best that has been known and thought in the world." As expert teachers of these canonical writers, we replicate, for example, the received casting that Coleridge is a "Romantic" writer or that "The Rime of the Ancient Mariner" is the most important of his works to teach. The most material manifestation of that expertise, of course, is the anthologies that we select (which seem to get heavier and heavier with the years). Less obviously, our own graduate training has set the stage for how we teach; for example, in the easy availability of Keats's "Negative Capability" letter to teach alongside the "Ode on a Grecian Urn." There is a tremendous amount of accumulated scholarly apparatus that we began to master in graduate school, and as we have continued as scholars, we have perhaps contributed to that accumulation. The mastery of other scholars' work, and the making of such contributions ourselves, are what make us "experts," qualified to teach our subject matter to the undergraduate beginners in our classrooms.

With non-canonical writers, however, much of the stage hasn't been built yet. As a result, many of us feel like the circus roustabouts whose job it is to raise the tent in a few hours before the first performance. The essays in this section respond to this situation by allowing the students to see those processes of canonical stage-building that are usually hidden to them—in effect, they all give the students what Catherine Burroughs calls "a backstage tour" of institutional practices. Instead of accepting the instructor's traditional job description to impart his or her expertise to beginners, these teacher-scholars creatively exploit that very dearth of staging—easily available texts, commentary, scholarly apparatus, critical heritages—and seize the chance to make the apparent "beginners" the experts.

The first two essays present in-class strategies for sharing expertise with the students. There is so much pressure towards devoting all the air-time in a course to the primary literary works. This pressure may be due to the pedagogical triumphs that close readings often produce in one class period. And it may also be due to our own sense that, with the expanding canon, we need to cram in as many primary works as possible. But in her essay, Patricia L. Hamilton argues that it is worthwhile to devote classroom time to teaching students to evaluate critics critically and to differentiate the critics' facts, inferences, assumptions, and value judgments, so that the student can decide which parts to accept and which to reject. She presents a pedagogical approach for those writers we might consider semi-canonical: i.e., "minor" writers, usually women, who have received a substantial body of critical commentary. Hamilton identifies some of the anxieties undergraduates have as beginners in the realm of scholarship and their understandable impulse to employ critics' pronouncements. As Hamilton points out, much of this critical commentary on women is riddled with some version of the following double-bind: "Frances Burney is best suited to write a novel of manners, and it is too bad that she can write only a novel of manners." Teaching students to evaluate these pronouncements demystifies the mystique of the critic's power and gives the student a more precise vocabulary for the components of his or her own response. Hamilton offers a model assignment and some practical considerations for the teacher.

Like Hamilton, Catherine B. Burroughs presents the merits of sharing "expert" material with beginners. She opens her course with what she calls "a backstage tour" of the pedagogical and scholarly apparatuses before they get to the primary texts. Her essay, "In No-Woman's Land: Teaching Women Playwrights from the British Romantic Period," shows the enthusiasm generated in her classrooms when she discloses to her students her own pedagogical decisions and indecisions about the best chronological opening date for the material, so that they may see how the historical event that is chosen as "inaugural" for the period shapes their readings and perceptions. Burroughs shows her students the scholarly backstage as well, discussing with them the scholarly assumptions in the prevailing discourse of binary oppositions between closet/stage, text/performance, and public/private. By raising these theoretical frames explicitly, Burroughs enables her students to "raise questions about how the narratives of theatre history are constructed" and to contribute to "the (feminist) project of revising [those] narratives." She also discloses scholarly tools to her students, tools usually reserved for experts—such as scholarly websites and calls for conference papers. Probably most important, Burroughs immediately "casts" her students as experts by requiring them to commit themselves early to a research project. This commitment provides the student with a corner of material on which he or she is the expert, and from which standpoint he or she can comment authoritatively on the material read by all the students. In a similar vein, Diane Chambers shows how she builds the stage for her presentation of Christina Rossetti. Instead of making her students a quick study, as Burroughs does, Chambers employs a strategy reminiscent of Claude Lévi-Strauss's *bricoleur*, the bricklayer who uses whatever materials are already at hand. Chambers begins with the surprising fact that her students' religious commitments already provide them with a doorway into liking and identifying with Rossetti, and grafts the scholarly content of her teaching onto this beginning. What is important about Chambers's essay is that it corrects the overgeneralization of one of the founding texts in the recovery of Rossetti, Jerome McGann's 1981 article, "The Religious Poetry of Christina Rossetti." McGann, assuming that much of the poet's religious context was obscured for the present-day secularized reader, exhumed variations of the doctrine of the Resurrection to bring to bear on "When I am dead, my dearest." As widely true as McGann's assumption of secularity might be, there are pockets of conversant readers, such as the students in Chambers's sectarian college. Chambers thus shows the importance of regarding the situation of specific students in devising an effective teaching plan for women writers.

The second group of essays in this section creates student-scholars (or beginner-experts) by stressing the context of the individual research project. Another province of expertise usually hidden from the beginning undergraduate student is the archive of rare books, those works often by women that were not deemed worthy of re-editing and re-publication after their authors' deaths. E. J. Clery and Peaches Henry outline the research assignments they give their students based on exposing them to such archives. In "Canon-Busting: Undergraduate Research into Romantic-Era Women's Writing in the Corvey Collection," Clery capitalizes on the excitement generated by her university's acquisition of a specific archive, the Corvey archive of popular literature (including 92% of all novels written in English from 1818 to 1829). Clery's honors undergraduates participated in an independent study project called "Adopt an Author," that required them to read rare material by one author available on microfiche (a headache-producing technology usually reserved for expert graduate students and faculty scholars). Based on their research, they wrote a critical analysis, a keyword description and bibliography to be entered on the Corvey Website. Thus these undergraduates had a chance, in adopting an author, to become the world's expert on her.

In a similar vein, Henry outlines, in "Teaching 'Recovered' Victorian Female Intellectuals," a research assignment in which the students do the kind of preliminary work (survey of oeuvre, collation of contemporaneous critical responses, catalogue of papers and so forth) that has already been done for canonized authors. Moreover, Henry assigns a research journal, which enables the instructor to evaluate work that does not pan out in a discovery—one of the major features of this kind of archival research. Rather than taking a specific archive, such as the Corvey, for its focal point, Henry's students' projects crystallize around a genre, Victorian nonfiction prose, and around the polemical goal of debunking the myth of exclusive male domain over the role of Victorian sage. Clery, too, notes the wider polemical reach of her project in redefining Romanticism, which, she writes, has carried with it "certain assumptions about what and who genuinely *matters* in the literary history of the years c. 1780–1830." Both teacher-instructors give their students firsthand knowledge of how a manageable anthology (and manageable syllabus) truncate the cornucopia of the archive, and "confront students' skepticism about [those] writers" excluded from the Norton (as Henry says).

Taking the research project to the culmination usually reserved for experts:,the publication of a new edition, Nicole Meller Beck and Beth Sutton-Ramspeck describe their editorial collaboration while Beck was a student and Sutton-Ramspeck an instructor at a small college. Sutton-Ramspeck discloses the scholarly isolation that helped to motivate their project: "In my situation (the only Victorian literature person at a small school, at a fairly great physical distance from other institutions with Victorianists, the alternative to working with a student wasn't working with another scholar: it was working alone." This is the condition of many scholars who work on non-canonical women writers. Scholars who work on Dickens or Wordsworth can usually be assured that their colleagues have at least read *Bleak House* or *The Prelude*. But, with non-canonical women writers, if only two or three scholars in the world are working on a figure, it is a long time between conferences. Beck and Sutton-Ramspeck's experience discloses both the rewards and difficulties of such a collaboration: Beck, as an undergraduate student, knew what kinds of questions undergraduates would want answered in the annotations. Beck's experiences editing and giving conference papers helped her get into graduate school. But the collaboration also caused some difficulties due to the fluidity of Beck's role as sometime student, sometime collaborator. In the classroom situation, Sutton-Ramspeck's other students envied the closeness that she had developed with Beck. And Beck did go on to graduate school, so that Sutton-Ramspeck was left with the professional responsibility of completing the edition. While other research projects described in this section mention the limits of the student's semester on accomplishing a substantial scholarly project, this essay reveals that an undergraduate's time span in college also places limits on completing a long-range scholarly project.

What is striking about all these means of according the beginning students a relatively rapid expertise is the degree of ownership, pride, and/or affiliation or identification that the instructors record. Henry notes too that "by the middle of the semester, students began to claim these authors as their own." Clery's report seems to summarize the experiences of all these scholar-instructors: "Their enthusiasm for the task was remarkable. It was clear that the opportunity of going where, in most cases, no critic had gone before, and making a genuine contribution to what was known about women's literary history was inspiring for them."

The final group of essays in this section on making a student a scholar involves the self-criticism of showing them the poles that support our own circus tents. One way to begin is to help them examine the limits of the enabling moves already in place. For example, Gina Luria Walker shows the limits of a concept that feminist scholars have inherited, often without question, from older models of authorship. The received, often unarticulated scaffolding our students use is a version of the Romantic ideal of the solitary poet, exemplified in P. B. Shelley's description in *A Defence of Poetry* (1820), "A Poet is a nightingale who sits in darkness, and sings to cheer its own solitude with sweet sounds." Luria Walker shows the fruitfulness of a counter-model, baptized as the "subterraneous community of women" by Claire Clairmont, Mary Shelley's step-sister. Luria Walker's pedagogy articulates both the proximate communities surrounding and informing individual authors, such as the coterie of William Godwin, Mary Wollstonecraft, and Mary Hays, and the wider concentric circle of the subterranean community of women that includes authors from other centuries and nations, such as Sor Juana de la Cruz. Inviting her students to become what they behold, Luria Walker constructs an internet community of women scholars with whom her students can regularly converse, and thus get a sense of writing and thinking formed in the crucible of the coterie.

A further example of assessing existing scaffolding for teaching women writers, David Latané's essay interrogates the apparently unproblematic concept of "popularity." He charts a taxonomy of its possible meanings—being inoffensive to most readers, going into numerous editions, achieving best-selling status—as a preliminary to questioning one of the master narratives of teachers of women writers, namely, that we are rescuing once-popular women writers from undeserved neglect. This narrative has been influential since Jane

Tompkins's 1981 essay on Harriet Beecher Stowe, and Latané's essay indicates that the scaffolding we have used for some time may be in need of replacement.

Our collection ends with a meditation on an overridingly important structural component of specific, situated classroom environments: the instructor. William B. Thesing's memoir addresses the impact of his early patriarchal biases on his scholarship and the impact of his male body on the students who signed up for a "feminist" course. As teachers we know the workings of transference from lots of exposure. How many times have we ourselves, as students, taken a course just because it was taught by a certain instructor? How many of us have colleagues with a phalanx of loyal students who will register for any course under that instructor's name? Or, to name the obverse, how many times have we each had students we ourselves simply cannot teach, often, we have to surmise, for the simple but intractable reason that we evoke memories of a disliked Aunt Jobiska? Thesing's example of himself as the surprise male instructor of a course in women writers enunciates one of the crucial steps in making the student a scholar. Namely, it is crucial that at some point in the process, the student must reassess the preliminary scaffolding of transference he or she has erected to uphold an interest in women writers. This scaffolding may be those prediscursive attachments and dislikes for specific instructors or the essentialist assumption that only a woman can understand, much less teach, women's writings. For the student to become a scholar, Thesing's essay suggests, the scaffolding must be reassessed, and perhaps dismantled, in favor of something more enduring.

CHAPTER TWELVE

Beyond "Great Crowds" and "Minor Triumphs": Teaching Students to Evaluate Critical Pronouncements

Patricia L. Hamilton

Imagine with me for a moment that you are an undergraduate English major taking an upper-division course in the eighteenth-century novel. For your term paper, you have chosen to study Charlotte Lennox's *The Female Quixote* because you are curious about early women novelists, and besides, it beats having to spend a single minute more on Richardson's *Pamela* than is absolutely necessary. One afternoon, you head to the library to do some preliminary research, and from the first reference work you consult, you learn that Charlotte Lennox "was in her lifetime one of the most widely admired among a great crowd of minor female writers." As you read on, you discover that "a few twentieth-century commentators...have suggested that the continued recognition of *The Female Quixote* is owing primarily to its author's connections with such friends or admirers as Richardson, Johnson, Fielding, and Austen," but the critic you are reading tells you that "the estimate of merit implied by the approval of these writers of genius and taste should not be taken lightly." The critic concludes that "The lively story of the quixotic Arabella, though no masterpiece, is the ably crafted work of a gifted writer. It still repays close reading, and it fully deserves its status as a minor triumph of eighteenth-century fiction."[1] I wonder—as you read these remarks, will you pick up on the critic's anxiety to fix Charlotte Lennox's position in the eighteenth-century canon? You might at least notice his efforts to carve out a space for her when he asserts that "Lennox's overall achievement as a novelist deserves rather more attention than it has received." However, after reading the critic's pronouncement that "the remainder of Lennox's fiction is decidedly inferior," will you ever be tempted to read any of her other novels?

Probably not. Like most of us, you may be unconsciously influenced by what Walter J. Ong calls the "oracular" quality of texts: "The author might be challenged if only he or she could be reached, but the author cannot be reached in any book."[2] Suppose you wanted to ask the critic what he meant by "decidedly inferior" and what he based his judgment on. How on earth would you find him? Even if you somehow managed to discover his e-mail address, he would probably delete your message without reading it, thinking it contained an Internet virus. So as far as you are concerned, he might as well be the Delphic Oracle. After all, he is unquestionably knowledgeable about Lennox, and there is nothing in his tone to suggest that his judgments are cantankerous or unreasonable. He must know what he is talking about. He is a critic, isn't he?

Precisely because of such influences, you might not notice that this particular critic takes away with one hand from Lennox what he gives with the other. He asserts that *The Female Quixote* is "ably crafted," but it is not an inspired "masterpiece"; Lennox is a "gifted" writer but not a "genius." What is troubling, of course, is that the critic does not specify his criteria for determining what "genius" is or what constitutes a "masterpiece." In the absence of such criteria, it is hard to dispute the implication that the novel's "triumph" will only ever be "minor."

I do not mean to suggest through the foregoing illustration that a typical upper-division English major naively accepts every pronouncement he or she encounters. Students of literature tend to be perceptive readers and probing thinkers. Undergraduates, though, have a limited range of experience on which to draw or, if you will, a circumscribed cognitive map on which to locate not only the facts of literary history but also the interpretation of those facts by "experts." Thus, although students in an eighteenth-century novel course would probably have acquired some background in the development of the novel as a genre, it is unlikely that they would be steeped in the history of criticism or of the ongoing canon-expansion debate. However, it is in the unfolding chronology of Lennox criticism that we find a clue to the sympathetic but somewhat dismissive stance our critic takes toward Lennox. In 1985, the year the reference article we have been considering was published, the small torrent of feminist criticism that changed the way scholars view *The Female Quixote* was still barely a trickle. That trickle swelled considerably, however, with the availability starting in 1989 of an Oxford World Classics paperback edition of *The Female Quixote* and has since shown no signs of abating. My point here is not that the reference article is somehow suspect for not being aggressively feminist in its orientation. Rather, I want to highlight a fact that scholars take for granted but that students seldom recognize: Critics' assumptions about texts often mirror prevailing intellectual currents. For this reason, criticism—even a biographically focused reference article—needs to be read in a broad context. Unfortunately, few undergraduates are prepared to read criticism in this manner.

As part of their cognitive development, students need to learn to weigh the interpretive judgments that literary criticism is in the practice of making and defending. This is a complex process that requires skill in reading attentively, asking questions, identifying assumptions, and weighing evidence. Complicating the process even further is the bewildering array of theoretical orientations that students today must confront. Unquestionably, the evaluation of criticism requires high-order critical thinking skills, but undergraduates are often still struggling to master lower-order skills such as synthesis. When faced with incorporating criticism into a term paper, some students are suspicious and resistant, while others are inclined to practice what I fondly refer to as the "dining-table" method of research: With half a dozen sources spread out before them like so many dishes at a buffet, they will take a generous helping from each critic—never mind that certain critical orientations do not settle any better together than would anchovies with jalapeños. Let me emphasize that students do not necessarily take this approach to research out of laziness. Many are painfully aware of the limitations of their knowledge on a given subject and thus are eager to embrace "expert opinion." Such students may be temporarily lodged at a developmental way-station on the road to cognitive maturity, not yet ready to travel onward without a guide. In any case, the dining-table method brings to light an important assumption that most teachers of literature share: although criticism provides us with useful facts and insights that enrich our reading experience, criticism is no substitute for our own responses to literary texts. Our challenge as teachers, then, is to help students draw useful insights from criticism without letting it dominate their reading.

The issue of prompting students to read beyond critical pronouncements is important, given the power that criticism has to shape our perceptions and judgments about literary texts. This is true for canonical as well as non-canonical texts. The point was driven home to me when I taught two novels from the long eighteenth century in a sophomore literature survey. For the first work, *Moll Flanders*, I ordered the Norton Critical Edition because I wanted to give my students a taste of literary scholarship. What I found captured in the array of critical excerpts in the back of the text was the lively debate over Defoe's artistic abilities that erupted after the publication in 1957 of Ian Watt's *The Rise of the Novel*. Responding to charges by one group of critics that Defoe's novels are inferior to those of his successors because Defoe was hasty and slipshod in his composition or unskilled at handling irony, another group of critics argues that *Moll Flanders* is shaped by an organic unity and stylistic consistency that had previously gone unrecognized. While I found the artifacts of the debate fascinating, my decision about which articles to assign to my students was a bit trickier than I had anticipated. I could not use any of the selections I had in mind without setting aside classtime to address how some of the critics were directly responding to, and in some cases challenging, the assumptions of others.

When I selected criticism on *Sense and Sensibility* later in the term, I encountered an interesting variation of the same problem. Two out of the four articles I chose open with negative statements. One critic proclaims, "*Sense and Sensibility* is Jane Austen's least loved and least respected novel," while the other one declares, "No one would wish to argue that *Sense and Sensibility* is Jane

Austen's greatest novel."[3] When I first read these judgments, I automatically supplied a context: Both critics were arguing about the relative merits of major works within Austen's opus—works that are without question canonical—and both were employing a common rhetorical strategy to situate their finely nuanced readings of *Sense and Sensibility* in the stream of Austen criticism. However, in my students' panel presentations on the criticism, I heard a few of my young scholars simply parrot the sentiment that *Sense and Sensibility* is an inferior novel, as if they had taken the introductory sentence of each article as its thesis and had disregarded everything that followed. Fortunately, the presentations were sequenced so that the fourth panel discussed an article that overtly challenged the assumptions of the other three, thereby providing a platform for class discussion of the critics' criteria for their judgments. I wanted my students to recognize that experts often disagree, but even further, that disagreement can stimulate new insights and generate new knowledge.

Gender was not particularly a factor in either the Defoe or the Austen criticism that my students read, but assumptions about gender—stated and unstated—are frequently at issue in the critical assessments of women writers of the eighteenth and nineteenth centuries. Thus, in the context of canon expansion, the need for teachers to help students evaluate critical pronouncements takes on particular importance. Let me illustrate. If we turn to the Twayne series volume on Fanny Burney, which would be a likely place for an undergraduate to begin doing research on *Evelina*, we read that "Fanny's inability to detach herself from her heroine and also to handle the first person narrator ironically" results in flaws in the novel that a greater artist, Jane Austen, might have overcome. "But," the critic continues, "Fanny had neither the heart nor the head for such complexities."[4] Most teachers I know, feminist or not, would raise their eyebrows at such an unsupported assertion, especially because of its patronizing tone. The insinuation behind the critic's dismissal, of course, is that Burney is not worthy to stand in the ranks of canonical authors such as Austen. More notably, the critic's use of Burney's first name instead of her last, as is conventional in scholarship, suggests that Burney's sex is a factor in the critic's judgment of her abilities. Unfortunately, I am afraid that a number of my students would accept the statement about Burney's heart and head without question, simply because a critic said it.

The good news is that problematic critical statements can be a gold mine for teaching important critical thinking and research skills. What we need to do, more often than not, is build bridges to what students already know. Specifically, we should take the study of argument beyond the current events and controversial issues that serve as fodder for most freshman composition courses and extend rhetorical analysis to literary criticism. Students need to learn how to weigh the evidence a critic offers in support of his or her thesis.

Students also need practice at detecting critics' unstated assumptions and evaluating the validity of their inferences. The problem is that we barely have enough time in undergraduate courses to cover important primary texts—so how can we sacrifice any time to teach criticism? While there is no easy answer to this question, let me suggest that any time we can devote to students' need for guidance in interpreting criticism can pay big dividends in the quality of students' thinking, class discussion, and written work.

With all of these concerns in mind, I designed a short writing assignment that seeks to develop students' critical thinking skills by asking students to analyze, compare, and evaluate two pieces of criticism on Burney's *Evelina*. I grouped critical essays into three categories (labeled simply "Group One," "Two," and "Three") based on their differing assumptions about the author and her work. The first group of critics perceived flaws in *Evelina* that they believed to be evidence of Burney's inferior writing ability, as in Lord David Cecil's contention that Burney's plots are "clumsy as well as improbable."[5] These critics' assessments of the novel were more or less dismissive of Burney's talent or achievement. The second group, feminist in orientation, saw not "flaws" but features that could be explained by the writer's conscious or unconscious intentions. These critics' articles were committed to finding ways of explaining anomalous aspects of *Evelina*, as in Judith Newton's argument that Evelina cannot go anyplace "without being forced, intruded upon, seized, kidnapped, or in some other way violated" because Burney is depicting the predatory nature of the marriage market.[6] The third group mediated between the nonfeminist and feminist ideologies of the first two groups by interrogating Burney's achievement of her aims in the novel without dismissing her overall ability. Because the articles I selected for the first two categories were divided rather too neatly according to the gender of the authors, I made sure that the third group encompassed both male and female critics.

My assignment asked students to select two articles from different groups, then give an overview of each critic's argument about *Evelina*, assess the credibility of each argument, and finally evaluate whether one piece was more fair, useful, enlightening, or convincing than the other. To help students complete the assignment, I provided brief definitions of terms and gave them a worksheet keyed to those terms.[7] The first part of the worksheet invites students to record important assertions the critic makes about the author and the work and then to list what the critic offers as support for those assertions. Identifying an author's supporting evidence is a skill that freshman composition courses emphasize as students are studying argument and persuasion, but students often receive too little reinforcement of this skill once they leave the composition classroom. The second part of the worksheet asks students to distinguish between facts, inferences, assumptions, and value judgments and to identify the author's biases regarding gender. I suggested to the students that they might want to highlight each type of statement with a different colored marker as they read.

Let me add here that before they began the assignment, I stressed that they should finish reading *Evelina* before reading any criticism. I wanted them to solidify their own responses to the text before being influenced by the perceptions and opinions of "experts." Moreover, I always find it enlightening to hear what puzzles or bothers students as we proceed through any given work. A recent class, for example, could not fathom why Evelina is totally unnerved by being seen in the company of a pair of prostitutes. The students' questions opened up a useful discussion about eighteenth-century attitudes toward virtue, reputation, and marriageability as well as about the way public spaces in London triggered cultural anxiety about class boundaries.

In response to the assignment, one student, Sara, chose the pieces with the earliest and latest dates—1949 and 1994. Sara identified the author of the more recent article, Beth Kowaleski-Wallace, as a feminist, but she argued that the article was neutral in tone and not unfairly biased by the author's feminist perspective. By contrast, she found the older piece by Lord David Cecil to be "condescending and not a little sexist." In her summary of Cecil's argument, Sara enumerated what Cecil presents as Burney's strengths. Then, posing a zinger of a question, she uncovered an unsupported value judgment: "With these considerable gifts, why then does Cecil proceed to call Burney 'hardly an artist at all in the fullest sense of the word'?" Sara pointed out that Cecil makes "sweeping generalizations about women, such as 'by nature, women are observers of those minutiae of manners in which the subtler social distinctions reveal themselves,'" and then she perceptively noted that Cecil faults Burney for just this "type of close examination of social situations." Sara easily picked up on the double-bind that Cecil and many of the older critics create for Burney: She is best suited to write a novel of manners, and it is too bad that she can only write a novel of manners. Sara called this "unfair and unfounded." However, then she argued, "*Evelina* may not be a masterpiece, but it certainly is an important step in the development of the novel, and particularly for the contributions to the female voice in literature."[8]

Sara's own assumptions about what constitutes a masterpiece would be a perfect topic for follow-up discussion in class. Did she have any specific criteria in mind, such as universality or aesthetic complexity? Had she encountered anything in the novel that, in her view, disqualified it from being considered a great work of literature? More broadly, did the class harbor survival-of-the-fittest notions about texts based upon, say, their high school curriculum? For instance, that *Romeo and Juliet* and *Animal Farm* must be masterpieces because everybody reads them, but *Troilus and Crisseyde* or *Clarissa* or *Ulysses* could not be all that important because no one in the room is familiar with them?

A second student, Kate, read articles by Toby Olshin and Gina Campbell dated 1980 and 1991, respectively. Whereas Sara favored the feminist criticism she read, Kate preferred the nonfeminist piece by Olshin. She concluded that Olshin's "more traditional" criticism makes "few unfounded connections, and his logic is rooted in the facts of the novel." Campbell, though, "begins with the assumption that psychobiographical examination is a valid way to find meaning in literature" and then "makes broad inferences based on Frances Burney's supposed emotional reaction to events in her family." Kate found that Campbell's argument "is based on little support."[9] Part of the issue here is that Campbell's interpretation of *Evelina* springs from earlier work by critics such as Joyce Hemlow and Margaret Anne Doody, but that work was opaque to Kate, who had never read any other Burney criticism. However, Kate's reaction would provide the opportunity to explore in-class discussion to the extent to which it is permissible to interpret a text based on biographical data or speculation about an author. Such a discussion might also be a convenient point at which to clarify the tenets of psychoanalytic criticism for students who were unfamiliar with that approach.

A third student, Rhiannon, chose two articles published in 1975, one by Waldo Glock and the other by Susan Staves. Rhiannon noticed that both writers challenge earlier critics' assumptions about the significance of *Evelina* as a serious piece of literature. She responded positively to the vigor and assertiveness of Glock's arguments but upon consideration felt that Staves develops her discussion more carefully and thus more convincingly. Rhiannon noted in her evaluation that Staves's references to "other comparable literature of the time period" and to Burney's personal writings help to place the novel in its historical context. Glock, however, "seems to ignore the historical context of the novel and the writer's own position in that society," causing him to attribute "the 'problems' of the novel to a flaw in Burney's own ability as a writer." Clearly, reading the two articles together allowed Rhiannon to form her own judgment about the importance of a work's socio-historical context. Moreover, in her conclusion Rhiannon went beyond simply synthesizing the critics' viewpoints to offer a perceptive critique of their assumptions. While Rhiannon thought that Glock does not adequately take gender into account, she believed that Staves "attributes too much to gender": "Staves's assumption that women know more about women leads her to the error of concluding that Burney's ability to depict 'Female Difficulties' as 'real' is due to the author's gender," rather than to her skill as a writer. Rhiannon suggested that a balanced view of Burney would be "both aware of Burney's circumstances as a writer and respectful of her genius as a writer in some ways independent of her sex."[10]

Sara, Rhiannon, and Kate were all honors students—admittedly neither a representative nor a random sample of students taking the eighteenth-century novel course for which the assignment was designed. Not all students would be able to negotiate the assignment as successfully as these three did. For this reason, I would recommend that instructors provide additional support for the assignment, both during the writing process and after it. For instance, it might be useful in introducing the assignment to talk about areas of life in which people make informed judgments. Some students, for instance, consult their friends or read reviews before buying CDs or attending movies. Similarly, people often obtain advice from others before planning a trip, buying a car, or investing money. In the professional arena, doctors and lawyers draw on the professional judgment of their colleagues and predecessors when they make diagnoses or prepare cases. A consideration of what comprises expert opinion in various areas may help students willingly to engage with literary criticism, which admittedly can be quite demanding.

Some students may lack experience in rhetorical analysis. If this is the case, the instructor may need to provide illustrations of facts, inferences, assumptions, and value judgments. A review of a popular movie would be a ready source of examples, as would a magazine ad or a newspaper editorial. Additionally, most students would benefit from a structured pre-writing activity designed to clarify their understanding of the articles they have selected. One useful activity might be to group together three or four students who have studied different articles and ask them to answer a series of questions based on their completed worksheets. A good starting place would be for them to compare among themselves any assertions of fact that their critics make about the author and work. In theory, the factual data should not be contradictory, but by comparing notes, students might uncover instances of selection and slanting. A second task could be for students to contrast the value judgments that their critics make about the work and author and then to identify the inferences and assumptions that drive their critics' viewpoints. Ideally, by comparing and contrasting several pieces of criticism in a small group setting, students would refine their sense of how well their own particular critics support their arguments. Moreover, students could be prompted to wrestle with whether the date of an article or the sex of its author has any correlation to the article's ideology.

After students have completed their papers, some type of summary activity in class would be beneficial. Being required to do something in a public forum with their writing generally prompts students to take an assignment of this nature seriously. Individual or panel presentations on the articles would help the whole class comprehend the wide spectrum of critical responses to the work under consideration. Follow-up discussions would allow the instructor to probe students' conclusions and reinforce important concepts. Depending on his or her own interests, the instructor could direct discussion toward a specific end, such as exploring the degree to which gender influences critical judgments.

From a pedagogical standpoint, the strongest selling points of the assignment are its flexibility and adaptability. I originally conceived of the project to spotlight the uneven and sometimes capricious critical treatment that novelists such as Lennox and Burney—and by extension, a host of other early women writers—have received. However, because critics of all persuasions and eras are liable to make assumptions, reason from inferences, and offer value judgments, the assignment could easily be tailored to fit any canonical writer such as Defoe who had undergone a shift in critical estimation at some point. The assignment could stand alone or be tied to a larger project such as a research paper. Certainly it could be shortened or expanded to fit the course's time constraints, although my attempts at teaching undergraduates to decode criticism prompt me to recommend allocating several portions of class time to the project over a one- or two-week period.

The primary drawback to the assignment is that it requires considerable preparation on the part of the instructor. He or she must find a half-dozen to a dozen pieces of criticism that can be read in useful opposition to one another—meaning that they must reflect a shift in the critical reception or understanding of the work that has come about through a change in assumptions about its author, its genre, or its cultural significance. In all probability this means spending time reading and eliminating articles that are too abstruse or clogged with jargon for undergraduates to grasp. A related problem is that an adequate array of criticism may not yet exist for recently recovered women writers. If criticism is scarce, one option is to have students compare the work's original reception with present-day assessments.

Happily, students sometimes surprise us with how much they comprehend about the tendency of critics to pontificate. Once when my Advanced Composition class was studying slanting, one of the students—without any prompting—brought in a photocopy of a page from a 1973 anthology of Victorian poetry and prose to share as an example. The page in question, titled "Other Victorian Poets," contained a seven-sentence biographical sketch of Elizabeth Barrett Browning. Bracketed between Barrett Browning's birth and death dates was the following information:

> Her unfortunate father, who has been immortalized as the villain in the most famous literary love affair of the 19th century, carries the stigma in addition of having derived his income from West Indian slave plantations. Educated at home, Miss Barrett became an invalid (for still mysterious reasons) from 1838 to 1846 when, Andromeda to Browning's Perseus, she eloped with the best poet of the age. Her long poem *Aurora*

Leigh (1856) was much admired, even by Ruskin, but is very bad. Quite bad too are the famous *Sonnets from the Portuguese*, dedicated to Browning (who thought she looked Portuguese). Though the Brownings' married life was reasonably happy, Mrs. Browning's enthusiasms for Napoleon III, spiritualism, and dressing her only child, a son, as though he were a toy, all gave her husband much pain.[11]

I read the passage aloud to the class, and when I reached the critic's pronouncement that *Aurora Leigh* and *Sonnets from the Portuguese* are "bad," I was heartened to hear the students burst out laughing—not because any of them had formulated their own judgments about either work, but because the critic's opinion was so blatantly unsupported.

Ultimately, though, it is not the blatant cases we have to worry about. Students are more likely to be taken in by subtle statements that appear to be couched in the language of reasonableness but that do not, upon examination, argue convincingly from evidence or reasoning. If we can encourage students to read beyond such pronouncements, we will be helping them to develop sound interpretive strategies of their own. Who knows? Maybe some of our students will discover enlightening new ways to view texts by that "great crowd of minor female writers"—ways that suggest the "triumphs" of works such as Lennox's *The Female Quixote* are not quite so "minor" after all.

Notes

[1] Jerry C. Beasley, "Charlotte Lennox," *Dictionary of Literary Biography*, ed. Martin C. Battestin, vol. 39 (Detroit: Gale Research, 1985), 306.

[2] Walter J. Ong, *Orality and Literacy: The Technologizing of the Word* (London: Routledge, 1982), 79.

[3] Claudia L. Johnson, "The 'Twilight of Probability': Uncertainty and Hope in *Sense and Sensibility*," *Philological Quarterly* 62.2 (1983): 171; and R. F. Brissenden, "The Task of Telling Lies: Candor and Deception in *Sense and Sensibility*," *Greene Centennial Studies: Essays Presented to Donald Greene*, ed. Paul J. Korshin and Robert R. Allen (Charlottesville: UP of Virginia, 1984): 442.

[4] Michael E. Adelstein, *Fanny Burney* (New York: Twayne, 1968), 37.

[5] David Cecil, *Poets and Story-Tellers* (New York: Macmillan, 1949), 92.

[6] Judith Newton, "Evelina: or, The History of a Young Lady's Entrance into the Marriage Market," *Modern Language Studies* 6.1 (1976): 50.

[7] See all assignment materials as appendices to this chapter.

[8] Sara Elizabeth Campbell, interview by author and course materials produced for "The Eighteenth-Century Novel." Cited with permission of student.

[9] Kate Virostko, interview by author and course materials produced for "The Eighteenth-Century Novel." Cited with permission of student.

[10] Rhiannon Brusco, interview by author and course materials produced for "The Eighteenth-Century Novel." Cited with permission of student.

[11] *Victorian Prose and Poetry*, ed. Lionel Trilling and Harold Bloom (New York: Oxford UP, 1973), 689.

The Eighteenth-Century Novel: Course Syllabus
Dr. Hamilton

Course description:
This course will focus on the period in literary history that saw the rise of an important new genre, the novel. Because early novels are notoriously long, we will have time to read only a sampling of moderate-length, representative works by both male and female writers. However, this sampling, along with the research-based paper you will write on an additional novel, will give you a feel for the richness and variety of the period. We will focus our attention on defining the characteristics of the genre as well as examining the cultural contexts that inform the themes explored in the novels.

Course objectives:
1) become familiar with the characteristics of eighteenth-century comic and sentimental novels;
2) study the history and conventions of the genre;
3) consider the social, economic, political, and religious context within which 18th-century novelists wrote and explore the cultural/spiritual values they supported or challenged;
4) develop critical thinking and research skills through discussion, research, and writing.

Reading Schedule:

Week 1	Introduction to the novel	
Part 1: Marriage, Money, and Social Class		
Week 2	*Moll Flanders*	*Moll Flanders*
Week 3	*Moll Flanders*	*Moll Flanders*
Week 4	*Evelina*	*Evelina*; preliminary bibliography for research paper due
Week 5	*Evelina*	*Evelina*
Week 6	*Evelina*; group work on criticism	Mid-term exam
Week 7	Analysis of criticism due: discussion	
Part 2: Journeys, Quests, and Identity		
Week 8	*Joseph Andrews*	*Joseph Andrews*
Week 9	*Joseph Andrews*	Conferences: draft of research paper due
Week 10	*The Female Quixote*	*The Female Quixote*
Week 11	*The Female Quixote*	*The Female Quixote*
Week 12	*The Female Quixote*	Research paper due; oral presentations
Week 13	*Humphry Clinker*	*Humphry Clinker*
Week 14	*Humphry Clinker*	*Humphry Clinker*

Figure 1. Patricia L. Hamilton, Sample Syllabus

The Eighteenth-Century Novel
Dr. Hamilton
Assignment: Evaluation of Criticism of *Evelina*

Write a 500- to 750-word summary and evaluation of two pieces of literary criticism on Frances Burney's *Evelina*. (Please choose pieces from two different groups below.) Give an overview of what each critic argues regarding Burney's novel, and then assess the credibility of each critic's argument, comparing and/or contrasting the two pieces as applicable. Be sure to give enough supporting details or examples so that someone who has not read the literary criticism for himself/herself will be able to follow you.

In your summary, make sure to identify the "who" and "when" as well the "what" of the pieces you are reviewing. Items for discussion in your evaluation might include: the tone of the piece (positive, negative, neutral); the critic's biases and critical orientation (e.g., historical, feminist, Marxist, and so on); the kind and degree of support the critic offers for his/her interpretation of *Evelina*; any facts or arguments you think the critic overlooks. In your judgment, is one piece more fair, useful, enlightening, and/or convincing than the other?

Group One
Adelstein, Michael E. "A Young Lady's Entrance into the World." *Fanny Burney*. New York: Twayne, 1968. 28–44.

Cecil, David. *Poets and Story-Tellers*. New York: Macmillan, 1949. 77–96.

Glock, Waldo S. "Appearance and Reality: The Education of Evelina." *Essays in Literature* 2.1 (1975): 32–41.

Olshin, Toby A. "'To Whom I Most Belong': The Role of Family in *Evelina*." *Eighteenth-Century Life* 6.1 (1980): 29–42.

Group Two
Campbell, Gina. "Bringing Belmont to Justice: Burney's Quest for Paternal Recognition in *Evelina*." *Eighteenth-Century Fiction* 3.4 (1991): 321–40.

Kowaleski-Wallace, Beth. "A Night at the Opera: The Body, Class, and Art in *Evelina* and Frances Burney's Early Diaries." In *History, Gender & Eighteenth-Century Literature*. Ed. Beth Fowkes Tobin. Athens: U of Georgia P, 1994. 141–58.

Newton, Judith. "*Evelina*: or, The History of a Young Lady's Entrance into the Marriage Market." *Modern Language Studies* 6.1 (1976): 48–56.

Staves, Susan. "*Evelina*; or, Female Difficulties." *Modern Philology* 73.4 (1975–76): 368–81.

Group Three
Greenfield, Susan C. "'Oh Dear Resemblance of Thy Murdered Mother': Female Authorship in *Evelina*." *Eighteenth-Century Fiction* 3 (1991): 301–20.

Oakleaf, David. "The Name of the Father: Social Identity and the Ambition of *Evelina*." *Eighteenth-Century Fiction* 3 (1991): 341–58.

Rogers, Katharine M. "Evelina." *Frances Burney: The World of 'Female Difficulties.'* New York: Harvester Wheatsheaf, 1990. 25–40.

Vopat, James B. "*Evelina*: Life as Art—Notes Toward Becoming a Performer on the Stage of Life." *Essays in Literature* 2.1 (1975): 42–52.

Figure 2. Patricia L. Hamilton, Sample Assignment (instructions)

Patricia L. Hamilton, Sample Assignment

The Eighteenth-Century Novel
Dr. Hamilton
Assignment: Evaluation of Criticism of *Evelina*

Critical Analysis Worksheet

Title: _____

Author: _____ Year: _____

I. Data

    1.   Assertions about the work   Support for assertions

    2.   a. Assertions about the author   Support for assertions

        b. Put an * beside any assertions about the author's gender.

II. Analysis

    1. Which assertions are facts?

    2. Which assertions are inferences?

    3. Which assertions are assumptions?

    4. Which assertions are value judgments?

    5. What are the critic's biases regarding gender?

Some Useful Definitions

1. *Facts*: Data that can be objectively verified through the testimony of witnesses, through observation, or through records or documentation.
    Example: This morning's earthquake registered 7.0 on the Richter scale.

2. *Inferences*: Conclusions made by reasoning from evidence; chains of reasoning that link known facts with missing or presumed facts in order to arrive at an explanation.
    Example: We can expect aftershocks in the next forty-eight hours.

3. *Assumptions*: Ideas that are taken as a given but may not have any basis in fact or conscious reasoning; unquestioned beliefs.
    Example: For the last week we've been having typical "earthquake weather."

4. *Value judgments*: Opinions about worth, importance, aesthetic value, utility, or morality arrived at through reasoning and based on personal or collective codes of values or beliefs.
    Example: The media did a poor job in reporting this morning's earthquake.

Figure 3. Patricia L. Hamilton, Sample Assignment (worksheet)

CHAPTER THIRTEEN
Teaching Women Playwrights from the British Romantic Period (1790–1840)

Catherine B. Burroughs

This brief essay outlines an approach for teaching pre-twentieth-century British drama, which (excepting Shakespeare) is often neglected in English and theatre departments. It is more about methodology than the texts in question, for, in courses that feature eighteenth- and nineteenth-century women playwrights, one is particularly challenged to orient students to the historical, theoretical, and literary terrain. How to help students appreciate that a study of British women dramatists between 1700 and 1900 is inevitably an exploration of those biases that still control the industry of theatre history? My answer has been to bring undergraduates directly into debates that occupy the scholarly community. While one does not want to lose sight of where college students are in their academic and intellectual development, I believe that professors demonstrate their respect for students and encourage appropriate ambition by viewing them as apprentices who are rehearsing to become scholars themselves—even if they are not.

In courses on Romantic women playwrights, my ultimate goal is to help students perceive scholarship as a *developing* enterprise, for this is indeed the situation in the field; it is unfolding and expanding in fascinating ways. Thus, in addition to sharing with students the reasons behind my decisions to design reading assignments, course requirements, and writing exercises in particular ways, I also introduce them to issues currently structuring the field—on Websites, in e-mail, at conferences, in academic journals. Relying on available online bibliographies, I have students familiarize themselves with the current conversations in romantic drama, so that they can see the work we do in the class as constructive as well as simply instructive.[1]

One of these issues is how perceptions of Romantic theatre have been shaped by a critical vocabulary that draws heavily on oppositions like closet/stage, text/performance, public/private. This information is important for students to have right at the start of the course, for only then will they understand the relevance of my raising questions about how narratives of theatre history are constructed. And it is this information, in turn, that helps them see how the act of studying women in Romantic theatre can contribute to the (feminist) project of revising narratives of theatre history in the first place. Because undergraduates often enjoy being given a "backstage" tour of courses, during the first few days of class, I share with students some of the challenges I have already faced when constructing the syllabus. For instance, while it strikes me as logical to conclude a class on Romantic women playwrights with the seven-year stretch that saw the publication of Joanna Baillie's last collection of plays in 1836 and the Theatres Regulation Act of 1843, I find the issue of where to begin more difficult. How far back into the eighteenth century must one go in order to have a context for assessing the situation of women in British theatre in the 1790s?

This question elicits a range of answers from students. However, I believe they are more invested in exploring this question when it is framed by discussions of students as researchers—and when posed after students have started to come to terms with the fact that theoretical frameworks determine how and what we learn. As I have described elsewhere,[2] while the American and French Revolutions mark a convenient starting place for British romantic studies, other events are more crucial for conceptualizing women's position in theatre during this time: the Stage Licensing Act of 1737; the changes in theatre administrations in the late eighteenth and early nineteenth centuries; the rise of female-controlled theatre spaces in the first four decades after 1800.[3] Certainly one could argue that a course on women in romantic theatre must start with the 1770s, which inaugurated a generation of female playwrights whose achievements partially account for a proliferation of dramatic writing by women between 1788 and 1800. (Hannah Cowley wrote the comedy, *The Runaway*, which was produced at Drury Lane in 1776; Hannah More's tragedy *Percy* at Covent Garden in 1777 was one of the most popular tragedies of the eighteenth century; and Sophia Lee's comedy at the Haymarket in 1780, *The Chapter of Accidents*, was performed yearly until 1824.) From the perspective of performance history, the 1770s are significant because Sarah Siddons made her second London debut in 1782, six years after David Garrick's retirement in 1776. The point of rehearsing this information here is not so much to underscore the idea that the dating of a theatrical period changes in response to the perspective featured but that this concept is demonstrated more dramatically and effectively, I believe, when students are engaged with historical information *as research apprentices*.

Thus, to create the stage for this mode of learning, during the first several weeks of the course I make short assignments using appropriate Websites and archival materials that encourage students to think about how they might contribute to the field. By familiarizing themselves with the current scholarship and taking the time *at the start of the course* to survey the critical contours of this area of study, students are then fairly quickly positioned to formulate projects that chart ways to make a contribution to the research, rather than only rehearsing someone else's discoveries.

These research projects first appear as abstracts and prospectuses, turned in within the first several weeks, and, eventually, they will result in one paper, an oral presentation, and a "creative" production scattered throughout the semester. These early formulations are crucial, in my view, for providing students with a framework for engaging with the primary texts subsequently assigned. That is, only after students have contemplated the structure of the syllabus, done some fairly intense reading in the field, gotten a sense of the terrain that they will be processing, and described projects for which they will then do research, do they proceed to look at actual play scripts and other texts written between 1790 and 1840.

As one can imagine, this part of the course—the first two weeks or so—requires a great deal of attention, for this approach runs the risk of confounding students accustomed to studying drama in more traditional ways. One of the things I find most nerve-wracking about operating in this manner is that I cannot know whether the process has been successful until *the moment* (in the third week, let's say) when students start to discuss the primary texts in class. For only then, if they explore the plays *in the context of their research projects as well as of the critical issues that emerged during our analysis of the syllabus,* can we be said to have achieved a level of commitment to the course materials that will result in students doing work as if it matters.

I have designed an additional exercise both to measure the success of my pedadgogical endeavor and to make students self-conscious in a positive way about how scholarship is done and about how the field of women in British Romantic theatre is evolving, and I present this toward the end of the course. Students fill out a questionnaire (appendix), which asks them to reflect on their experience of studying the material. In contrast to evaluative instruments issued at most colleges and universities, this questionnaire does not require students to assess teacher or student performance (although this is implicit in the questions) but rather to think about how pedagogical approaches can determine one's relation to a body of reading. I ask students to assess the kinds of information that seemed most crucial to their understanding of the field, the in-class and homework activities that most greatly benefited them. I also ask students to describe their impression of the field, so I can link their learning processes to the material that was most effectively communicated and most completely retained.

In an upper-level British drama course in the fall of 1999, in addition to the questionnaire, I reprinted the prospectus for the essay I planned to write for this edited volume so that students could see that their reflections on pedagogy would (and did) influence my own attempts to wrestle with how to represent my field—as I move between scholarship and the classroom. The comment below is representative of the class's general reactions to reading current scholarship, especially by women. One student reported:

> I think what impressed me the most, right from the beginning about the scholarly research we read was that the authors didn't just state…feminist issue[s] and argue…their impact on British literature but rather looked at the roots, the history of the issue [the context]. I found that to be SO interesting and what truly separated "college" feminism from "high-school" feminism. There was a maturity, an intelligence to every argument, and a NEED to understand it, rather than just to argue it.[4]

This response made me understand more fully that the idea of "representation" as initiated and controlled by an individual—a professor—can be desirably balanced by a community of students who have been given skills that help them question the process of representation in the first place. Indeed, as this essay indicates, it has been my experience that students who develop a strong incentive to deal carefully and responsibly with factual information, critical interpretation, and theoretical assumptions, and who are also challenged to think of themselves as helping to shape a field—even on a small scale—emerge as highly invested in processing material that might otherwise seem esoteric and precious. Moreover, for those of us who believe this area of study is crucial for understanding a wide range of periods and playscripts, encouraging students to participate in the larger scholarly community—as well as to form scholarly communities of their own—can make teaching much less adversarial and even speed up the process of recovering information about pre-twentieth-century female theatre artists.

As I have continued to work Romantic women playwrights into my courses on British drama and nondramatic literature since 1999, I am continually challenged to think critically about the ways in which my syllabi represent the contributions to theatre history of Hannah More, Hannah Cowley, Joanna Baillie, Elizabeth Inchbald, Jane Scott, and others. Additionally, writing essays alongside my students—with the difference that mine may find a more public venue (through publishing)—has turned out to be another effective method for helping students to gain more respect for their own critical abilities. Such a practice also pushes me to keep learning new ways to tell "the story" of women who wrote plays between 1770 and 1840.

Notes

[1] For a listing of this bibliography and recent developments in the field, see "British Women Playwrights Around 1800," *Romanticism on the Net* [Website], available from http://www-sul.stanford.edu/mirrors/romnet/wp1800/essays.html.

2 See my "Uncloseting Women in British Romantic Theatre," in *Women in British Romantic Theatre: Drama, Performance, and Society, 1790–1840*, ed. Catherine Burroughs (Cambridge: Cambridge UP, 2000).

3 Ellen Donkin's elegant and lively study of women playwrights in London, which starts with a chapter that goes back to the Restoration, is invaluable for providing information about some of these trends. *Getting into the Act: Women Playwrights in London 1776–1829* (London: Routledge, 1995).

4 Christie Perfetti, interview by author and course materials produced for English 367, "The Erotics of Home: Early British Drama, 1550–1800." Wells College, Fall, 1999. Cited with permission of student. For other thoughtful comments to this questionnaire, I would like to thank the members of the class enrolled in ENGL 367 ("The Erotics of Home: Early British Drama, 1550–1800)" at Wells College in fall 1999: Karen LoParco, Freya Mercer, Christie Perfetti, Vanessa Rom, and Julie White. Christie's comment is representative of the class's general reactions to reading current scholarship, especially by women.

6 The Oxford UP project I refer to in my sample syllabi, under contract between 2001 and 2002, unfortunately had to be abandoned.

Early British Drama: "The Erotics of Home"
Dr. Burroughs

Course Description:

This course will be taught in two parts—as ENG 367 and ENG 368, and it may be the first ever devoted to "the closet play" taught at the (under)graduate level. Because I am creating a two-volume anthology for Oxford University Press on British closet drama, the aim of these sequential courses is to test the structure of the anthology with undergraduates like you who will actually be reading these plays. [6] Thus, the anthology that will eventually result will, in most senses, be the product of what happens in these two semesters and classrooms. By taking this course (and/or its sequel), you will apprentice yourself to a research project that teaches you how to: do archival research; research material for annotations; emerge with original research projects that (perhaps) require more than one semester to complete.

This course examines British theatrical culture and playwrighting from 1642 to 1820. Our focus is the women dramatists and actors of the period as we explore the kinds of fantasies about "the home" and "the family" encoded in plays and performances. Where does one find "desire" in the dramaturgy—and in descriptions of actual play productions of the period? What are some of the strategies that women playwrights used to confront issues such as (pre)marital sex, virginity, female sexuality, and childbirth?

Required Texts:
- Burroughs, Catherine, ed. *Women in British Romantic Theatre: Drama, Performance, and Society, 1790–1840* (Cambridge: Cambridge UP, 2000)
- Donkin, Ellen. *Getting into the Act: Women Playwrights in London, 1776–1829* (New York: Routledge, 1995)
- Finberg, Melinda C., ed. *Eighteenth-Century Women Dramatists* (Oxford: Oxford UP, 2001)
- Rogers, Katharine, ed. *The Meridian Anthology of Restoration and Eighteenth-Century Plays by Women* (New York: Penguin, 1994)
- Selected Xeroxes

Recommended:
- Burroughs, Catherine. *Closet Stages: Joanna Baillie and the Theater Theory of British Romantic Women Writers* (Philadelphia: U Penn P, 1997)

Course Approach:

The syllabus will be revised periodically to reflect the evolution of the dynamic and performance of the individuals in the class. Much of our class time will be spent in "workshop mode"—that is, we will practice "close reading" in collaborative and autonomous exercises both in and out of class. Specific passages to "close read" in preparation for class discussion will be assigned, and students will be held accountable for these passages through oral exchange, quizzes, small group exercises.

Figure 1. Catherine Burroughs, Sample Syllabus (continued on next page)

> **Early British Drama: "The Erotics of Home," 1640–1820**
> Dr. Burroughs
>
> **Reading Schedule:**
>
> **Week One:** Introduction to the Course
>
> **Week Two:** "Introduction" to *The Meridian Anthology of Restoration and Eighteenth-Century Plays by Women*; Aphra Behn's *Sir Patient Fancy* (1678); Donkin, Ch. 1 of *Getting into the Act*
>
> **Week Three:** "Introduction" to *Eighteenth-Century Women Dramatists*; Mary Griffith Pix's *The Spanish Wives* (1696) in *Meridian*; Mary Griffith Pix's *The Innocent Mistress* (1697) in *Eighteenth-Century Women Dramatists*
>
> **Week Four:** Catharine Trotter's *Love at a Loss; or, Most Votes Carry It* (1700)
>
> **Week Five:** Susanna Centlivre's *The Busybody* (1709) in *Eighteenth-Century Women Dramatists*; and *A Bold Stroke for a Wife* (1718) in *Meridian*
>
> **Week Six:** Elizabeth Griffith's *The Times* (1771) in *Eighteenth-Century Women Dramatists*; "Introduction" to *Women in British Romantic Theatre*; selected photocopies
>
> **Week Seven:** Frances Burney's *The Witlings* (1779) in *Meridian*; Ch. 6 in Donkin
>
> **Week Eight:** Sophia Lee's *The Chapter of Accidents* (1780); Ch. 4 in Donkin; Burroughs's article on Sophia Lee from *European Romantic Review*
>
> **Week Nine:** Hannah Cowley's *The Belle's Stratagem* (1780) in *Meridian*; Ch. 3 in Donkin
>
> **Week Ten:** Elizabeth Inchbald's *Such Things Are* (1787) in *Meridian*; Ch. 5 of Donkin; Ch. 8 in *Women in British Romantic Theatre* (Marvin Carlson)
>
> **Week Eleven:** Joanna Baillie (TBA); Ch. 2 of *Women in British Romantic Theatre* (Greg Kucich)
>
> **Week Twelve:** Elizabeth Inchbald (TBA); Ch. 10 in *Women in British Romantic Theatre* (Jane Moody)
>
> **Week Thirteen:** Joanna Baillie (TBA); Ch. 7 in Donkin; Ch. 6 of *Women in British Romantic Theatre* (Susan Bennett)

Figure 1. Catherine Burroughs, Sample Syllabus

Later British Drama: The Tradition of British Closet Drama, 1750–1900
Dr. Burroughs

Course Description:

This course will be taught in two parts—as ENG 367 and ENG 368 ("The Tradition of British Closet Drama, c. 1550–1900"), and it may be the first ever devoted to "the closet play" taught at the (under)graduate level. Because I am creating a two-volume anthology for Oxford University Press on British closet drama, the aim of these sequential courses is to test the structure of the anthology with undergraduates like you who will actually be reading these plays. [6] Thus, the anthology that will eventually result will, in most senses, be the product of what happens in these two semesters and classrooms. By taking this course (and/or its sequel), you will apprentice yourself to a research project that teaches you how to do archival research; research material for annotations; emerge with original research projects that (perhaps) require more than one semester to complete.

Required Texts:

- Photocopies of playscripts and essays—on reserve.
- *Closet Stages: Joanna Baillie and the Theory of British Romantic Women Writers*. Catherine Burroughs. University of Pennsylvania Press, 1997.

Course Requirements:

Each of you will choose a particular play on the syllabus on which to become an expert—that is, to research, to annotate, to comprehend. You will produce a series of short writing assignments, make a series of oral presentations on "your play" and create a 7- to 10-page paper that grapples with the theoretical and practical challenges your play presents as a closet drama. In addition, you will annotate a copy of the play.

The rest of your grade will involve other oral presentations, informal writing exercises, and assignments designed to help you refine the paper and annotation assignment described above. In addition, you will be asked to turn in "reflections" once a week. These reflections should take the form of a 250- to 500-word, typed essay in which you "reflect" upon the class that has just occurred; raise questions about issues and commentary voiced by your peers and professors; and comment upon the readings that you have processed for the previous class. In addition, you can comment upon the class dynamic and what is and is not working for you in the class. Most of all, you should regard the reflections as a chance to convey what you are learning from the course and to comment upon anything that you may not have had a chance to comment upon in class. However—most importantly—the reflections should "reflect" what has MOST ENGAGED you about the course material during the past week.

Figure 2. Catherine Burroughs, Sample Syllabus (continued on next page)

> **Later British Drama: The Tradition of British Closet Drama, 1750–1900**
> Dr. Burroughs
>
> **Reading Schedule:**
>
> **Week One:** Introduction to the Course
> **Week Two:** Marta Straznicky, "Closet Drama," forthcoming in *Blackwell Companion to Renaissance Drama,* ed. Arthur Kinney (with kind permission of the author—not to be cited without permission); Jonas Barish's "The Problem of Closet Drama in the Italian Renaissance," *Italica* 71 (1994); Jonas Barish's "Language for the Study; Language for the Stage" *The Elizabethan Theatre,* ed. A.L. Magnuson and C.E. McGee, 1993.
> **Week Three:** Papers produced by the seven members of ENG 367—the first part of the closet drama course offered last semester
> **Week Four:** Elizabeth Griffith, "Amana"; "Introduction: How the Drama Disappeared" from Susan Wiseman, *Drama and Politics in the English Civil War* (Cambridge, 1998); Cynthia B. Ricciardi and Susan Staves, "Introduction" to *The Delicate Distress* by Elizabeth Griffith (University Press of Kentucky, 1997); Betty Rizzo's essay on Griffith in Mary Anne Schofield and Cecilia Macheski, eds., *Curtain Calls: British and American Women and the Theater, 1660–1820* (Ohio University Press, 1991)
> **Week Five:** Samuel Taylor Coleridge and Robert Southey, *The Fall of Robespierre*; William Jewett, "The Fall of Robespierre and the Sublime Machine of Agency," *ELH* 63 (1996): 423–52; Daniel Zalewski, "Coleridge Regained" *Lingua Franca* 5.4 (1996): 70–73
> **Week Six:** Percy Shelley, *The Cenci*; Selections from Stuart Curran's *Shelley's Cenci: Scorpions Ringed with Fire* (Princeton University Press, 1970)
> **Week Seven:** George Gordon, Lord Byron, *Cain*; Younglim Han, Ch. 1 from *Romantic Shakespeare: From Stage to Page* (Fairleigh Dickinson Univ. Press, 2001); William Brewer, "The Diabolical Discourse of Byron and Shelley" *Philological Quarterly* 70.1 (1991): 47–65
> **Week Eight:** Presentations of Papers-in-Progress
> **Week Nine:** Joanna Baillie, *The Bride*; Preface, Ch. 1 and Ch. 3 of Burroughs's *Closet Stages: Joanna Baillie and the Theory of British Romantic Women Writers*; Slagle's "'Like a burnt child': Theatre Theory and the Price of Fame (1791–1805)" in *Joanna Baillie: A Literary Life*
> **Week Ten:** Robert Browning, *Pippa Passes*
> **Week Eleven:** Thomas Lovell Beddoes, *The Bride's Tragedy*; H.W. Donner, Introduction to *Plays and Poems of Thomas Lovell Beddoes*
> **Week Twelve:** Matthew Arnold, *Empedocles on Etna*; Karen Raber's Introduction and Conclusion to *Dramatic Differences: Gender, Class, and Genre in Early Modern Closet Drama*
> **Week Thirteen:** Frances Anne Kemble, *An English Tragedy*; Burroughs's "'Be Good!' Acting, Reader's Theatre, and Oratory in Frances Anne Kemble's Writing" in *Romanticism and Women Poets: Opening the Doors of Reception*, eds. Harriet Kramer Linkin and Stephen Behrendt; Kemble, "On the Stage"; Claire Luckham, *The Dramatic Attitudes of Miss Fanny Kemble*

Figure 2. Catherine Burroughs, Sample Syllabus

Women Playwrights from the British Romantic Period (1790–1840)
Dr. Burroughs

Student Questionnaire

1. Please name the courses in British drama you have taken or are planning to take.

2. In each of the courses, what kind of information has helped you most in understanding the cultural position and accomplishments of British women playwrights?

   - historical background in readings and class discussion?
   - overviews of theatre history?
   - timelines?
   - other chronological devices?
   - the syllabus itself?
   - the professor's organization/presentation of information?
   - class discussions?

3. What specific impression of the situation of British women playwrights (1700–1900) have you received from my courses? That is, what would you feel comfortable saying that you know for sure about the period (to a layperson)?

4. Which writers and plays do you remember most vividly? (Please name titles and authors, even if unsure of them.)

5. What other details about British women playwrights do you recall most vividly?

6. Which exercises that you did in and out of class assisted your memory?

   - oral presentations?
   - constructing timelines?
   - exams?
   - paper assignments (informal and formal)?
   - secondary sources/literary criticism?
   - professor's own essays?
   - peer essays?
   - conferences with professor?
   - other?

7. Describe the first and clearest impressions you have of the field of feminist theatre history. Name any scholar or scholarly research that you recall from any of these courses.

Figure 3. Catherine Burroughs, Sample Student Questionnaire

CHAPTER FOURTEEN
Working within a Community of Learners: Teaching Christina Rossetti at a Christian College

Diane Chambers

Christina Rossetti is one of the most popular writers in the upper-level English classes that I teach. While researchers debate Rossetti's placement in feminism and in the canon and the influence of her Christian beliefs on her poetry, my students find in her poetry space for identifying the intersection of faith with both her secular and religious poetry and for discussion of faith issues and women's role within a Christian context. For successful teaching, it is vitally significant that I recognize the evangelical Christian community that is Malone College and that I learn about my students' background and what they have experienced. Most students have relatively conservative backgrounds, sometimes based on the churches they attend but also on the rural and small-town communities within which they grew up. By beginning with them and their culture(s) as central to their interpretation of texts, I can empower them to be readers and interpreters of text, help them see the value of literature in their own lives, help them see how their ways of making meaning may be different from that of others, and open them up to different readings of texts. More specifically, I can get them to read and discuss the works of women writers, most of whom they have not encountered in other classes. Christina Rossetti works well for me because many students identify with her spiritual walk and her willingness to take "the lowest place."

Malone College describes itself as a Christian college for the arts, sciences, and professions. It is associated with the Evangelical Friends Church, and although "Friends" appears in the name, the "Evangelical" marks it as distinctly different from the Society of Friends (Quakers). The founders of the college were a husband and wife team, Walter and Emma Malone, and much is celebrated, especially during women's history month, about Emma's accomplishments. Nevertheless, a tension exists between recognition of the accomplishments of women and the conservative tradition of women's place found in evangelical churches, and this tension often manifests itself in the classroom. Many of the women have been raised to follow what they have been taught are biblical mandates for women's roles and behaviors, and although women outnumber men, those women who have been brought up to be passive, humble people wait for someone else to take charge of the discussion and prefer to be active listeners instead of speakers. Although their faces may register alarm at what someone says, they will not speak up and offer an alternative viewpoint. One of my goals is to encourage and promote the importance of speaking one's thoughts, even when they might be disagreeable to someone else. I work to establish a classroom environment that is supportive and encouraging, one in which the women students in particular can move both within and outside of the cultural influences that have helped shape them. While not all students are deeply committed Christians, to varying degrees the Malone classroom environments remind students that they are learning within a Christian context and that faith is not compartmentalized. Large numbers of students come to the school with a knowledge of the Bible and biblical tradition, and all students are required to take Old and New Testament classes; yet they have many different understandings of what it means to be a Christian. The faculty also come from a wide variety of Christian backgrounds, but all are encouraged to provide an environment in which students can come to terms with integrating their faith with their learning.

Gender issues are a significant topic on the campus, but the arguments take place in a context that may seem odd to the secular world. Much debate is given to "appropriate" gender roles, with biblical citations and Christian commentaries used to support both sides of the issue. Guest speakers on campus argue from a variety of Christian perspectives. Women professors meet students in the dorms to talk about their lives and provide insight into how they intersect their faith with the choices they have made. Because most of the focus is on women's roles, the Woman Question of the nineteenth century is alive and thriving on the Malone campus. Many women major in the traditional professions for women—nursing and education—although other students have made career decisions that would have been difficult for their grandmothers to make. While most of my female students would never call themselves feminists, they have not been unaffected by the feminist movement. A few of the less passive women have become outspoken advocates on women's issues. They are often outraged at how women are treated both at the school and in society. They are stunned by the misogyny in some of the literature they read, and they are confused about who they should be. Although many students may not speak up in class, they will talk to me or take strong stances in their writing. Some female and even male students deliberately select paper topics that will force them to explore gender concerns because they know that my classes are a safe place in which to inquire.

The students see Christina Rossetti as a woman who struggled with her placement in the world and as a woman whose poetry addresses them and their needs. They find something compelling in her writing that makes them listen and think. After several years of teaching Rossetti at Malone, I see that "something" as her ability to speak to a variety of Christian students about faith. Her poetry has helped them examine their own beliefs and roles at the same time that they learn about a poet who demonstrates an extraordinary use of language and a distinctive poetic voice. The questions they ask about her and her poetry and the answers they provide to each other reveal the influence of their faith on their interpretations of Rossetti's poems.

In designing my classes, I consciously position myself, the students, the writers, and their works because I want the students to understand that the knowledge produced is developed within a particular community of knowers and to understand the role of specific contexts in shaping their own voices and identity as well as their understanding of texts. I have learned to choose authors and texts carefully in order to meet students and move them: what to read, when to read it, how to read and discuss it, and why, have become vitally integrated aspects of how I design a course. I seek to provide a multiplicity of voices in the literature that the students read and work to have them acknowledge the multiplicity of their own voices, especially when they assume a certain sameness about themselves as learners and knowers. The example that follows of how students at Malone College respond to Christina Rossetti is from my Victorian Writers class in the fall of 1998, but their experiences are typical of the ones I have whenever I teach Rossetti.

Sharon Smulders claims that Rossetti "personified, for her contemporaries, the voice of faith in an age of doubt and so appeared to be estranged from her own time and place."[1] This description of Rossetti also fits many of my students who see themselves as the solitary faithful in an age of doubt and who feel "estranged" from their own time and place because of their faith. They find themselves Christians in a post-Christian culture. The most conservative women dress modestly and speak softly. Some students are highly offended by what the secular world takes for granted—nudity, public sexual discourse, swearing, drinking. Their tradition of piety leaves them feeling marginalized and counter-culture. Even more "mainstream" Christians, who may be offended by some aspects of modern culture while embracing other aspects find a Christian college a safe place to be faithful. As someone who has taught at secular schools, I find a Christian campus one of the few places where students can openly talk and write about the interaction of faith with anything in their lives, including their education. Instead of being encouraged to set faith aside, they are encouraged to grow in faith in meaningful ways.

In addition, most of my students have the religious background and language needed to read and discuss Rossetti without much difficulty. As Jerome McGann notes, "almost all of [Rossetti's] best work is generated through a poetic grammar that is fundamentally religious in origin and character."[2] In addition, McGann theorizes that one of the reasons Rossetti fell into disfavor among New Critics was because her particular religious belief differed from the Broad Church or High Church and Anglo-Catholic filters through which most of the interpretation of religious poetry is done. He argues that reading Rossetti's poetry requires readers "to willingly suspend not only our disbelief in her convictions and ideas but also our *belief* in those expectations and presuppositions about religious poetry which we have inherited from those two dominant ideological lines."[3] However, not only do most of my students come to the study of Rossetti equipped to understand her grammar, but they also have no need either to suspend disbelief in her convictions or to suspend belief in other ideological lines of thought. Indeed, I need to work in the *opposite* direction, carefully moving them from their own ideological religious lines to the ability to suspend them and be receptive to other critical interpretations.

My classes are heavily discussion-oriented, and students are taught how to discuss literature with one another and not just with me. Early in the semester I divide them into small groups of five or six, giving careful consideration to placement. Randomly assigning students to groups results in more ineffective functioning than when I consider who gets placed together. They are given a task to accomplish within the group that is related to the assigned reading for the day. Depending on the assignment, groups either report back to the entire class or turn in written work either that day or the next. I provide more direction early in the semester and gradually provide less as the semester progresses. On the days when I have groups, part of the class may be given to group discussion and part to whole class discussion or short lecture. Small groups give quiet students an environment in which they feel more comfortable speaking out. While some never move far beyond the comfort of their group, others make the transition to whole class discussion. The group activities I set up to train them in how to respond—for example, citing page numbers or lines of verse or responding to what another person says before continuing with one's own ideas. The same tactics used in small groups are expected in class discussions. When they look to me for an answer, I ask if anyone else wants to say something first. This particular class responded well to less teacher-centered learning and performed well in groups.

Thus, by midpoint in the semester, this particular group of students was able to sustain discussion and ask thought-provoking questions without much prompting. I became a facilitator, frequently a listener, and occasionally a clarifier. Christina Rossetti gave them additional confidence in their abilities because they put their backgrounds to use in discussing and interpreting her work. She appeared "easy" to them. They quickly identified her poetry's deep religious sensibility and the Christian beliefs by which her many themes seemed united. Students understood the elements of Rossetti's faith as exemplary of what they themselves believed, describing her weakness and helplessness, for instance, as evidence of a spiritually mature and necessary lack of pride in the face of God. Rather than critiquing her for her apparent lack of independence, students responded sympathetically and favorably to what they saw as the resignation and humility appropriate to a child of God.

During our discussions, one of the key issues students identified was Rossetti's focus on death, specifically death related to her faith and to remembering. Several of them said that because of her faith, her portrayal of death is more joyful throughout her poetry than what they expected. One student said Rossetti explores death but not in the somber manner of Emily Brontë. Instead, the way she writes, specifically her meter, resists interpretation as depressing. Rather, they identified contentment, peace, and death as just another stage of life, nothing to get excited about, and nothing to lose faith over. Indeed, to some students she seemed rather complacent about death, and her descriptions of the peacefulness of the grave raised questions. Specifically, they wondered why she focused so much on the grave instead of on heaven. Their questions sent me searching for answers, and I returned with Jerome McGann's theory about how Rossetti's belief in Soul Sleep (psychopannychism) influenced her poetry.[4] As McGann notes, "the *OED* defines psychopannychy as 'the state in which (according to some) the soul sleeps between death and the day of judgment.'"[5] They understood quickly, requiring far less of me than a class full of students unschooled in Christian teaching. While they might not have known much about the concept itself, they could compare it to their understanding of and/or their beliefs in the afterlife. Poems such as "Song" ("When I am dead my dearest"), "Up-Hill," and "The Bourne" became readily comprehensible within the concept of Soul Sleep. No longer were the students concerned with her inattention to heaven. Instead they focused on what they interpreted within their understanding of Rossetti's beliefs. It was a remarkable display of tolerance for someone else's beliefs, displaying more acceptance of Rossetti than some of them have for one another.

"Goblin Market" easily resonates with Christian students. While there is much background I had to supply in classes at secular schools, some of Malone's students were far more knowledgeable than I, finding biblical allusions and providing specific verses that amazed other class members, who scribbled notes as students spoke. Instead of being bogged down in basic plot or diction problems, this class could move quickly to higher level questions such as whether or not women could be Christ figures, whether the story was secular using biblical allusions or indeed religious, where were the men located in the poem, and what did the poem say about women's roles.

I wanted my students to consider other possible readings of Rossetti's poetry and let them know that Christian readings of Rossetti were not the only kinds of interpretations. We had discussed briefly one Victorian view of "Goblin Market" as a moral fable for children and what kind of messages it might be thought to send to young girls. I had intended to provide them with alternative readings. However, before I had an opportunity to broach the subject with them, one student with a used book came up to me with questions before class; during class I asked if she would share with the others the question she asked of me. Although turning red from embarrassment, she told the class that the notes someone else had written about "Goblin Market" contained all kinds of references to sex, and she wondered what was going on. Thus, we were able to begin examining alternative readings of Rossetti's most famous poem. First, I once again moved the students into their groups. Each group was assigned a perspective: social, economic, sexual, or gender. After coming up with ideas in the groups, we got together with each group reporting on their perspective. After that, I provided some critics' views, and students could think about the overlap. Dolores Rosenblum's "Christina Rossetti: The Inward Pose" worked particularly well as a feminist reading that intersects with students' previous learning about Victorian women's lives.[6] They also opened themselves up to Elizabeth Campbell's "Of Mothers and Merchants: Female Economics in Christina Rossetti's 'Goblin Market'" and Terrence Holt's "'Men sell not such in any town': Exchange in *Goblin Market*."[7] Campbell presents a reading of the economics in the poem and declares, "this reading will...attempt to show how 'Goblin Market,' charmingly cast as a fairy tale, asserts the vital socioeconomic function of women despite their marginalization by the Victorian market economy."[8] By starting from their faith positions and then moving to other readings of the poem, I have found the students more willing to listen to and consider alternative readings such as Campbell's. Indeed, many of my students who are interested in the roles and lives of women are more open to feminist readings when they are introduced to those positions after first affirming their own views; they find that some of the readings are close to their own interpretations and that their interests in women's issues span a multiplicity of voices.

One of my goals is to get students to see connections between writers rather than seeing isolated voices. For example, earlier I noted one student who compared Rossetti to Emily Brontë. In the weeks after we finished Rossetti, the students continued to refer to her. When we read Gerard Manley Hopkins, we discussed why Hopkins became part of the literary canon in the twentieth century while Rossetti was neglected until recently. One student suggested that on the surface Rossetti seems simple, and her poetry may not appear to contain much depth while Hopkins is obviously difficult from the start, yet when it came to issues of faith and doubt, the two seemed to have something in common. Another suggested that Rossetti's Christianity is too severe for some to handle and that she demands too much in terms of a spiritual walk with God. Other students decided it was because she was writing from a woman's perspective, and if men were deciding on the canon, then she was definitely out. As one student pointed out, men never seem to be able to understand women and why should this be any different. (Indeed, as the semester progressed, students recognized and debated how they responded to one another from a gendered perspective, probably as a result of my particular critical stance.) I asked if it could be a combination of what they said, and they agreed. I then went on to provide them with summaries of commentary made by critics such as Isobel Armstrong, Angela Leighton, Jerome McGann, Sandra Gilbert, and Susan Gubar. We could discuss the ways the critics intersected with and departed from the students' thoughts.[9]

The students' interest in Rossetti continued. Several of them chose her for their long research project. One student, fascinated by what he discovered in answering his test question on "Goblin Market," learned more about the Tractarians and Rossetti's involvement with High Anglicanism; he also told me that while studying for his exam, he had his mother read the poem, and the two of them got involved in finding biblical allusions. He and others borrowed books and articles that I had in my file and began sharing them with one another. When he discovered something that just mentioned potential heroism in "Goblin Market," he came in to ask what I thought. I talked about the work I did on sisterly heroism for my dissertation, and I also referred him to Dorothy Mermin's "Heroic Sisterhood in *Goblin Market*."[10] Another student wrote about the sister relationship in "Goblin Market" while yet another explored women in several Rossetti poems. She and two others met with me for a lengthy discussion of "The Lowest Room." Another of the men in the class shocked one of our librarians when he asked her how he would learn more about sex and fruit in literature. Yet another student from a previous year worked on a creative writing independent study in which he retold "Goblin Market" as a futuristic horror story. A year after the class, an English major taking a course in playwriting turned Rossetti's most famous poem into a play.

The work we did with all the women writers as well as Hardy's *Tess of the d'Urbervilles* led two female students to projects related to women's lives in the Victorian period. One commented that she had always idealized the Victorian period, but after reading and discussing the literature as well as working on her project, she no longer wanted to be Victorian. For many of them, the work we did with women writers as well as with the Woman Question opened up opportunities to discuss women's lives and the relationships of men and women in a way that was different from opportunities in the past. They could make connections and note changes between the lives of Victorian women and their own. The literature provided an avenue by which they could explore their own concerns. Another faculty member in our department sat in on one of the classes and observed that students felt comfortable enough with one another to raise serious issues and challenge one another to explain their positions. He was impressed at the large number of students who spoke out and that men did not dominate the discussion (as so often happens at Malone), how all the students appeared to be listening actively, even if they did not speak, how they had learned to tell one another to look at specific passages in the text, and how I was able to ask them questions that integrated literary criticism (e.g., Gilbert and Gubar suggest...) with their own discussion of the text, especially that students had learned to respond thoughtfully to that criticism.

What is particularly exciting about these students and their intellectual endeavors is that this was not a class of only English majors and minors. Indeed, less than one-third of the 28 students fell into that category. All students at Malone are required to take an upper-level English class to fulfill their general education requirements, and Victorian Writers is one of the unrestricted classes. The students who intellectually engaged with the study of Victorian literature included accounting, nursing, history, ministry, and communication arts majors. However, the success in getting students to think carefully and critically about what they read happened because I recognized that students come to my classes *not* as blank slates or empty vessels but as people with cultural heritages and contexts that influence them as learners. David Bleich writes that it is important to him to remember that no matter what group of students he addresses,

> it is membership of these students in various communities that is most pertinent to their studies of language and literature, rather than what formal sorts of knowledge they have already been exposed to before they entered my classrooms. If we acquire the courage to eschew our patronizing task of "introducing" students to "our" style of study, and instead ask all our students, younger or older, to introduce their own ways and thoughts for mutual sharing, we will have begun a productive response to the many voices now seeking to educate for an authentically just society.[11]

I taught in secular secondary and post-secondary institutions before coming to Malone, and I learned quickly that if I was to succeed in teaching the students at this comparatively conservative school, I needed to reconsider any assumptions

I might make about them as a community of learners that were based on previous experience and learn again myself.

A tension exists between what we want students to know, what we have read and want to pass on, our sense of ourselves as authorities, and what students themselves can develop on their own. We also make choices about the way we spend our time in the classroom based on what we believe about why we read literature, but none of what we decide will make any difference if the students are not receptive to our choices and if they cannot be challenged to become invested in the intellectual endeavor.

Notes

[1] Sharon Smulders, "Woman's Enfranchisement in Christina Rossetti's Poetry," *Texas Studies in Literature and Language* 34 (1992): 568.
[2] Jerome McGann, *The Beauty of Inflections: Literary Investigation in Historical Method and Theory* (Oxford: Clarendon Press, 1985), 246.
[3] McGann, 240–41.
[4] McGann, 242–47.
[5] McGann, 242.
[6] Dolores Rosenblum, "Christina Rossetti: The Inward Pose" in *Shakespeare's Sisters: Feminist Essays on Women Poets,* eds. Sandra M. Gilbert and Susan Gubar (Bloomington: Indiana UP, 1979), 82–98.
[7] Elizabeth Campbell, "Of Mothers and Merchants: Female Economics in Christina Rossetti's 'Goblin Market,'" *Victorian Studies* 33 (1990): 393–410; and Terrence Holt, "'Men sell not such in any town': Exchange in *Goblin Market,*" *Victorian Poetry* 28 (1990): 51–67.
[8] Campbell, 394.
[9] For a lengthy discussion of why Hopkins was privileged over Rossetti, see McGann's "The Religious Poetry of Christina Rossetti" in his *The Beauty of Inflections.*
[10] Dorothy Mermin, "Heroic Sisterhood in *Goblin Market,*" *Victorian Poetry* 21 (1983): 107–18.
[11] David Bleich, "Reading from Inside and Outside of One's Community," in *Practicing Theory in Introductory Literature Courses,* ed. James M. Cahalan and David B. Downing (Urbana, IL: National Council of Teachers of English, 1991), 21–22.

Victorian Writers
Dr. Chambers

Course description:
The purpose of Victorian Writers is to increase your knowledge and awareness of significant writers of the Victorian period as well as to increase your understanding of Victorian literature's contributions to literary history. We will examine the interplay between their writing and the culture in which they wrote as well as try to understand why Victorian literature remains popular in the twenty-first century—why Victorians are still read and/or why their works have been adapted to contemporary media such as movies.

Objectives:
- an understanding of some of the writers of the Victorian period in Britain, including their place as part of the literary canon; of significant cultural and aesthetic issues as they pertain to the literature.
- an ability to examine, analyze, and write about literature; to understand a piece of literature as a whole, noticing the relationship of parts to the entire work and the work to literature in general; to discuss the interrelationships among the texts; to deal critically with topics, issues, and ideas that are found in a work of literature.
- an appreciation of the relationship between literature and culture; for the contributions of the Victorian writers to our literary heritage.
- an awareness of how literature provides opportunities to learn about ourselves, the world we live in, and our relationship to others.

Expectations and requirements:
You should think of this course as discussion-oriented, not as a series of lectures. Your educated analysis of the works is an important element in the study of literature because no story, poem, or play will mean the same thing to all persons. You are, therefore, expected to participate in small group and class discussions. This includes asking questions when you are perplexed or when someone's interpretation does not agree with your own. Your approach to the course will determine how much you will learn this semester. If you bring interest and a positive attitude to the work, you will be receptive to what a particular text is saying to you as an individual.

Readings:
- Intro to the Victorian period
- Emily Brontë: selected poems
- Charlotte Brontë: *Jane Eyre*
- Alfred Lord Tennyson: selected poems
- Robert Browning: selected poems
- Elizabeth Barrett Browning: selected poems
- Elizabeth Gaskell: *Cranford*
- Matthew Arnold: selections
- Christina Rossetti: selected poems
- Gerard Manley Hopkins: selected poems
- Oscar Wilde: *The Importance of Being Earnest*
- Thomas Hardy: *Tess of the d'Urbervilles*

Figure 1. Diane Chambers, Sample Syllabus

CHAPTER FIFTEEN
Canon-Busting: Undergraduate Research into Romantic-Era Women's Writing in the Corvey Collection

E. J. Clery

A number of critical and theoretical developments are now beginning to alter and expand the selection of Romantic-era literature for teaching purposes. A growing number of important critical studies on writing by women, accompanied by new scholarly editions, has encouraged many instructors to include the work of at least two or three female authors: Mary Shelley, Dorothy Wordsworth, Ann Radcliffe, and Charlotte Smith are themselves close to achieving canonical status. However, with the best revisionist will in the world, instructors are still faced with obstacles when they try to broaden the canonical horizon of their courses. The two most obvious problems remain: access to texts and the limits of course-time. Recent editions and anthologies have greatly extended the range of available texts, but they are still only the tip of the iceberg, and trying to construct a course "a la carte" can still prove an expensive business for departments (in terms of photocopying) and/or students. In addition, then there is the inevitable limits of any course, particularly acute in the case of the romantics: how to do justice to the "Big Six" and the critical history which lies behind their canonization, while providing a more inclusive understanding of the literary period?

What follows is an account of one strategy we have initiated at Sheffield Hallam University to involve undergraduate students in the rewarding work of recovering forgotten texts of the Romantic era while circumventing the problems just mentioned. Our aim has been to allow the students themselves to become front-line researchers, specialists in the career and writings of a single author, and then contribute their findings to a database available on the Internet. The benefits of such a project, we found, go far beyond solving the problems of available resources; by exposing the students to the practices of archival research—the nuts-and-bolts of recovery—we make available a deeper understanding of literary research, especially biographical and bibliographical. By publishing their findings on the Internet, students become more invested in their work as a significant contribution to a growing field. Ultimately, students see themselves as scholars in ways that dramatically affect their educational experience. The "Adopt an Author" option, as we call it, is now in its sixth year, and this is a good moment for review and reflection.

The experiment was made possible in the first instance by the acquisition of an important collection of Romantic-era literature in a microfiche edition by the Sheffield Hallam University library. This is the "Edition Corvey," a collection of approximately 3,000 literary works in English, part of a private library in Westphalia, Germany, consisting of a total of 72,000 volumes in German, French, and English, most published between 1790 and 1835. The library at Schloss Corvey was the creation of the bibliophile Landgrave of Hesse-Rotenberg and his wife. What is remarkable about the collection, from the point of view of the English scholar, is its popular, nonhierarchical nature. These collectors apparently bought novels, poetry, drama, travel writing, and memoirs unselectively and in bulk. As a result, it is a treasure trove of "minor" or neglected literature; it includes 92% of English-language novel production for the period 1818–29, several texts can be found nowhere else, and the representation of writing by women is outstanding.

In 1994 Sheffield Hallam became the first British university to purchase the "*belles letters*" section of the "Edition Corvey." In 1996 the Sheffield Hallam University Corvey Project was begun, with funding from the British Academy Research Fellowship Scheme. The outline of the project (drawn up by Professor Judy Simons with Dr. Robert Miles and Dr. Philip Cox in English, and Dr. Noel Williams in computing), defined the principal aim as follows: "to create a descriptive and analytic survey of women's writing in the Edition Corvey using hypertext technology." In the first stage of the four-year project, the appointed Research Fellows, I and (successively) Dr. Glenn Dibert-Himes and Dr. Julie Shaffer, in collaboration with database specialist Chris Venuss, worked on establishing a Corvey Project Website with a hypertext database that would serve as a gateway to the holdings of the collection. The database contains biographical, bibliographic, and analytic material including newly researched accounts of the careers of women writers, a large number of contemporary reviews, synopses of novels, and lists of keywords describing each work that will eventually allow detailed searches. Over the initial period of the project a wealth of women's writing has become available on the Internet and in new editions, but the need for navigational tools to this previously neglected material is more vital than ever. The Corvey Project continues, with the support of the University and currently under the directorship of Dr. Mary Peace, with regular seminars related to the collection, an e-journal linked to the site, and updates and additions to the database.

At the beginning of the 1997–98 academic year we launched a teaching/research initiative to encourage undergraduate use of this valuable resource, and to try to integrate the pedagogic and research ideals of the English Subject Group. As in many departments elsewhere, final-year English students undertake a course of independent study over two semesters, resulting in a dissertation on the subject of their choice. Most choose to look at works of twentieth-century literature, or take the option of creative writing (a subject group strength). At the end of the 1997 summer terms, second-year students considering what to do for their "Independent Study Unit" were invited to participate in the "Adopt an Author" scheme in conjunction with the Corvey Project on Romantic-era women's writing. This involved selecting a little-known female author represented in the collection holdings; reading two or three of her works; and writing a critical dissertation, a synopsis, and a keyword analytical description of each work for use in the online database, an annotated bibliography of critical and reference works used, and, where information was available, a biographical sketch and an account of the critical reception of her work (using, for the most part, contemporary reviews). Although the course of study remained independent, they would receive more guidance at the outset than usual, some extra training in research skills, and the opportunity to consult the Corvey research fellows as they required.

To our surprise and delight, sixteen undergraduates (all female, as it happened) chose to work with us in excavating the forgotten publications of almost unknown writers. We began by providing them with a list of 150 writers (about half the number of female authors who feature in the *belles letters* Edition Corvey). All of these could be found in *The Feminist Companion to Literature in English* edited by Virginia Blain, Patricia Clements, and Isobel Grundy.[1] Reading through the entries helped give students a sense of the extent and diversity of women's writing at the time, as well as providing some information on which to base their choice. Thirty of the authors were also represented in the Royal Literary Fund (RLF) Archive, a marvelous resource which the SHU library bought on microfilm to support the Corvey Project. From 1792, when the RLF was founded, needy authors and their sponsors wrote detailed letters of application to the trustees of the Fund, including life histories and lists of publications. Once students had made a short list of writers, they could then browse through examples of their work in the Edition Corvey before making a final decision.

In three group orientation sessions, the students learned about catalogues and other research available on the World Wide Web. They were given annotated reading lists, with information about standard biographical dictionaries and bibliographies, as well as works of criticism on literary production in the Romantic period, and on women's writing in particular. The students seemed to be variously equipped: only a few had used the Internet before (this was back in 1997!) and not all had previously studied the Romantic period, but already their enthusiasm for the task was remarkable. It was clear that the opportunity of going where, in most cases, no critic had gone before, and making a genuine contribution to what was known about women's literary history was inspiring for them.

The most exciting part of the experiment for the staff was the glimpses of the students' initiative afforded by supervisions, such as the day one student burst into the office to tell me that she'd found a description of her author in the correspondence of Elizabeth Gaskell, having followed up the link from a case file in the Royal Literary Fund Archive. Another study based on a particularly thorough examination of the RLF and other sources was that on Hannah Maria Jones. The student in this instance was able to propose a new date of birth for the author; she has since gone on to make a career in librarianship. Many participants have traveled far afield, to look at periodical reviews in collections in Leeds and Manchester, or to visit local archives connected with their authors. They took to the use of specialized reference tools with impressive alacrity. One or two students in the first year, when the option was an unknown quantity, underestimated the commitment required. However, most have embraced the challenge of becoming research pioneers.

Inevitably, there were some technical teething problems. We promised each student the loan of paper printouts of two texts from the microfiche edition, but printing out works of four, five, six volumes is a laborious business, and technical breakdowns, staff shortages, and a funding crisis delayed provision. The students seemed to cope: They could always resort to the trusty microfiche reader, but it was an anxiety nonetheless. In subsequent years we have made the students responsible for the printing out of their own work, which they then borrowed without charge. The resulting photocopied texts now fill a large bookcase and are being transferred to the Sheffield Hallam library for the benefit of future researchers.

At the halfway point, the students submitted a "pro-forma" with a brief account of their work to that point and a plan of action for the next stage. These were encouraging and sometimes quite heartwarming: One participant explained at some length how the author had become "part of my life." Personal identification has subsequently led a number of students to choose authors who lived in their own part of the country, and the novelist Sarah Green was selected by her undergraduate namesake. However, while we are aware that energies might, in some cases, have been channeled into the biographical detective work at the expense of the critical/interpretative aspect of the research, this has not happened to the extent that it was necessary to alter the rubric of the scheme. In supervisions, a major part of our input is focused on helping students identify critical issues and themes in the texts as the basis for the dissertation element. Valuably, this process remains more egalitarian than is usual with undergraduate dissertation preparation: The students are the real experts on their chosen works; we take our lead from them.

It seems safe to say that the participating students finished their undergraduate careers feeling they have made a difference. Items from their portfolio have been added each year, with permission and acknowledgment, to the student e-journal within the Corvey Website entitled *Corinne*, and in the case of the best work, to the Corvey database. They have brought to light facts and provided a critical apparatus, where little or nothing existed before. We receive frequent inquiries from academics and nonacademics alike relating to the student projects. Where possible we forward messages to the former students themselves. The Website represents a permanent connection with them and many have stayed in touch. At least six that we know of have gone on to graduate studies, most within the field of Romantic-era women's writing. A remarkable trio, close friends who encouraged one another's research and produced the best projects of the year 2000, have all ultimately subscribed to graduate degrees. One of them is part of a cohort of five M.A. students at Sheffield Hallam this year pursuing an advanced "Adopt an Author" option. However, what is most important to us is that all participating students have gained the experience of exploring an uncharted field, and have learned how to make maximum use of a library in order to pursue interests they have largely defined for themselves. The success of the Virago Press in the 1980s showed the interest that could be generated among a nonacademic readership in forgotten works by women writers of the past. One benefit of the Internet will be that research resources will become more readily available to nonacademics; as rare texts become digitized, scholarly research will cease to be the rarified activity it is at present, confined of necessity within the walls of the institution. Our hope is that involvement in the Corvey Project will have encouraged in the students not only a taste for lifelong learning, but for active, lifelong research.

Note

[1] Blain, Virginia, Patricia Clements, and Isobel Grundy, eds. *The Feminist Companion to Literature in English*. London: B. T. Batsford, 1990.

CHAPTER SIXTEEN
Teaching "Recovered" Victorian Female Intellectuals

Peaches Henry

The teacher needs to admit what everyone knows: that the best literature of the Victorian period was written by men and that's why the women have not survived to make it into the Norton.
—An English major

This comment from a student evaluation of a course focusing on the prose writings of Victorian women writers represents one of the most damaging and insidious obstacles facing faculty who wish to teach "recovered" female writers: the incorrect impression that such authors have been rightly forgotten and overlooked due to the inferiority of their work. Untutored in the historical, literary, and cultural contexts which influence how texts are valued (or not) and thus which texts get published (or not) in the anthologies that constitute their textbooks, students accept constructed canons as natural ones, believing that they perpetuate texts that have demonstrated excellence over time. Women's texts that have not made the cut for such anthologies as the long standard *Norton* series, students reason, do not deserve to be studied, because they simply are not good enough. Not only do students perceive of these writers as inferior, but they also view their presence on syllabi as blatant tokenism. Like the one quoted above, students are unconvinced of their merit, and one finds oneself in the unenviable position of defending these writers rather than discussing their ideas or impact on their contemporaries, much less their enduring importance to Victorian studies.

In the face of such skepticism, I needed to develop pedagogical responses that spoke to this mind-set. Rather than teach from the weak position of justification, I determined to make a frontal attack on students' facile acceptance of stereotypes and myths about women's writing. To break the hold of such long-standing and entrenched attitudes, I had to create a paradigm that forced unwilling students to engage with these authors and the sociopolitical institutions out of which they emerged and through which their texts have passed during the twentieth century. Through such engagement, I was convinced, students would develop discernment about the literary traditions, history, and marketplace influences at work in the world of literary production. Such encounters would enlighten students about a variety of complex issues that influence the production of knowledge, who gets to produce it, how it will be disseminated, and how it is valued. Armed with this understanding, students would be equipped to make intelligent judgments about the authors and texts they encountered in my courses and those of my colleagues.

The strategy I employed to combat students' negative attitudes about women's prose writing, then, was to convert the obstacles I faced into strategic opportunities. That is, rather than defend these authors' claim to a place at the academic table, I chose instead to give students the opportunity through independent research to substantiate their position that these women writers did not deserve one. Thus, my pedagogical strategy was to use students' biases and suspicions to educate them about the impact of competing critical traditions and histories, to expose the effects of the literary marketplace on the publication of works by non-canonized writers, and to teach them about the underlying values that have determined the aesthetic principles by which authors and texts are canonized or not.

In the late 1990s, when I initially began integrating prose by Victorian women into the already crowded syllabi of such courses as the British Literature Survey, I encountered resistance from students, generally sophomore and junior English majors, who thought that I was stealing space from legitimate (read "canonized") authors in order to "force" lesser known and therefore inferior writers into the curriculum. This attitude was reinforced by the fact that these women were not represented in the standard anthologies or, if they were represented, appeared at the end of chronological periods in issues sections such as "The Woman Question" or "Victorian Ladies and Gentlemen," relegating women's writing to the margins as little more than an afterthought. Equally damning from the perspective of students were the specialized collections devoted to recovering women's writing such as Andrea Broomfield and Sally Mitchell's *Prose by Victorian Women, An Anthology*, amounting to special pleading.[1] Moreover, students cited my use of photocopies of out-of-print texts as evidence of the illegitimacy of these texts, because of course any text worthy of the academy would have remained in print—an indirect reference to the "test of time" standard. Students viewed women writers as interlopers undeserving of their attention or time. In light of these views, I challenged students to test their thesis that the presence of these women on the syllabi of my courses was a feminist plot to give undeserved credit to inferior artists. Put this way, our approach to these women writers took me off the defensive and put my students on the offensive in a manner that would lead them to a deeper understanding of how literature is valued, preserved, and disseminated.

Consequently, I designed a semester-long research project that required students to research and accumulate the information which for female nonfiction prose writers is unavailable. Designed with upper-level English majors in mind, the semester-long project was individualized and research driven. Each student selected an author on whom he or she would conduct research throughout the semester. This semester-long research project required each student to discover additional primary texts by our authors (that is, in addition to those featured in our anthologies) and to unearth biographical, literary, historical, social, and cultural information about them. Also, our objective was to reconstruct the impact these women writers made on their contemporaries. Secondarily, we attempted to discover why women writers whose work had been so popularly and critically accepted during their lifetimes should have practically disappeared by the twentieth century.

The research project was intended to facilitate the following objectives: First, as a result of their own research, students would develop an interest and engagement with at least one Victorian woman writer. Second, students would gain an understanding of the social, political, and critical processes involved in canon formation. Third, students would re-create and critique the literary critical history of one Victorian woman writer. Fourth, students would write their own assessment of one Victorian women writer's literary accomplishments.

This paradigm for teaching recently recovered Victorian women writers became a powerful tool which allowed me to counteract a classroom phenomenon that I refer to as "submerged resistance." Submerged resistance is the contemptuous or dismissive attitudes that students hold toward marginalized texts like those of under-represented female writers but that they have learned to conceal behind acceptable politically correct façades. While they dutifully listened and took notes during lectures and class discussions about women writers and their texts, students revealed their contempt for these writers in venues which they felt were risk-free such as in reading journals (lightly graded half-page responses to assigned essays) or where they could remain anonymous such as in end-of-the-semester teacher-course evaluations (TCEs). In the reading journals students expressed dismay at the lack (in their opinions) of quality of the female writers especially in relation to a male writer whom they thought had probably been displaced by a woman: "I don't see why we're studying [Eliza Lynn] Linton. All she does is complain about how girls dressed [in 'The Girl of the Period']. I can't believe we're wasting space on her when we could be reading a real writer like Dickens," or "When are we going to read some important writers?" Students challenged the legitimacy of writers in terms of their subject matter: "So far all the writers we have read talk about women's issues. I think the Victorian period was about more than just women's stuff."

If criticisms in reading journals were coded, they were direct and vociferous in teacher-course evaluations. In the TCEs, students attacked authors on the basis of their lack of name recognition, the infrequency with which they are taught, their exclusion from popular anthologies, and their absence from high school advanced placement (AP) courses and standardized tests such as the Scholastic Aptitude Test (SAT):

> I'm an English major and I've never heard of Edith Simcox. I think that says a lot about the quality of her writing.
>
> Most of the writers on our syllabus this semester don't even show up in the *Norton Anthology*. If they do, like Cobbe, it's in that special topics section that we never got to in the survey [British Literature Survey required for English majors in most programs].
>
> I've had a lot of English courses and none of them had any of the women we read this semester. I liked reading them but I wonder if we should have been reading some more important writers like Mill or Ruskin.
>
> In high school I took advanced placement classes. We studied Dickens, the Brontës, and George Eliot. We never read anything by Helen Taylor, Vernon Lee, or Eliza Linton and those courses were supposed to be preparing us for college English. I don't think we should have wasted time on these no-name writers when we shoulda been studying the important people. I don't understand why we studied all these women nobody ever heard of.

Because the objections expressed in TCEs, which I received months after my course was completed, rarely surfaced in class discussions, I did not have the opportunity to address them with students.

However, because it invited students to state openly their reservations about the female writers they were studying, the research project provided a meaningful and timely method to respond to students' submerged resistance. Rather than work to convince students of these writers' merit, I invited them to prove their hidden judgment that the course was merely an "affirmative action class for Victorian women" by conducting the requisite research. For students who considered these writers interlopers, here was their chance to show the professor that she was "forcing these inferior writers on to the syllabus where they didn't belong." Told that they were not required to "promote" their writer but instead to assess her work, contemporary status, and her literary legacy honestly, students were enthusiastic about the opportunity to voice their "real" opinions about their writer. They delighted in the prospect of demonstrating their foregone conclusion.

After presenting the project to students, I offered a one-hour lecture on the history of women's absence from the canon of Victorian nonfiction prose, including the familiar argument about separate spheres and highlighting John Holloway's model of the Victorian sage and the pioneering work of Mitchell, Broomfield, Susan Hamilton, and others.[2] I informed students that by the 1950s an elite group of Victorian nonfiction prose writers were signaled by scholars who designated this all male group as "sage" writers. Since then, an elite group of male sages, including Thomas Carlyle, Thomas Macaulay, John Ruskin, John Stuart Mill, John Henry Newman, Matthew Arnold, and Walter Pater, have given a skewed view of the nonfiction prose genre. Though such prose has come to be represented by five or six male writers in texts such as Holloway's influential *The Victorian Sage*, in actuality hundreds of men and women participated in its production. I noted that the Victorian periodical press's practice of publishing articles anonymously created an obstacle to women's recognition since scholars have been unable, until recently, to identify the authors of many Victorian prose pieces and were more likely to assume that women did not write for learned journals and reviews. Women essayists published mostly in the periodical literature of the day; their work is thus more difficult to find. In addition to the transference of periodicals to microform, other material difficulties remain; few literary scholars have been willing to perform the necessary archival research to uncover this genre. Though some Victorian women's essays were collected in volumes after their original appearances, most are still only available in the original nineteenth-century periodicals. The vast majority of material produced by Victorian women writers remains buried in crumbling periodicals. I pointed to the work accomplished in the *Wellesley Index to Periodicals* (1966–1990) where thousands of unsigned periodical essays have again found their authors, resulting in several valuable anthologies featuring women nonfiction prose writers. I indicated to students that the historical critical situation of Victorian nonfiction prose by women has resulted in courses devoid of female voices from the period. I informed them that new anthologies have given me the opportunity to introduce these forgotten writers to the academy. I concluded the lecture by inviting students to join the scholarly discussion about these writers. I encouraged them to study a single author and judge her merit for themselves.

After this lecture, each student selected an author and embarked on an independent recovery project. Throughout the semester, students continued to read work by a variety of women writers as well as more of that by the writers on whom they had chosen to focus. In addition, they read numerous critical and theoretical articles and chapters on Victorian nonfiction prose and women's writing. Moreover, they were encouraged to discuss their work in class and in research journals throughout the semester, raising questions, expressing frustrations, and sharing information as well as concerns. Although I allowed my students a great deal of independence, I was careful to direct their work by providing specific tasks and objectives (discussed below). From the start, I told students that they might not be successful in discovering all that they set out to find, and in light of that eventuality, I explained that I would measure their success by their efforts. To familiarize students with research techniques and tools, I had a reference librarian give the students several training sessions which included teaching them about such texts as the *Dictionary of Literary Biography (DLB)*, the *Dictionary of National Biography (DNB)*, *Poole's Index to Periodical Literature*, the *Index to the London Times*, and the *Wellesley Index* as well as numerous Internet databases such as *Periodical Contents Index*.[3] Students were also alerted to library features such as interlibrary loan, microform, and the rare book room.

Presented with clearly stated objectives designed to meet the broad aims listed above, the project consisted of three parts with the third serving as a final exam (see appendix). Part I of the research project required students to create a bibliography of the author's primary works, using the *Wellesley Index* and *Periodical Contents Index*. In addition to the bibliography, students were required to write a survey of their author's work in prose format. First, they did a study of the periodicals in which she published establishing the following facts:

1) periodicals publishing her work
2) the editorial stance of each periodical
3) whether her subject matter coincided with the editorial stance of those periodicals.

Second, they analyzed their author's bibliography, considering these issues:

1) her subject matter
2) the relation of her subject matter to the public debates of the day
3) the evolution of her subject matter over time
4) the genres she wrote—reviews, social critiques, political treatises, manifestoes, travel literature.

During class meetings, students discussed their findings, informing each other of their discoveries and disappointments. As they worked on Part I of the project, many were surprised and impressed by the prodigious and varied output of their authors. Also, students began to reassess their responses to these writers as they learned that these writers had been widely published and read:

> [Eliza Lynn] Linton burst into the genre of the Victorian periodical, creating a place for her writing and personal development. Beginning with the fiction pieces published in *New Monthly* and *Temple Bar* and ending with her witty, cutting "Wild Women" articles, and including the shorter reviews, essays and necessary travel and personal experience connected to the articles, Linton's career was both prolific and involved. It is relevant to understand that Linton was published in over thirty periodicals in a fifty-two year

writing career because, as a woman and as a writer, the reading culture found Ms. Linton lively, enjoyable to read, and witty and extremely well informed.[4]

Through fiction and nonfiction prose, [Harriet] Martineau established herself as one of the prominent social critics of her time. She stands as one of the most widely published women of the Victorian period. Her works competed successfully with the writings of authors like Charles Dickens and Charlotte Brontë.[5]

As they discovered that these women had been fully integrated into the intellectual life of the period, their conversations evinced growing admiration for these forgotten writers as evidenced by this passage from Part I of a research project done on Helen Taylor: "Whether she was fighting for the enfranchisement of women or debating a finer point of Parliamentary policy, Taylor was on the cutting edge of the issues of her day, and could well be considered on the cutting edge today."[6] Moreover, students gained an appreciation of the difficulties involved in generating anthologies of material which is extant only in crumbling Victorian periodicals. Several students were dismayed when nineteenth-century journals owned by our library disintegrated in their hands as they tried to make photocopies. One student commented on this situation in her report on Martineau: "Her list of literary accomplishments is so expansive that it is hard to imagine that only a small number of scholars recognize the value and merit of her work. While a small portion of her works can be found in popular anthologies, the vast majority of what she created is deteriorating on dusty library shelves."[7] By the time they completed Part I of the research project, students began to show engagement with individual authors as well as some inchoate comprehension of the dynamics of canon formation.

Part II of the research project focused on contemporaneous critical responses to each author's work, with continued attention to recovering primary material as well as locating the author's papers (i.e, manuscripts, correspondence, diaries, and so on.). Here, students were forced to move beyond the *Wellesley Index* to such sources as *The Times of London* for obituaries or the *DNB* or the *DLB* as well as the letters of canonized writers such as Tennyson or Darwin, both of whom wrote to and about Cobbe, for example. Thus, there were four goals for Part II of the research project:

1) to compile a bibliography of contemporaneous critical responses to each author's work
2) to determine the location of her papers
3) to compile a supplementary primary bibliography
4) to maintain a research journal.

In their research journal, students were required to keep a written account of their research experiences: descriptions of encounters with research librarians, observations on using the interlibrary loan system; adventures in the rare book library; and descriptions of tantalizing yet ultimately dead-end leads.

Like Part I, Part II revealed new insights about individual authors and exposed fresh difficulties involved in researching a non-canonized figure. Students experienced some of the frustration associated with archival work. These comments from one student's research journal chronicle the ups and downs of such work:

> Some of my efforts were successful; others were abject failures. I found this part of our research project in many ways frusterating (sic) yet in others rewarding. I was unable to locate any contemporaneous reviews of Taylor's work. If I were doing further scholarly research, I have a feeling that I would have to begin to consult indexes of the journals that Taylor published in one by one following her articles in order to find any responses. I also believe that her letters and papers would be a very valuable resource...[8]

In their research journals, students described their efforts to cope with the disappointments of investing time and effort in the library while garnering few, if any, solid results:

- 10/29—Checked *British Archives: A Guide to Archive Resources in the UK* for information on the whereabouts of Eliza Lynn Linton's personal papers. Unable to locate the papers using this book.
- 11/4—Checked *Poole's Index to Periodical Literature* for additional primary works and secondary works. Found a great number of both, but the citations included only volume numbers and not dates for the articles. *Poole's* covers many more publications than the *Wellesley Index*, but offers much less information and is harder to navigate.[9]

> I spent quite a lot of time searching Victorian websites, but was not really able to unearth anything more. I found all of the sites very interesting (in fact, almost two hours slipped by without my noticing), yet was unable to expand my specific knowledge of Taylor.[10]

In addition to appreciating the hardships associated with researching these writers, students began to realize the critical respect these writers had garnered from their contemporaries and, at the same time, to question why these women had been excluded from the canon of Victorian nonfiction prose. They developed a growing discernment regarding conventional Victorian attitudes toward women that contributed to their lack of acclaim:

> In the end, when attempting to evaluate the impact which Helen Taylor had on her

contemporaries, all opinions must be settled upon using moderation. Though she received much criticism for her strident positions, there were still those in the intelligentsia that appreciated Taylor. Many agreed that Taylor was lacking in certain social graces; however, the fact that she made an impact on public policy and public discourse is undisputed.[11]

Respected for her diction yet controversial for her views, Linton remained an enigma to the literary circle of the time, including George Eliot, Sarah Grand, Mona Caird, Charles Dickens, Herbert Spencer, Thomas Hardy, and Millicent Garrett Fawcett. The masses, however, thrived on her extremism and controversy, thus Linton's career flourished in Britain and America long past her death at the end of the nineteenth century.[12]

As these passages demonstrate, by the completion of Part II of the research project, students' disdain for their authors had evaporated and they had begun to claim these authors as their own, expressing their frustration that these noteworthy and intelligent women had been omitted from the canon.

Part III of the research project required students to organize, analyze, and synthesize the individual research they had completed in the context of the critical, theoretical, and primary essays we had read during the semester. This final exam required students to write a ten- to twelve-page analysis of at least four articles by their chosen author. Their primary purpose in the paper was to develop a broad view of their author's work and career based on the research they had done for the semester. They were to view this final report as an opportunity to share with interested colleagues their findings about the work and career of their selected author. Their analyses were to demonstrate an enhanced understanding of an author's work based on the knowledge provided by their research. Their analysis of an author's form, technique, style, and argument had to be informed by individual research into her publication history, her contemporaneous popular and critical reception, and relevant biographical, historical, social, and political issues. Finally, students' analyses were supposed to begin to answer the following questions:

1) Why should this writer, whose work was so popularly and critically accepted during her lifetime, have practically disappeared in the twentieth century?
2) What did the student's assessment of her work and influence in the nineteenth century lead him or her to conclude regarding her intellectual contributions and her current standing in the twentieth-century academic arena?

From the evidence of students' final papers, the research project was a transformative experience for students. Not only did they develop an interest and engagement with at least one Victorian woman writer that would never have resulted from a conventional lecture/discussion format, but they also gained an extraordinarily sophisticated sense of the process of literary canon formation, the literary marketplace, and the production of knowledge as demonstrated by their recognition that their participation in this course was also a part of the process of knowledge production and canon formation. This paper on Harriet Martineau shows the intellectual engagement of students in Part III: "Despite the relative obscurity into which many of her writings have fallen, Martineau's work still remains at the foundation of modern feminist thinking. The women writers of the Victorian period made possible the careers of people like bell hooks and Amy Tan."[13] Importantly, in Part III of the research project, students were analyzing and evaluating their authors' ideas, cultural impact, and literary legacies rather than doubting their literary pedigree as the student quoted above shows here: "Yet, because so many of her works focused on the social and political structure of her time, over the years they have begun to lose their social relevance."[14] Students completed the course with a meaningful appreciation of the individual writers they researched as well as the broader group of Victorian women prose writers and with an understanding of their importance to contemporary literary studies. Ultimately, students have recognized that the job of recovery engaged in by scholars (and by themselves) is not a feminist plot to unearth inferior women writers' texts and use them to undermine western civilization as we know it, but rather that scholars are recovering the voices of writers whose work enhanced and helped create Western civilization as we know it and that by restoring these lost voices to the literary canon, scholars broaden and deepen the dimensions of human existence. Arguably, most of the students would have found this comment about Cobbe applicable to all the writers they encountered in the course: "As a thinker of importance, as a leader of public debate, and as a stylist of merit, Cobbe deserves the revival she is receiving in the modern academy."

Thus, the results of this course for students and for me were overwhelmingly positive. My own assessment of the students' intellectual engagement, growth as scholars, and general enthusiasm throughout the course indicates the value of this pedagogical approach to teaching recovered Victorian women writers. The commentary in TCEs was also gratifying:

> I really had a unique experience with this class. When I signed up for it, I had no idea that it was so specialized—I read "Victorian Prose" in the [course schedule] and thought we'd read Dickens, Carlyle, the usual canonized stuff. Instead I got a world of information I didn't know existed, and "met" a whole lot of very interesting women. The research was engaging because it was so new and unpredictable.

Most telling of all is that the experience of the course remains with students, and they value it long after the course ends: "I have often thought about our Victorian Prose by Women class, and even told one of my co-workers the entire history of Eliza Lynn Linton! We don't forget projects like that!"[15,16]

As the gratifying results of this course demonstrate, innovative approaches can turn the pedagogical difficulties that accompany teaching "recovered" women writers into transformative learning experiences for students. Faculty must be unafraid to confront students' skepticism about these writers. Moreover, they should develop teaching methods that will lead students to question their own misconceptions and biases about marginalized texts. Creatively conceived methodologies will explode the myth that Victorian women wrote only domestic and sensational fiction and will reveal instead the fact that they also wrote smart and authoritative prose.

Notes

[1] New York: Garland Publications, 1996.

[2] John Holloway, *The Victorian Sage: Studies in Argument* (New York: Norton, 1953); Andrea Broomfield and Sally Mitchell, eds. *Prose by Victorian Women, An Anthology* (New York: Garland Publications, 1996); Susan Hamilton, ed., *"Criminals, Idiots, Women and Minors": Nineteenth-Century Writing by Women on Women* (Orchard Park, NY: Broadview Press, 1995).

[3] Periodical Contents Index (PCI) is a Web database that currently indexes the tables of contents of over 1900 major US and Western European journals dating from 1770 to 1993.

[4] Crunk, Shannon. "Eliza Lynn Linton on Writing, Wild Women and Mother England." Part I: Research Project for English 464B: Victorian Prose by Women, Fall 1997. Cited with permission from student.

[5] Lillard, Qiana. "Harriet Martineau: Research Project for Victorian Prose." Part III: Final Exam for English 464B: Victorian Prose by Women, Fall 1997. Cited with permission from student.

[6] Rimmelspach, Rene. "Helen Taylor: Author, Activist, Feminist." Part I: Research Project for English 464B: Victorian Prose by Women, Fall 1997. Cited with permission from student.

[7] Lillard, n.p.

[8] Rimmelspach, Rene. "Helen Taylor: Through Others' Eyes." Part II: Research Project for English 464B: Victorian Prose by Women, Fall 1997. Cited with permission from student.

[9] Crunk, Shannon. "Research Journal for Part Two, Research on Eliza Lynn Linton." Part II: Research Project for English 464B: Victorian Prose by Women, Fall 1997. Cited with permission from student.

[10] Rimmelspach. Part II, n.p.

[11] Rimmelspach. Part II, n.p.

[12] Crunk. Part II, n.p.

[13] Lillard, n.p.

[14] Lillard, n.p.

[15] Crunk, n.p.

[16] Because the graduate population represents our future teachers of British literature surveys and nonfiction student writer courses, they also need to be introduced to these writers and

encouraged to pursue dissertations on them. When I taught this course at the graduate level, I addressed the students as teachers and scholars. Thus, they were asked to engage with the writers from both scholarly *and* pedagogical perspectives. With this population, I emphasized the absence of critical or theoretical paradigms with which they can align themselves or against which they can react. In addition to completing the tasks assigned the lower-level students, graduate students were required to familiarize themselves with the Victorian periodical press and with Victorian publishing in general. Moreover, they were encouraged to approach the primary texts from generic, aesthetic, and formal perspectives in article-length seminar papers. Like the undergraduates, these students selected a single author on whom to concentrate. The success of the graduate course was comparable to that of the undergraduates. Graduate students who took this course are planning dissertations in which women they researched figure prominently.

Victorian Prose by Women
Dr. Henry

Course Description and Objectives:
This course is structured around the idea of recovery and revaluation. Such an undertaking is a profoundly complicated one because it includes attempting to do many associated but differently demanding tasks. Among them are assignments such as locating and reading texts; evaluating their literary, social, historical worth; discovering the underlying values that have determined the aesthetic principles by which texts/authors are included or excluded; becoming familiar with established critical and theoretical approaches while developing alternatives; delving into archives; and creating research tools where none exists. Given the complexity of our undertaking this semester, our effort will be multipronged and we will keep all prongs moving forward simultaneously. Ultimately, my aim is to give you an opportunity to engage in individualized original research on a nineteenth-century female prose writer.

Required Texts:
"Criminals, Idiots, Women, and Minors": Nineteenth-Century Writing by Women on Women 2nd ed., ed. Susan Hamilton (Orchard Park, NY: Broadview Press, 1995).
Norton Anthology of Literature by Women, 2nd ed., ed Sandra M. Gilbert and Susan Gubar (New York: W. W. Norton, 1996).
Prose by Victorian Women, eds., Andrea Broomfield and Sally Mitchell (New York: Garland Publications, 1996).

Sample Syllabus:
- Critical History of Victorian Nonfiction Prose (lecture).
- "The Epic Age: Part of the History of Literary Women," in *Literary Women* by Ellen Moers (New York: Doubleday, 1976).
- Introduction to *The Woman Question: Society and Literature in Britain and America, 1837–1883: Defining Voices* by Elizabeth K. Helsinger, William Veeder, Robin Lauterbach Sheets (Chicago: U of Chicago P, 1989).
- "The Literary Life: Some Representative Women," in Moers.
- "Victorian Sage Discourse and the Feminine: An Introduction," *Victorian Sages and Cultural Discourse: Renegotiating Gender and Power*, ed. Thais E. Morgan (New Brunswick: Rutgers UP, 1990).
- Linda H. Peterson, "Harriet Martineau: Masculine Discourse, Female Sage"; in Morgan Harriet Martineau, "Female Industry" in Hamilton.
- Anna B. Jameson, "The Milliners" in Hamilton.
- Carol T. Christ, "'The Hero as Man of Letters': Masculinity and Victorian Nonfiction Prosen" in Morgan.
- George P. Landow, "Aggressive (Re)interpretations of the Female Sage: Florence Nightingale's *Cassandra*," in Morgan.
- Florence Nightingale, *Cassandra*, in Hamilton.
- Frances Power Cobbe, "Criminals, Idiots, Women, and Minors" in Hamilton.
- Margaret Oliphant, "The Condition of Women" and "The Grievances of Women."
- Mona Caird, "Marriage" in Hamilton.
- Eliza Linton, "The Wild Women: As Politicians" and "As Social Insurgents" in Hamilton.
- Mona Caird, "A Defense of the So-Called Wild Women" in Hamilton.

Figure 1. Peaches Henry, Sample Syllabus

Victorian Prose by Women
Dr. Henry

Research Project Part I

Objectives:
1. Compile a bibliography of your author's primary work
2. Write a survey of your author's work (5–7 prose pages)

Our semester-long research project in Victorian Prose by Women is the discovery of primary texts by our authors and the unearthing of biographical, literary, historical, social, and cultural information about them. We may not be completely successful in discovering all that we set out to find. However, we will measure our success by our efforts.

Your first task is to create a two-part bibliography, using the *Wellesley Index to Victorian Periodicals* and *Periodical Contents Index* (a Web database). The first part of the bibliography will list (in chronological sequence rather than normal alphabetical order) one author's primary work; the second part will list contemporaneous secondary material (in alphabetical order).

Once you have developed part one of the bibliography, you will complete a survey of your author's work, which you will present in prose format.

First, do a study of the periodicals in which she published, establishing the following facts:
1. Which periodicals did she publish in most often (did she publish in foreign periodicals, especially American ones)?
2. What was the editorial stance of those periodicals?
3. Did her subject matter appear to coincide with the editorial stance of the periodicals in which she published?

Second, analyze your author's bibliography, considering the following issues:
1. What was her subject matter?
2. Did it appear to be related to particular debates of the day?
3. How did her subject matter change over time?
4. Was she writing reviews, social critiques, political treatises, manifestoes, and so on?

Overall, you want to get a sense of your author's work over her career.

Your work for Part I of the Research Project should produce about 5 to 7 pages of prose plus the first part of your bibliography. You should feel encouraged to discuss your work in class, raising questions and sharing information as well as concerns.

Figure 2. Peaches Henry, Sample Assignment (continued on next page)

Victorian Prose by Women
Dr. Henry

Research Project Part II

Objectives:
1. Compile a bibliography of contemporaneous critical responses to the author's work
2. Determine the location of her papers
3. Compile a secondary primary bibliography
4. Maintain a research journal

In Part II you will create the second part of the bibliography you began in Part I. In alphabetical order, you will list contemporary secondary (that is, critical theoretical) sources about your author's work. In addition, your bibliography will include the location of your author's papers (which might include material such as her manuscripts, correspondence, diaries). Also, you will complete a supplementary primary bibliography of your author's work; that is, unearth as many additional primary pieces by your author as you can. This supplementary primary bibliography will carry you beyond the *Wellesley Index* (WI) and *Periodical Contents Index* (PCI), because the scope of these indices does not fully cover some of our authors.

Accomplishing the objectives listed above will require a great deal of work which will not always yield results. The fact that we are conducting such research means that other scholars have not done this work. Therefore, you will become literary detectives. All good detectives know that the first rule of detection is to make good use of your resources. In your case, your first source will be me, and below I have provided you with some general ideas about how to begin your search. Your most valuable resource will of course be the reference librarians, some of whom have been working with us already this semester and some of whom can be brought on at any time. For Part II of the research project, I would like you to maintain a research journal detailing the progress of your work, including your successes and your failures.

To get started I suggest that you consult the *Dictionary of National Biography (DNB)* and the *Dictionary of Literary Biography (DLB)*. The *DLB* often lists the whereabouts of an author's papers. Both *DNB* and *DLB* may also provide bibliographies that might be helpful. Another place to start might be the obituary section of the *Times of London*. Some authors wrote for newspapers as well as periodicals: the *DLB*, *DNB*, and *The Times* might be helpful in locating those pieces.

Return to the *WI* and consider the periodicals for which your author wrote in this way: *Blackwood's Edinburgh Magazine* was started to compete with the *Edinburgh Review*, so if your author published in one or the other, you might attempt to determine whether a particular article received any response in the rival magazine. Another tack to try is to consider your author's circle of friends, associates, even enemies. Study indexes to the letters, writings, and papers of canonized writers for references or connections to your writer or her work.

The report of the results of your work in this phase of the research project should take the form of a two-part bibliography with a note on the whereabouts of your author's papers, your research journal, and a five- to seven-page assessment of your author's work based on contemporaneous reviews and criticism.

Figure 2. Peaches Henry, Sample Assignment (continued on next page)

Victorian Prose by Women
Dr. Henry

Research Project Part III—Final Exam

Objectives:
1. To write a 10- to 12-page analysis of at least four articles by your author
2. To write a final report of your findings about the work and career of your author
3. To answer (as far as possible) this question: Why should this writer, whose work was so popularly and critically accepted during her lifetime, have practically disappeared in the twenty-first century?

The third part of your semester-long research project in Victorian Prose by Women requires you to read and analyze several of your author's essays in the context of the critical/theoretical material we have read and discussed during the semester, the primary essays we have read from the textbook for the course, and, most importantly, from the individual research you have been engaged in throughout the semester.

Thus in Part III (the final exam) you will write a ten- to twelve-page analysis of at least four articles by your chosen author. The primary purpose of this paper will be to develop a broad view of your author's work and career based on the research you have done this semester. Consequently, you are free to consider and use material from the critical and theoretical texts we have discussed in class. Also, any critical and theoretical texts that you have discovered in your own research may be used as you see fit. You are encouraged as well to engage with the primary essays in your textbook, referring not only to those by your author but to any by other authors in the text as well. That is, you are invited to be comparative in your paper.

Your most important resource should be the information you have gathered as a result of your research. This final report is your opportunity to share with interested colleagues your findings about the work and career of Harriet Martineau, Eliza Lynn Linton, Harriet Taylor, and Frances Power Cobbe, respectively. Your analysis of your author should demonstrate an enhanced understanding of her work based on the knowledge that your research has provided you. That is, you should be able to draw educated conclusions about the nature of her work because of your research. Thus, your analysis of her form, technique, style, and argument should be informed by individual research into her publication history, her contemporaneous popular and critical reception, and relevant biographical, historical, social, and political issues.

Finally, your analysis should begin to answer the following question: Why should this writer, whose work was so popularly and critically accepted during her lifetime, have practically disappeared in the twenty-first century? What does your assessment of her work and influence in the nineteenth century lead you to conclude regarding her intellectual contributions and her current standing in the twenty-first-century academic arena? Your conclusions should offer the reasoning which caused you to reach your determination.

Your paper should include endnotes (though you may use textual citations for your author's essays) and a complete bibliography. Consult the *MLA Handbook* for the correct formats. Remember that endnotes and bibliographical citations are single-spaced within and double-spaced between each entry.

Figure 2. Peaches Henry, Sample Assignment

Chapter Seventeen
Everybody Learns and Everybody Teaches: Feminist Pedagogy and Co-editing Mary Ward's *Marcella*

Nicole Meller Beck and Beth Sutton-Ramspeck

Nicole

One of my most distinct memories of student-teacher interaction took place on a weekday evening at a local grocery store. It was the second semester of my sophomore year and I was doing a bit of light shopping when I noticed one of my professors doing the same. Instead of saying hello, though, I ducked down the next available aisle, hoping he had not recognized me. The possibility of having to acknowledge a teacher in a non-classroom environment was deeply unsettling—even if he was only contemplating the calorie content of a Lean Cuisine entrée. It was not that I particularly disliked this professor, only that I was totally unprepared to encounter a teacher doing something as mundane as grocery shopping. As a student trained in the traditional classroom and the hierarchy it fosters, it had never occurred to me that teachers needed to eat. In fact, not only did teachers not eat, they did not pursue a family life, a social life, or professional development; they had no existence the twenty-three hours of the day when I wasn't in their class.

The rigid student-teacher hierarchy of the traditional college classroom is a well-respected and deeply entrenched facet of our educational system; the teacher imparts knowledge and the student absorbs it. Often, the boundaries are frightfully distinct. As Lynda Stone notes, "In spite of caring, cooperative, and connected classrooms, and a teacher education literature that includes 'critical feminist pedagogy,' schools are still bastions of traditional, masculinist epistemology."[1] It need not be that way. This paper addresses the ways those rigid distinctions are blurred when a teacher and a student collaborate on an editing project. Further, it demonstrates that a successful collaboration between a teacher and a student can foster individual growth, both professionally and personally, for those involved. Accordingly, we have chosen to retain our individual voices throughout.

Beth

Accounts of scholarly collaboration generally feature an autobiographical section, so in the spirit of the genre, here's our story. In the spring of 1997, Broadview Press awarded me a contract to edit the novel *Marcella*, by Mary ("Mrs. Humphry") Ward (1851–1920). After having studied Ward's work for several years, I was delighted at the opportunity to make this, one of her most compelling novels, available again. It had been virtually unavailable for the previous eighty years, aside from a brief period in the 1980s when Virago Press issued an edition. The novel had not always been so obscure. When it was originally published in 1894, the appearance of a new book by the best-selling author of *Robert Elsmere* was sufficiently newsworthy to be announced on the notice boards of most of London's evening newspapers. The story of its eponymous heroine's flirtations with socialism and Aldous Raeburn, the future Lord Maxwell, *Marcella* is of interest to today's readers both as a rich portrayal of late-Victorian socialism and as an important example of New Woman fiction. I believed—and subsequent course adoptions of the text have borne out—that the best-selling, politically engaged Marcella, apparently anomalous in the "aesthetic" 1890s, would offer a particularly teachable text for courses in which instructors were challenging traditional views of Victorian fiction, Victorian feminisms, or literature of the fin de siécle.

Completing this project would entail, among other things, gathering materials for appendices of contemporary documents, footnoting references in the text itself, and, perhaps most daunting of all, establishing a copy text for the novel. Because *Marcella* is not a canonical novel, no one had previously studied its publishing history in a systematic way: there was no information about the concrete differences between the two main editions published during the author's life, and thus there was no reliable basis for choosing between them. I therefore knew that I would have to "collate" these editions. I also knew that these systematic comparisons would require more than one set of eyes. What I didn't know was to whom those eyes would belong. At Millikin University, the small school where I was then teaching, I was the only Victorian literature specialist, and there are no graduate research assistants. However, there is a robust honors program, and for a year I had been advising an honors student who had been developing a project on Victorian women writers—and developing impressive knowledge and research skills in the process. That, of course, is Nicole.

Nicole

Luckily, at Millikin, we had access to funds to help support my participation in the project. After all, as I now know, research is part of the activity faculty get paid to do over their summer vacations, but the average student takes a summer job to pay tuition and fees. In the previous three years Millikin had developed a Summer Undergraduate Research Fellowship program: for eight weeks of research over the summer, generally research assisting a faculty member's scholarly project, students were paid (that year nineteen students were paid $2250 each) and provided free campus housing and a small expense allowance. Fortunately, too, the administration was far-sighted enough to recognize that collaborative research work is not exclusively the provenance of the sciences and social sciences; in fact, they were actively recruiting humanities faculty and students to the program. Beth and I successfully applied for the fellowship in March and began work shortly after classes ended in May.

Beth

When we started working together, we did not realize how progressive our collaboration is. As we have begun to study collaborative writing, however, we have come to understand that our enterprise is rather unusual. Studies of collaborative writing have generally looked at three typical circumstances: a few composition theorists, most notably Andrea Lunsford and Lisa Ede, have examined collaborative writing in the "real world" work place (i.e., outside of academia); another, much larger group, of whom the most prominent is Kenneth Bruffee, have written about "collaborative learning" in the classroom; and still another group have theorized about scholarly collaboration between academic colleagues.[2] What we did is something markedly different, something "betwixt and between," for in our case, one of us was a teacher and the other a student—at least according to the Millikin phone directory. When we sat down to edit *Marcella*, however, we were simply collaborators. Indeed, we worked on such an equal basis that I decided early on that the editing job was no longer "mine" but "ours" and that we would have equal billing as editors.

This liminal relationship, we believe, constitutes by its very nature a challenge—arguably, a feminist challenge—to the usual teacher-student duality. At best, academe occasionally smiles on mentoring and apprenticeship, but even these structures objectify—sometimes even exploit—the student. That is certainly not the model we are following. How is it a feminist challenge? In part because collaboration itself is relational, challenging what Patricia Sullivan has called the "myth of the independent scholar"—that traditionally solitary masculine authority figure.[3] Of course not all feminisms—or all feminists—celebrate or promote nonhierarchical relationships. My work on feminist history taught me that long ago. Furthermore, the challenging of hierarchies is not exclusively a feminist project. However, it is one significant branch of feminist thought and activism—and it has inspired my own efforts to develop a feminist pedagogy. More to the point, perhaps, our project offers a feminist challenge to traditional models of research and collaboration because it was empowering. As Constance Penley writes: The feminist teacher "carries out a very deliberate self-undermining of her own authority by refusing to be an 'authority' [authoritarian] at all."[4] Ideally, as in our case, everybody learns;

everybody teaches. Finally, our collaboration was a feminist one because we worked to make it that; along with Helen Cafferty and Jeanette Clausen, we have become convinced that "feminist collaboration does not 'just happen,' but is constructed...through conscious and unconscious choices affirming the feminist politics of inclusion, power sharing, egalitarianism, consensus, and trust in the context of shared feminist commitments."[5] In embarking on this project with a student, I made a conscious decision to dismantle an artificial and counterproductive hierarchy; since then we have worked together to create the equal partnership necessary to complete our project.

Nicole

We knew that the first tasks facing our partnership would be to compare editions, establish a copy text, and decide what we would need to annotate. Before we could do this, however, we needed to establish the criteria by which to make our decisions about the text. At this point, Beth and I were both ready to learn about an unfamiliar process. Accordingly, we began the summer by reading about the theory and practice of textual editing. This is when I, as a student, became aware of how innovative our project was going to be. Given the relative newness of the topic for both Beth and myself, the hierarchical teacher-student model was not going to work; it was not even a possibility. Rather, Beth's willingness to allow me to share my interpretations of the articles and theories—to teach, so to speak—enabled each of us to conceive our goals for *Marcella*, on an equal footing. Further, I was exposed to a world of professional scholarship that I hadn't seen before. My contributions and decisions would have a much greater importance than a mere semester grade; I was contributing to the academic discourse that I had previously only been able to observe.

The most important decision that we made together concerned the copy text. Through our earlier research, we had learned that most scholarly editors today seek to preserve the text as originally produced or created. Editors must choose between (among other options) a facsimile of one actual historical text, flaws and all, or a modern reconstruction that represents the editors' best insights into the author's actual intent—insights derived from analysis of manuscripts, published texts, and other evidence. As G. Thomas Tanselle notes, "Editors, like everyone else interested in the past, must decide whether we know the past better through artifacts or through our trained imaginations."[6]

To make this decision, we had to compare the two editions of *Marcella* published in Ward's lifetime. We spent five mornings a week taking turns reading aloud from *Marcella*, alternating whenever one of us was tired. In some ways, this activity most thoroughly demolished the student-teacher hierarchy, as, despite the need to concentrate, we read and laughed and remarked on the story, like Victorian sisters sharing a serial. Beth read from the 1911 Westmoreland Edition—volumes 3 and 4 of what were then the "Complete Works." I read the first edition, published in 1894; we both watched closely for discrepancies. In addition to noting numerous—sometimes questionable—changes of punctuation, we identified seventy-six substantive variations between the two editions, but none that changes meaning in any but minor ways. All but three, in fact, involve a single word; none changes a full sentence. Surprisingly, the later Westmoreland Edition contains two new errors of subject-verb agreement. Moreover, while we were able to analyze Ward's working notes (approximately 150 pages), and a nearly complete set of her drafts and heavily revised page proofs for the first edition, we could not locate the text from which changes were made to prepare the 1911 Westmoreland edition. Although most critics writing about *Marcella* have referred to the Westmoreland edition, following the convention of identifying the author's "last intention," we chose the competing approach of respecting the author's "first intention." Because of the new errors and lack of direct evidence that Ward completely controlled production details in the later edition, we selected the 1894 edition as our copy text.

Neither completely accepting nor rejecting a particular theory of editing, Beth and I offer a compromise: a nearly exact transcription of the 1894 text, making only small silent corrections, such as regularizing capitalization. Then, in footnotes, we alert readers to substantive variations. Perhaps the most important reason we selected the first edition was articulated by Ward herself, in her introduction to *Robert Elsmere* in the Westmoreland edition. There she explains her reluctance to revise substantially because "the book belonged to a particular moment both in my own life and in the life of my generation."[7] If Ward was so reluctant to revise, then as true collaborators, Beth and I needed to value her artistic and authorial perspective by choosing as copy text the version over which we knew she had exerted the most direct control. Our examination of Ward's writing process not only allowed us to learn from each other, but to learn from Ward what was truly her vision for *Marcella*.

Beth

As we read, we identified passages that might require footnotes. This was an area where Nicole's contribution was particularly valuable; despite her growing expertise, she had only two years distance from her first encounter with Victorian literature and could surmise what would puzzle her peers. As much as possible, we divided the material to be annotated by topic; for example, I got religion, nursing, and Parliamentary politics. Nicole got education, fashion, Fabianism, and phrases in foreign languages. We worked together on these notes at a table, surrounded by reference books, interlibrary loan materials, and sources we had borrowed on research trips to the University of Illinois library sixty miles away. We shared with each other the discoveries we made about "the boats at Oxford" or senna tea or Arnold Toynbee. In addition, like the collaborators we have read about, we spent a good portion of time talking. William Van Pelt and Alice Gilliam have identified four kinds of talk among collaborative writers: procedural talk, substantive talk, talk about the writing process, and social talk.[8] Ironically, although we did all four, the social talk may be the most progressive—and the most immediately relevant to the establishment of a distinctly feminist pedagogy. Of course social talk between students and faculty is hardly rare—between classes, at department functions, or when students seek advice through a personal crisis. However, ours was more frequent and sustained talk—at the beginning of each day's work, during daily breaks, in long car rides to the library, and over meals. We talked about family issues, about Nicole's graduate school plans, about my job hunting—our lives. Forming a friendship like this was perhaps "unprofessional," but that term presumes a profession based on hierarchy, distance, and unequal power. "Unprofessional behavior" was therefore essential for forming the relationship that would enable us to engage in the other kinds of talk on an equal basis— and thus to solve problems and make decisions as we carried out our project. Our "conscious...choices affirming the feminist politics of inclusion, power sharing, egalitarianism, consensus, and trust" in lieu of the traditional and "masculine" method of instruction was, then, a conscious dismantling of the student-teacher hierarchy.[9]

Beth

We've been asked frequently whether we think our experiment can be duplicated. We certainly hope so. Clearly, there are plenty of wonderful books—especially by eighteenth- and nineteenth-century British women writers—that merit careful editing and reissue. Granted, our collaboration could not be replicated in every situation; it was made possible by the advanced work of the "student" in our partnership and even, perhaps, by the fact that the "teacher" in our partnership was embarking on a type of scholarship that was relatively new to her. Although we feel quite positive about the experience, we recognize some significant barriers to such collaborations. First, as writers about collaboration often note, many institutions look askance at collaboration, valuing it less when assessing performance for professional advancement. This attitude is particularly notable in English departments, where the emphasis on the individual's "private" act of reading readily lends itself to the traditional and "masculine" methods of student-teacher interaction. This approach contrasts markedly with the scientific and social scientific model of large research teams compiling data. Given the persistent expectation that a scholar be, as Jeanne Moskal says, a "solitary, disinterested being in isolated contemplation," a prospective editor who is still in a probationary position would check how her institution views collaborative projects and editing projects at tenure time, and act accordingly. At some schools, the wise scholar will save the editing project until she is safely tenured. At others, however, a project in which teaching and research so obviously mesh might be viewed even more favorably than traditional literary critical scholarship. Moreover, many schools have budgets to facilitate research—including the hiring of "research assistants"—or to support innovative teaching methods. Our own early experience was very positive in this regard, for Millikin obviously supported us both, and Nicole was accepted by several graduate schools.

Perhaps a more serious objection to collaboration between a teacher and an honors student is that it could be considered elitist—weaker students do not get such valuable opportunities, and the already academically rich student gets richer. There is truth in this objection—up to a point—but the reward was well earned, and there are strong arguments that other students have benefited from the text that the collaboration produced, from what their fellow student contributed to the text, and from what their teacher has learned. Furthermore, as the editing progressed, other students have had the opportunity to share in the collaboration, albeit in smaller ways. After Nicole and I had completed most of the research and writing for the footnotes, and after the text had been scanned and the footnotes entered, I taught *Marcella* in an upper-level course on the nineteenth-century novel, using the typescript as the course text. The students in the class were offered extra credit for finding typos and scanning errors that Nicole and I had missed. I also invited their suggestions about the footnotes and introduction: information they thought should be added, deleted, or clarified. The students seemed excited about the opportunity to help edit, and several asked about obtaining the book when it was published. It was clear that they gained an awareness of the process of book editing and a recognition that not every edition is equally reliable. One student, Shannon Bohle, described it as "a wonderful opportunity where the class was able to feel that they became part of a discourse that extended beyond the classroom walls." This, then, is also a partial answer to the question of whether collaborative editing can be translated to a classroom situation.

Nicole

Talking about both process and product in one paper is a bit unwieldy, but we think it is justified by Ward's own views on writing and collaboration. Long before Bakhtin wrote about the dialogic, long before contemporary reading theory, Ward, in her introduction to *Robert Elsmere* in the Westmoreland edition, argued that "the public in a sense cooperates in the book...; and those who are drawn to read it, unconsciously lend it their own thoughts, the passion of their own assents and denials...; the reader's eager sympathy, or antagonism, completes the effort of the writer."[10] We like to think that in this sense, we as editors are collaborating with Ward to cooperate with her future readers.

Conclusion

Finally, *Marcella* is a novel of education. It describes its heroine's years in boarding school and hints at the reading and study she engages in under the diverse influences of Aldous Raeburn, Harry Wharton, and Edward Hallin. Even more importantly, Marcella overcomes certain class biases—flawed attitudes not only toward the working class but toward the aristocratic class, as exemplified by Aldous and Lord Maxwell. She learns the error of her "passionate ambition...to be the queen and arbitress of human lives"—especially the lives of working people and of Aldous. Early in the novel, the local villagers "affected her like figures in poetry or drama," and Aldous, she later admits, is "just a piece of furniture in my play."[11] However, as Ward wrote in a letter to her friend Mandell Creighton, Marcella learns "to see [Aldous] in & for himself." Student-teacher collaboration requires a similar transformation: Each of us needed to learn to see the other "in and for herself," not only as a person with a set "class" role—a teacher; a student—but also as a person who eats and shops and pursues career advancement. Just as Marcella's family, colleagues, and neighbors reinforce her class biases, so academe encourages authoritarianism, hierarchy, and competition rather than collaboration—especially between faculty and students. We like to think that the form our collaboration has taken is part of our contribution to the personal and political project that Ward's novel advocates.

Notes

We would like to express our appreciation for this help to Ohio State-Lima students in English 542, The Nineteenth-Century Novel, Autumn 1999: Melissa Adam, Shannon Bohle, Deb Chamberlain, Sherry Gossard, Michael Lianez, Mindy Schoonover, Debbie Sifuentes, Chad Sybert, and Sarah Timmerman; Sherry Gossard later helped us check page proofs.

1 Lynda Stone, "Introduction," *The Education Feminism Reader*, ed. Lynda Stone (New York: Routledge, 1994), 2.

2. See Lisa Ede and Andrea Lunsford, *Singular Texts/Plural Authors: Perspectives on Collaborative Writing,* (Carbondale: Southern Illinois UP, 1992), and "Why Write...Together?" *Rhetoric Review* 1 (1983): 150–57. See also Kenneth Bruffee, *Collaborative Learning: Higher Education, Interdependence, and the Authority of Knowledge,* 2nd ed. (Baltimore: Johns Hopkins UP, 1999).
3. Patricia A. Sullivan, "Revising the Myth of the Independent Scholar," *Writing With: New Directions in Collaborative Teaching, Learning, and Research,* ed. Sally Barr Reagan, Thomas Fox, and David Bleich (Albany: SUNY Press, 1994), 11–30.
4. Penley is quoted in Jamie Barlowe and Ruth Hotell, "Feminist Theory and Practice and the Pedantic I/Eye," in *Common Ground: Feminist Collaboration in the Academy,* eds. Elizabeth G. Peck and JoAnna Stephens Mink, (Albany: SUNY Press, 1998), 274.
5. Helen Cafferty and Jeanette Clausen, "What's Feminist About It? Reflections on Collaboration in Editing and Writing," in Peck and Mink, 83.
6. Carol J. Singley and Susan Elizabeth Sweeney, "In League with Each Other: The Theory and Practice of Feminist Collaboration," in Peck and Mink, 71.
7. Cafferty and Clausen, 83.
8. "The Varieties of Scholarly Editing," in *Scholarly Editing: A Guide to Research,* ed. D. C. Greetham (New York: MLA, 1995), 16.
9. Mary Augusta Ward, Introduction, *Robert Elsmere,* in *The Writings of Mrs. Humphry Ward* 16 vols, (London: Smith, Elder, 1911), vol. 1: xiii–xliv.
10. Mary Augusta Ward, *Robert Elsmere* (xxix)
11. Mary Augusta Ward, *Marcella,* ed. Beth Sutton-Ramspeck and Nicole B. Meller (Peterborough, ON: Broadview, 2002): 73, 75, 391. For more information, see http://www.lima.ohio-state.edu/english/marcella/index.html.

CHAPTER EIGHTEEN

"Can Man Be Free/And Woman Be a Slave?" Teaching Eighteenth- and Nineteenth-Century Women Writers in Intersecting Communities

Gina Luria Walker

On October 7, 1814, Percy Shelley recorded a conversation with Claire Clairmont from the previous night: "Mary goes to bed early. Sit up late talking with [Claire]. She states her conception of the subterraneous community of women."[1] Shelley's attention to Claire's idea provides a plumb line into his texts, particularly his feminist epic, *Laon and Cythna* (1817). It also suggests a useful prism through which to observe the interplay between sexuality, education, and conversation among a sextet of English avant-gardists. Claire's perception that, even as they are part of the larger human community, women share a separate, often sequestered, domain, continues to inform my thinking as scholar and teacher. I realized that an intriguing course could be constructed using Claire's artifact as the working rubric, reading through selected public and private texts of several members of the Wollstonecraft-Godwin-Shelley circle to trace the collaborative efforts between and among Mary Hays, Wollstonecraft, and Godwin as they consider gender relations, and continuing the inquiry into the second generation.[2] In the fall of 1998, I offered a new course at The New School in Manhattan, "Can Man Be Free/And Woman Be a Slave?" This is how I described the course in the New School bulletin:

> Percy Shelley's question poses the central dilemma in the attempt to graft the rights of man onto the wrongs of woman. This course traces the evolution of the idea of equality between the sexes in the aftermath of the Enlightenment. We examine the perspectives of six avantgardists: Mary Wollstonecraft, William Godwin, and Mary Hays, leading figures of the "revolutionary" generation in the era of upheavals in America, France, and England; and Percy Shelley, Mary Wollstonecraft Godwin Shelley, and Claire Clairmont, inheritors of the belief in the possibility of human regeneration. In their private and public texts, we hear the opening notes of the modern conversation between men and women about gender. We observe the fault lines that erupt as visions of "greater equality" collide with social conventions. We consider the women's efforts to make claim to a transfigured domestic female subculture in which women deliberately practice a solidarity that subverts things as they are. But despite their concerted efforts, both generations also attest to the impermanence of alliance between the sexes and the obduracy of gender that makes of all humans tyrants and slaves.

"*Can Man Be Free/And Woman Be A Slave?*" 191

Distinguished British scholars Nora Crook and Clarissa Campbell Orr join our discussions using an electronic meeting space.

The intellectual and erotic *pas de deux* between first, Wollstonecraft and Godwin, then Mary and Percy Shelley, formed the narrative structure of the course. These were complemented by our examination of the complex relations between and among the four women: the brief, intense intimacy between Wollstonecraft and Hays during the last twenty-one months of Wollstonecraft's life; the "shade of my mother," as Mary Shelley conceived Wollstonecraft's enduring presence, hovering over her life and imaginative representations, as well as Claire's; the equivocal relationship between Mary and Claire; their various responses to other significant female figures, including Fanny Imlay and Mary Jane Godwin; both women's convoluted quadrilles with Byron; and, finally, the spluttering communications between the men—Godwin and Shelley, Shelley and Byron—about the women.

Teaching the course was an education for me as well as for the students. In addition to the obvious challenges and benefits of providing informed access to the writers' texts, there was the composition of the classes which included both credit and noncredit students, all women, ranging in age from twenty to seventy-five, from diverse ethnic, racial, national, and religious backgrounds. A new and intriguing layer of complexity and enrichment was the distance learning component, allowing two distinguished British scholar/teachers to join our discussion by way of an asynchronous Internet site furnished by the New School Online University (NSOU). Overall, for both semesters in which I taught it, the course was a resounding success, with several instructive pedagogical lessons. In this account, I discuss the dynamics of the double classroom—real and electronic spaces—describing the difficulties as well as the unanticipated enhancements to learning which seem to contradict some of the current consternation about distance education. In addition, I consider the difficulties that arise in teaching non-canonical women writers whose texts blur the conventions between and among literary genres, as in Hays's novels, and the rationale for treating private texts with the same degree of serious scrutiny as public representations, as in Claire Clairmont's letters. Finally, I recount how this first course was transformed into a sequence of offerings on "The Learned Lady: Women Who Dared"—that is, struggled to be educated, and resisted cultural constraints by creating texts instead of, or as well as, textiles and babies.[3]

I structured "Can Man Be Free/And Woman Be a Slave?" to illustrate what I identified as the "chamber music" effect, arguing that the early modern discussion between men and women about gender is inherently collaborative, demonstrating how the texts of the two trios "talk" to each other. As the idea and practice of collaboration was crucial to the course, I decided to incorporate the approaches of others active in contemporary scholarship that bridges Gender, History, and Literature. There was a pedagogical imperative as well: by focusing the readings and discussion on individual figures rather than literary, historical, or theoretical paradigms, I anticipated that students would require a quantity of contextual background, some of which I was prepared to provide, but not all. It occurred to me that the NSOU technology might make possible a second, concurrent locus of teaching and learning. I invited two British scholars, both knowledgeable in relevant areas, to join the class. Expecting student curiosity about numerous related issues as I developed the course, I hypothesized that it would be helpful to add another layer of instruction and personality to create a multiple effect: the imagined, textual community of women supported by an actual, as well as a virtual, community of women made possible by the Internet.

I wanted the class to "hear" the conversation between and among the texts, and between the generations. In the first semester, the required readings included William Godwin's *Things as They Are; or, The Adventures of Caleb Williams* (1794) for both its political and formal influence; Wollstonecraft's *A Vindication of the Rights of Woman* (1792), as well as *Mary; A Fiction* (1788), *The Wrongs of Woman; or, Maria* (1798), and selections from her correspondence; Godwin's *Memoirs of the Author of 'A Vindication of the Rights of Woman'* (1798), then no longer available in the States, so I made do, awkwardly, with photocopies[4]; the Broadview edition of Mary Hays's *The Victim of Prejudice* (1799) edited by Eleanor Ty (1996), and my transcriptions of selected letters from the originals of Hays's unpublished correspondence in the Carl H. Pforzheimer Collection of Shelley and His Circle at the New York Public Library; Percy Shelley's *Laon and Cythna* (1817), and his prose and verse letters to Maria Gisborne (1822); Mary Shelley's *Matilda* (1818) and excerpts from her journals and letters; and selections from the journals and letters of Claire Clairmont.

This is what I chose; then I confronted the difficulty of putting these texts in the students' hands. In some cases, modern editions were readily available— Janet Todd's compilation for Penguin of *Mary, Maria,* and *Matilda* proved handy. *Laon and Cythna* was impossible to secure in a reliable text, so I resorted to a copy of the original in an early Oxford edition of Shelley's collected works. Marion Kingston Stocking's superb editions of the letters and journals of Claire Clairmont are still only available in expensive hardcover library editions; here, too, I made do with cumbersome photocopies.

By way of explaining the lack of academic uniformity in the texts the students had before them, I considered the publication and reception history of each work, and the combination of determination, luck, and inadvertency that their survival involved. One theme that emerged from class discussions was that marginality was not restricted to the women, but extended to the calumny heaped on Godwin for "stripping his wife naked"[5] in his *Memoirs* of her, and the strenuous efforts made to obliterate Percy Shelley's vivid evocation of visionary sexual love between brother and sister in the original version of *Laon and Cythna*.[6] Most students had never before considered the effects of gender on the politics of publishing. I found myself reiterating that our inquiry was an initial attempt to consider the six figures together, and that the texts that were available in modern form were the result of assiduous scholarship done in the past thirty years on previously ignored figures. Such academic explorations, I told the class, were made possible by myriad, ongoing acts of scholarly discovery, reclamation, and reconstruction. In their independent research and class presentations, the students discovered that they, too, were participating in, even contributing to, this process.

The second time around I modified the syllabus: In the first semester, we kept bumping into Milton's dominant representations of man and woman, so this time, we began with selections from *Paradise Lost*; the *Vindication* in the useful new Broadview edition of the two *Vindications*, edited by D. L. Macdonald and Kathleen Scherf; *Maria*; regretfully, I omitted Godwin's *Memoirs of the Author of 'A Vindication of the Rights of Woman'* until the Broadview edition was available; Hays's *Victim*; *Laon and Cythna*; *Matilda*; and excerpts of texts by Claire Clairmont. This proved to be a ragtag assortment, without uniformly rigorous editorial standards of annotations, attention to text, and biographical or critical contexts. I filled in the best I could. The students remained diligent and respectful of the difficulties with the readings, but their efforts, like mine, felt constricted by time-consuming tasks of copying photocopies, making sure that we all read from the same editions, and a general sense of disarray at the inaccessibility of some of the women's writings. At one particularly provoking moment, when the class was sorting through a mess of Claire Clarmont's journal entries, I sang a bowdlerized line from "My Fair Lady": "Why can't a woman's texts be more like a man's?"

The course requirements included an independent written project, with a short in-class presentation. Students were encouraged to choose a subject that particularly intrigued them from my general overview in the opening lecture. The students were required to meet with me almost immediately to frame their inquiry so they could get started on their research. The student topics were wide-ranging: among them, a reading of Rousseau's *The New Heloise* and its influence on the sextet, particularly the novels of Wollstonecraft and Hays; the historical bases for representations of the connection between women's condition and African slavery; and various analyses of Wollstonecraft's thought, including a reading through the "Letters to Imlay" to discern the tension between reason and sensibility, and her *Letters from Norway* in terms of its "journalistic" perspective, among others. The diverse experiences of individual students generated unexpected richness. A brilliant Korean student from Parsons School of Design, a division of New School University, had an extraordinary response to Wollstonecraft: in the first semester, she compared Wollstonecraft's thoughts on female education with the visual and textual representations of Mary Kennedy, a British feminist artist who chronicled her pregnancy and the first few years of her son's life in the 1970s. During the next summer, Kaori and her Chinese boyfriend traveled through Scandinavia to meet his family. In the fall, Kaori described to the new class how she took Wollstonecraft's *Letters from Norway* on the trip, clutching the book tighter and tighter as the couple ventured northward, meeting his older women relatives who tried to convince Kaori to give up her ambitions to be a graphic artist, and instead settle down to marriage and children.

The texts of the four female writers we studied do not emerge out of clear-cut traditions, nor do they share a common fund of knowledge. In an early lecture, I introduced the idea of the erratic appearance, autodidactict education, and ignorance of the others' existence among a sampling of "learned ladies" in the western tradition.[7] Beginning with the Ancient Assyrian *naditu* Enheduenna, *naditu* priestess-poet at the end of the Second Millennium B.C.; Sappho; Aspasia; and Hypatia; I mentioned Sor Juana Inez de la Cruz (1648–95). Natalie, a Mexican-American student from California, was astonished to learn that such a figure existed, and that she had never heard of her. In her conference with me, Natalie asked if she could study Sor Juana, examining her life and texts to see if the repetitive historical patterns I suggested of women's efforts and disabilities obtained in Sor Juana's experience, too. During her presentation to the class, Natalie read selections from several of Sor Juana's texts. One excerpt made a great impression on everyone: Sor Juana writes,

> From the moment I was first illuminated by the light of reason, my inclination toward letters has been so vehement that not even the admonitions of others....nor my own meditations...have been sufficient to cause me to forswear this natural impulse that God placed in me; the Lord God knows, and for what purpose. And he knows that I have prayed that he dim the light of my reason, leaving only that which is needed to keep his Law, for there are those who say that all else is unwanted in a woman.[8]

Students were struck by the kinship between Sor Juana's reflections and Mary Hays's bitter comments in letters to Godwin that she then incorporated into *Memoirs of Emma Courtney* (1796), a "fiction" based on her own experiences. They also compared the blighted aspects of Sor Juana's creative and emotional life with Hays's thwarted efforts for recognition. The poignancy of Sor Juana's unfulfilled quest for cultural authority and recognition led us to consider the dynamic of the eclipse of one woman by another—for example, Hays, a brilliant and ambitious female intellectual, overshadowed by Wollstonecraft, a major Enlightenment *femme philosophe*; and Claire Clairmont, still an enigma compared to her better educated, more professionally successful stepsister. We considered Hays's textual evolution—the origins of her radical feminism in the traditions of Rational Dissent, her lifelong epistolary relationships, her explicit desire to engage with learned men in order to educate herself, her determination to extend her own erudition to other women, and Wollstonecraft's ambiguous effects on Hays's life and thought.

This proved the appropriate time to examine teaching the non-canonical woman writer. The students were eager to explore Hays's determined intellectuality, and her vehement confessions of romantic and sexual failure as she tried to vivify her gloss on the "idea of being free" in imitation of Wollstonecraft. Such inquiry opened up discussion about the turbulent relationship between the thinking woman and her local community of women, as well as unchanging cultural assumptions about the inevitable nexus between female education and unconventional sexuality. We reflected that, historically, women were mainly self-taught, that is, not trained cognitively in masculine forms. Hays's novels incorporate material from actual letters, as well as elements from theology, philosophy, poetry, drama, she read on her own. As early modern women writers made their way with difficulty and equivocation into the republic of letters, their realities were expressed privately, like Claire's, or publicly in their "fictions."

Not all the students from other cultures responded positively to what they were learning. Two younger Asian students dropped the class soon after it began because, as one of them said to me, with obvious discomfort, in person, on behalf of both, "The ideas are too strange. I may not think this way." Their absence from class in the next week attested eloquently to the persistent hold of gender expectations in societies different from our own. The older, noncredit students expressed their amazement at the contemporaneousness of the issues raised by the texts, and at the evidence of recurring patterns in women's struggle for education and recognition. They also acknowledged bittersweet responses: excitement at discovering women writers of whom they were ignorant, regret at not having encountered them long before.

My colleagues in the cyber seminar, Clarissa Campbell Orr and Nora Crook, assumed crucial pedagogical responsibilities. Dr. Orr's lecture, "Current Perspectives on Mary Wollstonecraft," surveyed the intellectual history of female contemporaries of Wollstonecraft and Hays, complementing the class reading and discussion by reporting on new critical literature that examined groups other than middle-class "ladies," particularly recent historical research on aristocratic women. She described the function of the wider religious debate in the controversy over women's "proper role and education," briefly considering Elizabeth Hamilton, Maria Edgeworth, and Mme de Genlis, focusing on the similarities and differences between Wollstonecraft and Hannah More, and noting recent studies of Unitarianism and Gender. Students were encouraged to acknowledge in cyber discussions, Dr. Orr's suggestions for further reading, conferences with me, that there was a broader, more complex "community of women" than the radical feminists might suggest. With her encyclopedic familiarity with the texts and critical work on both Shelleys, and a more literary-historical approach than mine, Dr. Crook's lecture posed the fascinating question, "MWS and PBS: Collaboration, Complementarity or Competition?" She introduced the dilemma of "biographism," which she explained as "the interpretation of…works in terms of what we can learn from them about the writers' biographies, or (biographism being a two-way thing) how our knowledge of the writers' biographies can help us to interpret" their works, for example, the dense narratives of *Laon and Cythna* and *Matilda*. Learning in the virtual sphere was concurrent with onsite class meetings and discussion.

The online lectures were posted several weeks apart. After students read each lecture, they were required to post at least one question for the respective scholar. In the first semester, otherwise talkative students were suddenly tongue-tied and silent: No one responded. "Why?" I asked, when we next met in class. For several of the older students, the problem was insecurity with the Internet. Among the younger students, however, I was startled to recognize "performance anxiety" at interacting with two such erudite British learned ladies. It was as if the students perceived the enterprise of the course and the immensity of the questions raised by the "chamber music" effect of the Shelleys anew; as if the imaginative and intellectual world to which I was introducing them to suddenly expanded geometrically. In a rush, the dynamics of women's quest for erudition, their anxiety about assuming authority, and their need for encouragement that we had discussed became pressing realities to the students. Even the fluent writers in the class expressed anxiety about presenting their own texts for public scrutiny. As one otherwise confident young woman said, "I don't know enough about anything. I'll just be advertising my ignorance in cyberspace."

I proposed that, for the next in-class session, each student draft a question that we would review together. That worked: as I had anticipated, they were intrigued by the new venue, soon ready to test out their own perplexities and perspectives. When, later that week, the first flurry of questions were posted and answered, what I had dimly imagined, happened: the students' sense of participating in a new community, in which they and their texts were the medium as well as the message, took shape as shared discourse. The dynamic of texts talking to each other assumed new meaning as well, as students who sat across from each other in class now observed and responded to one another's postings in a layering of "voices" that reflected the preliminary impulse for the course. Even the hitherto intense contact between the students and me in the classroom mutated in the cyber seminar as they observed the visiting learned ladies responding to the students, to each other, and to me as their colleague. As teachers, we made a concerted effort to link our differing interests and approaches to the students' inquiries and confusions. The students, too, attempted a new etiquette, imitating the measured thoughtfulness of our guests, testing their new sense of themselves as fledgling learned ladies, collaborating, rather than competing. Reticence in the "public" cyber sphere made for greater intimacy in the "domestic" realm of the classroom when we reconvened there together.

Some texts worked, some did not. As always, there was a powerful response to the alchemy of Wollstonecraft's life and thought "because," as one student explained, "she was a woman who suffered like all of us, even though she was a genius." The class agreed that, in her novels and letters, Hays articulated a surprisingly modern skepticism about "things as they are" between the sexes. I observed that additional contextual materials were needed for deepening students' understanding: Milton and Rousseau; the unique influence of "Enlightened Dissent"[9] on Godwin, Hays, and Wollstonecraft; more of Percy Shelley's texts to enable students to appreciate the iconoclasm of *Laon and Cythna*; a bit of Byron, so that his talent, fascination, and reputation would be explicable. Although there have been major advances in recent scholarship on these figures, the familiar problems persist of the dearth of primary texts and nonspecialist critical analyses. This was a real problem, given the lacunae in students' knowledge and understanding of the past, in this case, the Revolutionary and Romantic periods. Students wanted to learn about women's role in the Enlightenment; the genesis of associationist psychology; the gendered disparities between educational opportunities for men and women. They were startled to encounter period-specific facts: that there was little scope for middle-class "ladies" to work so that economic independence was a fantasy rather than a reality; that the "rights of man" were limited to a small group of males, which both men and women resisted extending to women; that limitations of obstetrical knowledge and the gendered differences in practice between "medical men" and midwives had extreme effects on maternal and infant morbidity and mortality; that the legal impotence of wives under prevailing English law rendered them and their children the husband's property; and that British borrowing practices intensified the ever-present conflicts over money, including Percy Shelley's financial gyrations predicated on his "great expectations." Despite the students' discomfort over the ambiguities of the

Shelleys' relationship, a crucial leitmotif of the course was the complex presence of Godwin and Percy Shelley as "generous men" in the various women's intellectual development.

The difficulties presented by the uneven reclamation of texts by individual figures in "Can Man Be Free/And Woman Be a Slave?" subsequently inspired me to construct a sequence of courses dedicated to giving students a sense of the historical breadth of learned women, and access to the most recent productions of the process of recovery of such women and their texts, as these become available. "The Learned Lady: Women Who Dared," which I now offer each fall semester, eschews conventional periodization, punctuating the past by the emergence of the learned woman, either individually or in groups—for example, medieval conventual women, eighteenth-century "lady novelists," "the new women" of the late nineteenth century. We begin with Enheduenna—using Jane Hirschman's translation in her *Women in Praise of the Sacred* (1995); Sappho's poetry; Elizabeth I, now, for the first time, available as orator, poet, correspondent, translator, as well as female prince;[10] Hildegard von Bingen; Christine de Pizan; Anna Maria van Schurman; and Mary Astell's *A Serious Proposal to the Ladies* (1694).[11] I was delighted when a student about to leave the classroom turned back to say, "I can sense all those women in the room with us, urging me on!"

"The Learned Lady Tutorial: Did Women Have an Enlightenment?" offered each spring, begins with Fanny Burney as presented intriguingly in *A Known Scribbler*, edited by Justine Crump[12] and includes, variously, Marie Madeleine Jodin—reclaimed by Felicia Gordon, Phillis Wheatley, Hays, Wollstonecraft, Godwin's *Memoirs of the Author of A Vindication of the Rights of Woman*, in the new Broadview edition, and concludes with one of Jane Austen's novels in modern scholarly form. I integrate recently published works by women writers as they appear, adjusting the required reading and independent projects as necessary. Thus, the accumulation of newly accessible writers and/or their newly accessible works function as a constant, *because* changing, reminder to students—and me—of the moveable feast of emerging evidence of women's intellectual and imaginative productions. Teaching this shifting landscape of the female past demands agility and invention, by both teachers and students. Students frequently amaze with the astute linkages they make between and among writers and their works. "I know why Austen's heroines always refuse the men who propose marriage to them, at least at first," a student exclaimed last spring, "they are building on Hays and Wollstonecraft who came before"— a modification to F. R. Leavis's "great tradition" that scholars are still debating and documenting. Modern editions, like those produced by Broadview and the University of Chicago's series, *The Other Voice in Early Modern Europe*, that provide historical and contextual materials, make teaching even unfamiliar texts a relatively comfortable pleasure. Gradually, the artifacts of women's lives of the mind are coming to light—and together.

In retrospect, my great regret in teaching "Can Man Be Free/And Woman Be a Slave?" was that we gave short shrift to Claire Clairmont, although the vitality of her letters fascinated students. Without useful critical work to inform our discussion about her, she remains a potentially significant figure, but as yet unmined. I still don't teach her because the necessary pedagogical tools don't exist. Nonetheless, in reviewing what they had learned at the close of each semester, students in the classes judged that Claire's life and texts communicated most forcibly the disabilities of female life. My keenest pleasure was seeing—and hearing—the "chamber music" principle in operation, particularly in the voices of Godwin and Wollstonecraft as expressed in their letters and the *Memoirs*. Provocative conundrums were raised by integrating the texts and the experiences of Wollstonecraft, Godwin, and Hays, then Percy Shelley and Mary Wollstonecraft Shelley. Students were invigorated by access to Nora Crook and Clarissa Campbell Orr, but then frustrated by questions that still can't be answered: "Whose was the Italian baby?" They were incredulous that texts had disappeared, for example, Hays's autobiographical "Reflections," her correspondence with William Frend, and Claire's Russian journals.

An inadvertent lesson for me in teaching "Can Man Be Free/And Woman Be a Slave?" and The Learned Lady sequence is the recognition that through time and around the globe, for women there has been no continuous thread of cognitive training or imaginative continuity, either of remembrance or record. This explains, in part, the anguishing sense of disability and deficiency that women's texts often express. Each woman writer, in her ignorance of others, is condemned to reinvent the (spinning) wheel. Now, with the assiduous efforts of more than thirty years of the New Scholarship, we are poised to knit together the threads of community, piece of evidence by piece, to imagine a continuum of learned woman in the absence of a real one. As a corollary, I realize the importance of identifying and articulating useful connections between and among women from different cultures and historical eras, both those we teach and those being taught. Each semester, I am struck by the reflexive element in students' experience in these courses: As they examine the history of women's struggles for education and textual recognition, students reflect more deliberately on their own present efforts to become what one student dubbed, "learning ladies."

As teacher and scholar, I have come to appreciate the imaginative leaps necessary in experimenting with women's hybrid representations to provide students with contexts that make sense of these texts as these draw on idiosyncratic, noncontinuous influences from the past, in contrast to even the most autodidactic of the men. Similarly, in exploring the interchanges between the men and women, I have learned that it is imperative not to be constrained by traditional assumptions about the restrictions of genre, or to accept uncritically public/private as the only legitimate terms for assessment.

Finally, learning to teach "Can Man Be Free/And Woman Be a Slave?" and *The Learned Lady*, I am confronted with an essential question about gender: Are we ready to take women and their texts on their own, *sui generis,* terms?

Notes

1. *The Journals of Claire Clairmont*, ed. Marion Stocking (Cambridge: Harvard University Press, 1968), 48, footnote 80: "London, October 7, 1814. Shelley's entry in Mary's journal says, 'Jane states her conception of the subterraneous community of women.' This may have been inspired by a reading of Ludvig Holberg's *A Journey to the World Under-Ground by Nicholas Klimius* (London, 1742), which describes the underground province of Cocklecu, where the 'Order of Nature' is reversed, and the females behave like males, 'in Possession of all Honours and Employments sacred, civil, or military' (p. 119)."
2. An outgrowth of the course was a panel on "Chamber Music" that I curated for the "Writing Lives" conference that Robert Polito and I co-directed at The New School in October 2001. The panelists for "Chamber Music" included Pamela Clemit on Godwin, Jeanne Moskal on Mary Wollstonecraft, Michael Rossington on Mary Shelley, Gina Luria Walker on Mary Hays, Nora Crook as moderator; The "Chamber Music" papers were published as an ensemble in the *Praxis* section of *Romantic Circles* [Website] (University of Maryland, 2002); available from http://www.rc.umd.edu.
3. See Elizabeth Wayland Barber, Women's Work: The First 20,000 Years (New York: W. W. Norton, 1994).
4. Happily, Godwin's *Memoirs* is now available in the first modern scholarly edition that Pamela Clemit and I produced for Broadview (Petersborough, ON: Broadview P, 2001);
5. Robert Southey to William Taylor, July 1 1804, in *A Memoir of the Life and Writings of William Taylor of Norwich*, ed. J. W. Robberds, 2 vols. (London: John Murray, 1824), 1:507. I appreciate Pamela Clemit calling this to my attention.
6. See Donald H. Reiman, "The Composition and Publication of *The Revolt of Islam*, Shelley and His Circle (Cambridge: Harvard UP, 1973), V: 141–189.
7. I refer to Myra Reynold's useful paradigm in *The Learned Lady in England 1650–1760* (1920; reprint, Gloucester, MA: Peter Smith, 1964). *passim.*
8. Octavio Paz, *Sor Juana or The Traps of Faith*, trans. Margaret Sayers Peden (Cambridge, MA: The Belknap Press of Harvard UP, 1988), 416.
9. See *Enlightenment and Religion: Rational Dissent in Eighteenth-Century Britain*, ed. Knud Haakonssen (Cambridge: Cambridge UP, 1996). *passim.*
10. *Collected Works*, eds. Leah S. Marcus, Janel Mueller, and Mary Beth Rose (Chicago: U of Chicago P, 2000).
11. Patricia Springbord, ed. (Peterborough, ON: Broadview, 2002).
12. Justine Crump, ed. (Peterborough, ON: Broadview, 2002). The subtitle of the course pays homage to Joan Kelly-Gadol's pioneering essay, "Did Women Have a Renaissance?" in the suggestively titled book, *Becoming Visible: Women in European History*, ed. by Renate Bridenthal and Claudia Koonz (Boston: Houghton Mifflin, 1977).

The Learned Lady Tutorial
Dr. Gina Luria Walker

Course Description:
The Learned Lady Tutorial focuses on the intersection of gender, Enlightenment, and revolution in the early modern period. We consider the interplay of gender and genre, as well as the influence of class, race, religious persuasion, and political advocacy in the texts of several American, British, and French women—Marie Madeleine Jodin, Olympe de Gouges, Catherine Macaulay, Fanny Burney, Mary Wollstonecraft, Mary Hays, Phillis Wheatley, Jane Austen. We examine Enlightenment ideas as they supported and/or thwarted women, and the uses women made of these tensions. We trace representations of the emerging public woman intellectual and writer to assess how notions of gender differences were inscribed in the nineteenth century and beyond. We investigate how women learned what they knew, their efforts to transform both male and female education, and the lingering effects of the revolutionary debate on their creativity, recognition, and personal lives.

By looking back at individual women's experience as represented in their published and private texts (letters, diaries, memoirs), we consider such questions as, what religious, cognitive, and cultural assumptions have thwarted women's efforts to learn? Are there patterns in the dilemmas women confront when they seek knowledge? How did training in Latin and Greek serve to segregate aspiring women from their male contemporaries? Why have so few women participated in the scientific and mathematic advances of the modern period? This course allows students to design, research, produce, and share independent projects that focus on women's struggle for education as a litmus test of intolerance and alliance, spoken and unspoken.

Required texts:
- *Persuasion*, Jane Austen, ed. Linda Bree (Petersborough, ON: Broadview P, 1998.)
- *Evelina: or, A Young Lady's Entrance into the World*, by Frances Burney, ed. Susan Kubica Howard (Petersborough, ON: Broadview P, 2000.)
- *A Known Scribbler*, ed. Justine Crump (Petersborough, ON: Broadview P, 2002.)
- *Memoirs of the Author of A Vindication of the Rights of Woman*, by William Godwin, ed. Pamela Clemit and Gina Luria Walker (Petersborough, ON: Broadview P, 2001.)
- *Memoirs of Emma Courtney*, by Mary Hays, ed. Marilyn Brooks (Petersborough, ON: Broadview P, 2000.)
- *The Vindications*, D. L. Macdonald, Kathleen Scherf (Petersborough, ON: Broadview P, 2002.)

Short Papers:
A "thinking question" for the seven main readings will be posted on the Siteline. You will be expected to respond to each in turn by posting a short answer. We will emulate the Enlightenment concern for learning and "sociability" by continuing our conversations during the week between in class sessions. All responses should cite specific passages of the work(s) under consideration so that our discussions express textual vitality rather than generalities.

Independent Projects:
Credit students will be required to do an independent project on some aspect of the course content, in consultation with the instructor.

Figure 1. Gina Luria Walker, Sample Syllabus (continued on next page)

The Learned Lady Tutorial
Dr. Walker

Reading Schedule

Week 1   **Introduction: Did Women Have an Enlightenment?**
- Koeller, David W. *WebChron: The Web Chronology Project* [Website]. North Park University 1996–2000. Available from campus.northpark.edu/history/WebChron/index.html

Week 2   **Women and the Enlightenment Debate**
- Kant, Immanuel. "What Is Enlightenment?" *The Portable Enlightenment Reader*, ed. Isaac Kramnick, 1–7. New York: Penguin Books, 1995.
- Foucault, Michel. "What Is Enlightenment?" *The Foucault Reader*, ed. Paul Rabinow, 33–50. New York: Pantheon Books, 1984.
- Rousseau, Jean-Jacques. "Duties of Women." in Kramnick, 568–79.
- Kant, Immanuel. "The Fair Sex." in Kramnick, 580–86.
- Tomaselli, Sylvana. "The Enlightenment Debate on Women." *History Workshop Journal* 20 (1985): 101–24.
- Taylor, Barbara. "Feminism and the Enlightenment 1650–1850" *HWJ* 47 (1999): 261–72.
- Knott, Sarah et al. "Considering Feminism and Enlightenment." *Women: A Cultural Review* 12 (2001): 236–48.

Week 3   **Aristocratic Feminism: Bluestockings & Salonnières**
- Schiebinger, Londa. *Mind Has No Sex? Women in the Origins of Modern Science*. Cambridge. MA: Harvard UP, 1989. Introduction; Chapters 1, 4, 6, 10
- Astell, Mary. "Some Reflections Upon Marriage," in Kramnick, 560–67.
- Campbell Orr, Clarissa. "Rational Religion and Aristocratic Feminism c. 1700–1800: Some Themes and Contexts." Paper for Seminar on "Genealogies of Feminism," William Clark Andrews Memorial Library, UCLA, Oct 19–20, 2001.

Week 4   **Fanny Burney (1752–1840)**
- Burney, Frances. *Evelina: or, a Young Lady's Entrance into the World*, ed. Susan Kubica Howard. Toronto: Broadview Literary Press, 2000. Introduction, "Frances Burney: A Brief Chronology"; *Evelina*, Vol. I, 87–242
- Crump, Justine, ed. A Known Scribbler: Frances Burney on Literary Life. Toronto: Broadview Literary Press, 2002. "Introduction," Journals and Correspondence of Frances Burney (selections)
- Walker, Gina Luria. Rev. of *Faithful Handmaiden: Fanny Burney at the Court of King George III*, by Hester Davenport; *Fanny Burney: A Biography*, by Claire Harman; *Frances Burney: A Literary Life*, by Janice Farrar Thaddeus. *Women's Writing* 8 (2001): 347–52. IMAGE: At the National Library, London www.npg.org.uk/live/search/person.asp?LinkID=mp00120

Week 5   **Phillis Wheatley (1753–1784)**
- Hume, David. "Negroes...Naturally Inferior to the Whites..." in Kramnick, 629.
- Kant, Immanuel. "The Difference Between the Races," in Kramnick, 637–39.
- Diderot, Dennis. "Who Are You, Then, to Make Slaves..." in Kramnick, 640–44.
- Paine, Thomas. "African Slavery in America," in Kramnick, 645–49.
- Jefferson, Thomas. "On Indians and Negroes," in Kramnick, 657–68.
- Priestley, Joseph. "The End of Empire," in Kramnick, 1–7.

Figure 1. Gina Luria Walker, Sample Syllabus (continued on next page)

- Robinson, William H., ed. "Chronology of Important Dates." *Critical Essays on Phillis Wheatley*. Boston: G. K. Hall & Co, 1982. 13–15.
- Gates, Henry Louis Jr. "Phillis Wheatley on Trial." *The New Yorker* 20 Jan, 2003. 82–87.
- Caretta, Vincent. Introduction. *Phillis Wheatley: Complete Writings*. Ed. Vincent Caretta. New York: Penguin Books, 2001. xiii–xxxvii.
- Wheatley, Phillis. *Poems on Various Subjects, Religious and Moral*. London: A. Bell, 1773. *Poems on Various Subjects, Religious and Moral: A Machine-Readable Transcription*. 1997. The Digital Schomburg African American Women Writers of the 19th Century. New York Public Library. 25 Feb 2003 http://149.123.1.7/dynaweb/digs/wwm9728.
- Caretta, Vincent, ed. *Phillis Wheatley: Complete Writings*. New York: Penguin, 2001. (tba)
- Robinson, William H., ed. *Phillis Wheatley and her Writings*. New York: Garland Publishing, Inc., 1984. Appendices C, D, E, F, and I.

Week 6   Marie Madelaine Jodin and Mary Darby Robinson

- Gordon, Felicia. "*Filles Publiques* or Public Women: A Training in Citizenship. Marie Madeleine Jodin (1741–1790) and Mary Darby Robinson (1758–1800)." Lecture for *The Learned Lady* course, The New School, 2002.
- Jodin, Marie Madeleine Jodin. "Legislative Views for Women Addressed to the National Assembly." 1790. Trans. Felicia Gordon. *Marie Madeleine Jodin (1741–1790), Actress, Philosophe, and Feminist*. By Felicia Gordon and P.N. Furbank. Burlington, VT: Ashgate Publishing, 2001. 282–330.
- Robinson, Mary Darby. "A Letter to the Women of England, on the Injustice of Mental Subordination." 1799. *Romantic Circles Electronic Editions*. Eds. Adriana Craciun, Anne Irmen Close, Megan Musgrave, Orianne Smith. U of Maryland. 5 Feb. 2003 http://www.rc.umd.edu/editions/contemps/robinson/cover.htm.
- Setzer, Sharon M. "Mary Robinson: A Brief Chronology." *A Letter to the Women of England and The Natural Daughter by Mary Robinson*. Ed. Sharon M. Setzer. Toronto: Broadview Press, 2003. 33–36.

Week 7   Catherine Macaulay and Olympe De Gouges

- De Gouges, Olympe. "The Rights of Woman." *The Vindications: The Rights of Men, The Rights of Woman by Mary Wollstonecraft*. Eds. D.L. Macdonald, and Kathleen Scherf. Toronto: Broadview Press, 1997. 378–92.
- Macaulay, Catherine. "Letters on Education." *The Vindications*: 400–08.
- Scott, Joan Wallach. "The Uses of Imagination: Olympe de Gouges in the French Revolution." *Only Paradoxes to Offer: French Feminists and the Rights of Man*. Joan Wallach Scott. Cambridge: Harvard UP, 1996. 19–56.

Week 8   Spring Break

Week 9   Self-Writing: Hays (1759–1843) and Wollstonecraft (1759–1797)

- Foucault, Michel. "Self-Writing." *Ethics: Subjectivity and Truth*. Ed. Paul Rabinow. Trans. Robert Hurley et al. 3 vols. New York: The New Press, 1997. 1: 207–22.
- Walker, Gina Luria. "Selections from Mary Hays's Love Letters." *'The Emancipated Mind': A Mary Hays Reader*. Toronto: Broadview Press, forthcoming.
- Walker, Gina Luria. "Mary Hays's 'Love Letters.'" *Keats-Shelley Journal* 51 (2002). 94–115.
- Brooks, Marilyn L. "Mary Hays: A Brief Chronology." *Memoirs of Emma Courtney by Mary Hays*. Ed. Marilyn L. Brooks. Toronto: Broadview Literary Press, 2002. 30–32.
- Macdonald, D. L. & Kathleen Scherf. "Mary Wollstonecraft: A Brief Chronology." *The Vindications*: 29–30.

Figure 1. Gina Luria Walker, Sample Syllabus (continued on next page)

Week 10   **Wollstonecraft's *Vindications***
- "The French Revolution and the 'Spirit of Age.'" *Norton Anthology of English Literature*. 7th ed. 2 vols. Ed. M.H. Abrams. New York: W. W. Norton, 2000. Vol. 2.
- Wollstonecraft, Mary. *The Vindications*. Introduction and Chronology
- Selections from *Rights of Men*: 39–45; 62–63; 80–81; 86–87; 88–89
- Selections from *The Rights of Woman*: Letter to M. Talleyrand, Advertisement, Introduction, chapters II–IV; chapter V, section IV; chapters VI & VII; chapter VIII, from "The two sexes mutually corrupt and improve each other"; chapter IX; chapter XII; chapter XIII–chapter VI; Appendices A, B, and D
- Walker, Gina Luria. Rev. of *Rebel Writer: Mary Wollstonecraft and Enlightenment Politics* by Wendy Guther-Canada. *American Political Science Review* (June, 2002): 405–406.

Week 11   **Godwin's *Memoirs* of Wollstonecraft**
- Wollstonecraft, Mary. "Letters to Gilbert Imlay." *The Works of Mary Wollstonecraft*. Eds. Janet Todd, and Marilyn Butler, assoc. ed. Emma Rees-Mogg. 7 vols. New York: New York UP, 1989. 6: 372–438.
- Godwin, William. *Memoirs of the Author* of *A Vindication* of *the Rights of Woman*. Eds. Pamela Clemit, and Gina Luria Walker. Toronto: Broadview Press, 2001. Introduction; William Godwin: A Brief Chronology; All of *Memoirs*; Appendices A, B, C, and D
- Hays, Mary. "Letter to William Godwin." 14 Oct 1794. Mary Hays purchase, 22 Dec 1971. The Carl H. Pforzheimer Library, New York.
- Walker, Gina Luria. "The Two Marys: Hays Writes Wollstonecraft." *Chamber Music: The Life–Writing of William Godwin, Mary Wollstonecraft, Mary Hays and Mary Shelley*. Ed. Gina Luria Walker. Romantic Circles, 2001. Eds. Neil Fraistat, Steven E. Jones & Carl Stahmer. Univ. of Maryland. 19 March 2003. www.rc.umd.edu/features/features/chambermusic
- Jones, Vivien. "The Death of Mary Wollstonecraft." *British Journal for Eighteenth-Century Studies* 20 (1997). 187–205.

Week 12   **Hays's *Memoirs of Emma Courtney***
- Hays, Mary. *Memoirs of Emma Courtney*. Ed. Marilyn L. Brooks. Toronto: Broadview Press, 2000.
- Walker, Gina Luria. Rev. of *Memoirs of Emma Courtney by Mary Hays*, edited by Marilyn L. Brooks. *Women's Writing* 8 (2001): 483–485.
- Walker, Gina Luria. "Mary Hays: Lost and Found." Talk at the conference *Whose Life Is It Anyway? Writing Women's Lives*. Barnard College, New York. 1998.

Week 13   **Jane Austen**
- Austen, Jane. *Persuasion*. Ed. Linda Bree. 2nd ed. Toronto: Broadview Press, 2000. Jane Austen: Brief Chronology; *Persuasion*: Vol. 1; Appendices B–E & H-I

Week 14   **Jane Austen**
- Austen, Jane. *Persuasion*. Vol. 2, 145–258.
- Waldron, Mary. "Rationality and Rebellion: *Persuasion* and the model girl." *Jane Austen and the Fiction of Her Time*. Cambridge: Cambridge UP, 1999. 135–156.
- *Persuasion*. Dir. Roger Michell. Columbia/Tristar Studios, 1995.

Figure 1. Gina Luria Walker, Sample Syllabus (concluded)

CHAPTER NINETEEN
Who Counts? Popularity, Modern Recovery, and the Early Nineteenth-Century Woman Poet

David E. Latané Jr.

Our students come prepared to give Blake or Keats a hearing, because they are Romantic poets about whom they have already heard. For Felicia Hemans or Letitia Landon, our introduction of their work is (usually) the first impression, and frequently these poets enter the classroom and the consciousness of the students under the banner of their popularity. A number of questions arising from the somewhat oxymoronic epithet "popular poet" are thus the instigation of this essay. How do we define popularity? or popular with whom? How has popularity been used in recent discussions of nineteenth-century women poets? To what extent should popularity matter to us in determining what we read, study, and teach? I have found that discussing the background and the problems in defining popularity is useful for the students in my Romantic literature classes. Especially in the case of Hemans, understanding the nature of her fame can be a rewarding quest that might lead not only to a better understanding of her art, but also open a window on modes of consciousness that are more alien to the students than much we place in their hands under the rubric of diversity.

When we make assertions about "popularity," we are often unclear about what we mean, or even about exactly where we received our impression. "Popular" frequently was used in the early nineteenth century in its original political and legal sense, "of the people," and was generally pejorative—as in the epithet "popular fallacy," or in the title of Charles Mackay's *Extraordinary Popular Delusions and the Madness of Crowds* (1841).[1] Bentham's cautious definition of 1780 includes another register: "By popularity is meant the property of being acceptable or rather not unacceptable to the bulk of the people."[2] The "not un-" construction is a marker of mediocrity, and, in references to literature for at least a century after, "popular" is tainted with whiffs of mediocrity or *hoi polloi*. In the late-Romantic period this attitude is reinforced by the cross-currents from Germany, as when Sarah Austin chooses to excerpt a passage by A. W. von Schlegel to translate in the *New Monthly Magazine* (1830) as "On Popular Poetry": "It is not, however, easy to perceive why poetry, to which it is given to express to men all that is highest and noblest, should be condemned to adapt herself to mediocrity, instead of addressing herself to the most elevated and most richly endowed spirits, and leaving the others to come up with her as they may."[3]

The high line of Romantic aesthetics in both Germany and England was deeply suspicious of quick popularity, and took Milton's "fit audience find, though few" as its motto,[4] a tag quoted with "astonishing frequency" by the Romantics.[5] As I have argued elsewhere, the *non plus ultra* of this view may be found in Browning's *Sordello* (1840).[6] Hazlitt and Wordsworth, opposites in many manners, agree on the dubiety of "popular poetry":

> Away, then, with the senseless iteration of the word, *popular*, applied to new works in Poetry, as if there were no test of excellence in this first of the fine arts but that all Men should run after its productions, as if urged by an appetite, or constrained by a spell![7]

> For fame is not popularity, the shout of the multitude, the idle buzz of fashion, the venal puff, the soothing flattery of favor or friendship; but it is the spirit of a man surviving himself in the minds and thoughts of other men, undying and imperishable.[8]

The fame/popularity binary is echoed into the Victorian period. In the mediocre best-selling poem *The Course of Time* (1828), the Rev. Robert Pollok urges the poet to become "the minister of fame" who despises "much the idiot roar / Of popular applause."[9] By 1855, Keats has achieved the fullness of "fame," so that the popular poets "Hobbs, Nobbs, Stokes, and Nokes" can dine out on his leavings in Robert Browning's poem simply titled "Popularity." Tennyson's early poems, as well as Hallam's well-known review of them, enthusiastically embrace the notion that his (likely) unpopularity is a virtual guarantor of his poetic worth. The *Noctes Ambrosianæ* sound a more self-conscious, satirical version: When the success of *Queen Hynde* (1825) is mentioned, Hogg replies "Success! She's no had muckle o' that, man. Me and Wordsworth are aboon the age we live in—it's no worthy of us…," to which North replies, "Nay, James, you are far too popular at present to be entitled to posthumous fame."[10] The examples of this motif are almost endless.

When modern academic critics denote a poet as "popular," however, they refer to widespread dissemination—akin to the best-seller list—and to the definition of "popular" as "well liked." The pejorative usage is now rare, and too often, the "popular" label is used as if its meaning were self-evident, and not in need of precise definition or support. Of course much usage is common sense; Byron was popular—Blake was not. Ranking poets against each other, however, usually causes problems, for comparative numbers are hard to come by, and a count of print runs or numbers of editions does not correspond with numbers of readers or influence. Byron's great overnight fame came from a small print run of an expensive quarto sold to aristocratic readers; later, to generate buzz, Byron's publisher Murray apparently produced bogus edition numberings.[11] John Gibson

Lockhart's *Peter's Letters to His Kinfolk* (1819) began life as a "second edition," apparently as a joke. So even the "facts" of the title pages that we so assiduously check must be taken with a grain of salt.

What has mattered more in the annals of "literary history" has been with whom a poet has been well liked, or popular. We know that Wordsworth's poetry did not sell; as Hartley Coleridge put it in his parody, "his 'Milk White Doe' / With dust is dark and dim; / It's still in Longmans' shop, and oh! / The difference to him." However, Wordsworth (as "Hogg" notes above) was uninterested in "popularity," and he dictated that many of his works be produced in expensive quartos or in multivolume sets. It is hardly surprising that sales of copyright editions were light—according to one source, they amounted to a mere 12,000 copies during his lifetime.[12] Moreover, one finds him complaining to Maria Jewsbury about pirate editions from Paris usurping sales, and later of his astonishment at a 20,000-volume print run for a four-volume set printed in Boston.[13] Official sales, then, tell only part of the story. However, more importantly, what mattered for Wordsworth's ultimate "fame" was the extent to which his poetry was remembered, quoted, internalized by readers—especially readers who counted within the economy of culture. Hartley Coleridge also claimed that no poet ever enjoyed in his own lifetime the respect and admiration Wordsworth collected in the 1830s, and according to his most recent biographer, "By the 1840s adulation of Wordsworth was becoming absurd," with the chair he sat in at a London soirée put aside as sacred.[14] Wordsworth had more readers than purchasers, and his readers grew to be the "Wordsworthians" from whom Arnold set out to rescue the poetry. Furthermore, in addition to those interested in poetry as such, Wordsworth was important to people who mattered outside the literary world—proved by the testimony of Mill, Darwin, and Gladstone, et alia, in letters and autobiographies—and was more influential than a popular religious poet like Pollok even among theologians and clergymen.[15] Other, demonstrably better selling or more popular poets left no such afterwake, and traditional literary history has focused on those who did. That is, literary history values work valued by the literati. Literary works chiefly by non-literati, for mainly extra-literary reasons, have been ignored (Martin Tupper's *Proverbial Philosophy* of 1838, for example, with its scores of editions). Twentieth-century criticism had much less to do with establishing the nineteenth-century canon than is generally asserted, except for oddities like Blake, Hopkins, and Dickinson. Our canon has been shaped by the people who counted, primarily in the nineteenth century itself.

It appears, however, that early in the twenty-first century criticism will have altered our sense of who was who in nineteenth-century poetry, in part by bringing to the bar the charge that critics in the twentieth century distorted the nineteenth-century reception, decreasing the magnitude of certain stars in the literary constellations and increasing others for arbitrary (or pernicious) reasons. Cultural studies and feminist critiques of patriarchal canon-making contribute most to this revision, raising productively many new questions and issues. We are now more keenly aware of works purchased, read, and cherished beyond the ken of the cultural elite, works that were remembered in the past only to be dismissed. From this group it has generally been works by women that have been resurrected. However, are we in the process of adjusting the magnitude in arbitrary ways ourselves? Alternatively, perhaps, are we inserting stars from one constellation into another, more preferable one? Popularity is a crucial term in these revisions, and in the classroom it is an issue with reverberations from the off-campus pop culture our students inhabit, and from the on-campus cultural studies approaches now dominant in the humanities.

Cultural studies, which is driven in part by friction with the old "history of ideas" (seen as elitist) and suspicion of the old "popular culture studies" (a site of apolitical nostalgia), tends to valorize "popular" in both senses of the word. Thus if a writer is demonstrably "of the people," *or* if the writer has a wide dissemination, then the works are phenomena worthy of critique—all the more worthy if hitherto unconsidered or resigned to low rather than high art, or if the author can be made to represent a marginalized group. Cultural critique of poetry slights aesthetic criteria or regards aesthetic considerations as of historical interest only. Feminist critics, especially those within stronger humanist traditions, have been comparatively more interested in demonstrating how we can read and enjoy works by women writers, and in making critical discriminations that point towards the best, or at least the most interesting (and pleasurable) poems for us, now. These critics look to popularity as a sign of later exclusion based on interested principles, or as a clue to forgotten modes of reading or sensibility. Both groups, then, sometimes take "popularity" as *ipso facto* a good thing.

While the popularity of many previously non-canonical women writers has been the subject of conjecture and inquiry, the work of Hemans is a paradigmatic case for these issues. Without question she was one of the more popular (that is, well-liked and widely disseminated) poets of the nineteenth century, with some of her poems becoming extremely familiar. Equally true is her absence from the older lists of great poets. Her life and her work have recently attracted much excellent scholarship and high-quality criticism, with lively contestations—Nanora Sweet, Susan Wolfson, Jerome McGann, Tricia Lootens, Paula Feldman, and many others. Three recent scholarly editions of her work have appeared.[16] She is in the unique position of being represented in every new anthology of Romantic poetry, and based on the presumption of immense popularity and influence she has been selected for every new anthology of Victorian verse as well, though she died before Victoria came to the throne.

When Hemans first reemerged she was in a remarkable way defined and, if you will, marketed by her popularity. Duncan Wu, in *Romanticism: An Anthology* gives all writers very brief introductions. The paragraph on Hemans begins: "One of the most popular and versatile poets of the period...."[17] Margaret Higonnet, in *British Women Poets of the Nineteenth Century* (1996), also leads with the issue— "Few poets were more popular in her day than Felicia Hemans"—as do Susan Wolfson and Peter Manning in the new *Longman Anthology of British Literature*: "A best-selling poet in England and America through most of the nineteenth century, Felicia Hemans..."[18] Others go further. The curious first sentence of the introduction to Hemans in Anne Mellor and Richard Matlak's *British Literature, 1780–1830* is "Felicia Hemans was the most popular poet in England between 1820 and 1835, second only—if that—to Byron." They go on to note that "Although she died in 1835, her popularity continued unabated through the nineteenth century; she led all other poets in her appearances in American and British anthologies of poetry in this period, outdistancing even Tennyson."[19] Daniel Albergotti attempts to correct the traditional "ahistorical" approach "perpetrated" by Romantic scholars, by emphasizing how "Byron and Hemans were at the very heart of the British literary scene, the two most popular, successful poets of the day," although Hemans, he argues, had the greater "reputation" among the Victorians.[20] In a recent essay Nanora Sweet adds that Hemans was "the dominant writer of the decade after 1825"; Stuart Curran chimes in with the notion that by 1825 in the eyes of contemporaries "the indisputable major poet was Felicia Hemans."[21] Peter Cochran, whose *Times Literary Supplement* piece "Fatal Fluency, Fruitless Dower" is unfriendly to Hemans, asserts that she was "commercially the most successful English-language poet of the nineteenth-century."[22] McGann attacks traditional literary history for ignoring "unaccountables," or facts that do not fit the paradigms. He says, "I suggest we look—right now—very closely at a few of those unaccountabilities. For instance: Do we know (or remember) that Felicia Hemans was the most-published English poet of the nineteenth-century? Do we know, or even think that we know, what that might mean?"[23] The first wave of reconsideration of Romantic women writers to a large degree was accompanied by statements about popularity and influence of a large magnitude, with the assumption that, until the present, magnitude had been camouflaged.

Many scholars begin now with the a priori notion that, in the words of Behrendt and Linkin, traditional scholarship resulted in the "ossification of a narrow and often masculinist ideological paradigm of Romantic poetry, one that profoundly misrepresents historical and cultural reality."[24] In the same vein as McGann, Marlon Ross asks, "How is it that a poet like Hemans, so respected in the nineteenth century, can be obliterated so entirely from literary history, covered over by romantic ideology?"[25] And teachers such as Scott Simkins are challenging students with Mellor's famous question, "What happens to our interpretations of Romanticism if we focus our attention on the numerous women writers who produced at least half of the literature published in England between 1780 and 1830?"[26] These calls for a radical revamping of Romanticism are salutary, important ones—but we should add, I think, "if it is true."

We may also wish to ask, what happens to our attempts to reclaim women writers if we base them on notions of popularity and on statistics about the number of women writers which turn out not to be true? This too would be a "profound misrepresentation," caused in part by our never precisely defining what is meant by "most-published," "commercially the most successful," "most popular," "most major," or even "half of the literature." These are absolute statements, chiefly about quantities, and yet no numbers are given, and in the absence of such we should always suspect rhetorical hyperbole. McGann's, Mellor's and Ross's questions, in fact, are obvious examples of *epiplexis*, or the asking of a question in order to reproach. Of course, we are doomed to interpretive misprison when it comes to "reality," and perhaps doomed as well to rhetorical questions. So here is one more: should our students be absorbing a narrative in which twentieth-century Romanticists deliberately obscured or ignored the glaringly obvious presence of a poet of massive popular fame and critical reputation, chiefly because she was female?

First, though, it should be established that these statements are off the mark. Sweet's assertion that Hemans was "the dominant writer" in the decade from 1825 to 1835 is defensible, given the nature of writing during the years after the death of Byron and before the rise of Victorians such as Dickens, and presuming that one speaks only of imaginative writers who came to the fore precisely during those years. Without those qualifications, however, Byron and Scott must be considered—or in a different key, Professor Wilson. In a Johnsonian mood, one might refute Cochran's "most commercially successful" by traveling to the Isle of Wight and kicking the all-too-substantial stone of Farringford, Lord Tennyson's Baronial Manor.[27] Speaking of Tennyson, is it meaningful for Mellor and Matlak to compare appearances in anthologies, when Tennyson's works were in copyright, and Hemans's were (mostly) not?[28] As for McGann's "most published"—while he has probably forgotten more about Byron than most Romantic scholars have ever known, Byron's immense and unparalleled publication history across continents and languages should be remembered.

The search capabilities of electronic databases also help test assertions about Hemans and other writers' "popularity." Each measurement is beset with limitations, but taking them together, along with more traditional evidence, one can draw conclusions.[29] The WorldCat is the Online Computer Library Center (OCLC) database begun many years ago as a library cataloging tool. It links the catalogs of major research libraries. The holdings of these libraries are massive—but are biased toward the writers and books that librarians felt were worth collecting (or worth cataloging, if gifts). Books by truly unknown writers are often unknown to the OCLC. The database originates in the United States and reflects U.S. holdings. One of its strengths, however, is that it also includes listings for some of the cultural ephemera outside the world of the book, especially sheet music and song settings. Both Hemans and Moore have numbers increased by the musical popularity of their lyrics (see Figure 1, Table 1). Scott's poetry should probably be included, but separating his poetry from his fiction proved difficult.

A "subject" count for "L.E.L." turned up every title in the mammoth microfiche *Library of English Literature*, so it was abandoned. Finally, Campbell and Moore's numbers are somewhat fuzzy—without looking at the objects, a few items were hard to differentiate from publications by other men with the same names. The table confirms, however, Byron's position as a publishing nonpareil, though it contains, perhaps, other surprises. I would have expected a better showing by Campbell early in the century, and perhaps more entries for Keats after 1865. Moore's strong showing throughout the century can be attributed to his songs and to his status as national poet for Ireland. The table confirms claims that Hemans was a very widely published poet, though not close to being "the most."

The *Chadwyck-Healey Full-Text English Poetry Database* includes about 80,000 poems by some 450 nineteenth-century British poets. By searching for poets' names, one can create a kind of poetic "citation index," showing with what frequency poets use their peers for epigraphs, mention them in texts (Elizabeth Barrett's praise of Robert Browning in "Lady Geraldine's Courtship," for example), or dedicate to them individual poems. The database is limited, mostly, to books, and thus the many poems dedicated by admirers to the more famous in country newspapers, gift books, and magazines are not included. Individual works may also generate multiple references, and for this reason the number of different poets has been counted as well as number of references. One should also realize that, by and large, writers were more reluctant to satirize or attack a woman by name than a man. Chadwyck-Healey based their choice of poets on the *New Cambridge Bibliography*, and it consequently under-represents Irish, Welsh, and Scottish writers, as well as working-class, and women poets, though 63 are included (see Figure 1, Table 2).[30,31]

Again we see the fascination with Byron. Wordsworth, it is clear, was throughout the century a "poet's poet," though in the years from 1800 to 1835 many of the entries are satiric or abusive. The *Chadwyck-Healey American Poetry Full-Text Database* reveals a similar ratio: in the years 1810 to 1900, a total of 50 different poets name Byron, 36 Wordsworth, 29 Shelley, 25 Keats, 15 Hemans, and 12 Landon. These numbers demonstrate the extent to which the traditional canon owes its configuration to the poets themselves. At least among other poets, Hemans would not seem to be an "indisputable major poet" with popularity that never fell off throughout the century. In the 1870 to 1900 period Hemans was named only by Hardwicke D. Rawnsley in the second edition to his *Sonnets at the English Lakes* (1882). During the same years Keats is named by Wilde, Hardy, Swinburne, Meynell, "Michael Field," and 34 lesser lights. Another kind of citation index may be found by searching the online version of *Notes & Queries*, which is available from the Internet Library of Early Journals at Oxford. In the years available (1851–1866) there are 1181 hits for "Byron," 354 for "Wordsworth," and just 48 for "Hemans."

The *Nineteenth-Century Short Title Catalog*, which includes the British Library, catalogues only books, but unlike the OCLC is not cluttered with duplicate entries. It shows that as far as book publishing went, Byron and Moore were the trade's best friends. If Hemans's popularity or commercial success was in the same ballpark, it was not primarily through the medium of the book (see Figure 1, Table 3).

Finally, the British Library (BL) catalog online has features that enable us to test the validity of Mellor's statement "numerous women writers... produced at least half of the literature published in England between 1780 and 1830."[32] The chief source of fuzziness here is a familiar one: what counts as "literature"? Men overwhelmingly dominated in certain kinds of writing—classical scholarship, for example, or history—and Mellor's estimate must certainly exclude published sermons. In 1805 alone, the BL catalog includes 140 works with "sermon" in the title, presumably all by men. (Even without sermons, the all-male Church of England clergy supplied an enormous number of publications by literary amateurs.) By searching for genre-specific words in titles and subtitles at ten-year intervals in the BL catalog, one gets an estimate that belies the "at least half" assertion (see Figure 2).

While the survey of the BL calatog is not conclusive, it confirms that while women writers were much more prevalent than traditional literary history has represented, it is not true that they wrote "at least half" of the literature during the Romantic age. An examination of applicants by writers to the Royal Literary Fund during the period shows that they were overwhelmingly male (31 men and four women, for instance, in one three-year period).[33] In the Corvey Collection, which according to Behrendt is "relatively unfiltered" and particularly strong in writings by women, the titles by women make up 32% of the British books classified as *belles lettres*.[34] Nigel Cross estimates that of all writers during the century, about 20 percent were female, weighted toward the genres of prose fiction and children's literature.[35] While this includes nonliterary genres, the BL count and other data show that his estimate more accurate than Mellor's for writing in the Romantic period.

Showing the record of emphasis on and exaggeration of Hemans's popularity (and of women's writing in general) raises a number of issues relating to our efforts to teach newly recovered women poets, and especially Hemans. We first need to think about how we construct the history of the poet's reception. We next need to decide more consciously whether we should foreground a writer's presumed "popularity," and if we do emphasize this aspect, how to make it meaningful to a reading of the poems. Finally, we might ask whether or not, at this stage of teaching and learning about Hemans and others, close-reading of the poems is not more important than historical and cultural context. What follows are speculations around these issues.

We should assume that statements about Hemans's popularity are not entirely objective and disinterested—even the pose of such a stance has lost rhetorical effectiveness in the face of a relentless demonstration of the human subject as ideologically constituted and overdetermined—but the causes of the inflation are interesting in themselves. The misprisons may be, in part, an unintended (and ironic) consequence of the gender bias of the nineteenth century. Because the Romantic ideology so firmly favored unrecognized genius in the garret, those intent on denigrating women's poetry had every reason to exaggerate the popularity of "scribbling women." Lively misogynistic writing tends to be read and cited more frequently than duller or more neutral prose, and the bogey of popular female poets in the nineteenth century may have colored the evidence for the popularity of Hemans and others—evidence now regarded in a positive light. The modernists tended to reinforce the notion. Ezra Pound, in his attempt to remake the canon to include Crabbe, for instance, indicts the hated Victorians on several occasions by mentioning the popularity of Hemans, whom he says they "adored."[36] In discussing Barrett Browning, Woolf places her with other dusty popular writers, "in the servants quarters, where, in company with Mrs. Hemans, Eliza Cook, Jean Ingelow, Alexander Smith, Edwin Arnold, and Robert Montgomery she bangs the crockery about and eats vast handfuls of peas on the point of her knife."[37] Thus when the turn away from the pejorative apprehension of poetic popularity occurs, the evidence found in the most likely places may have been already exaggerated.

Recent critics, who are trained to take an adversarial stance toward the canon, or at least the history of its formation, have seized on this evidence and used it to attack the narrowness of the traditional "Romantic" canon—especially as they perceive it to have been constructed by mid-twentieth century New Criticism. In a recent essay in *ELH*, Alan Grob describes a "hermeneutics of disparagement" in contemporary Romantic studies, and charges that "a historical interpretation guided by adversarial presuppositions ... not only leads frequently to the meanest of judgments but is especially prone to errors, distortions, and misrepresentations of the most astonishing and sometimes inexplicable kind, at least if the critical practice now prevalent in Wordsworth studies is any indication."[38]

We might posit that in the recovery of women poets there exists a kinder corollary, a "hermeneutics of advocacy" that champions the non-canonical, and marches under the banner of democratizing or empowering, of rectifying unjust neglect. This hermeneutics does not distort or err so much as it puts the kindest possible light on the evidence, as the desire to right a wrong produces whiggish literary history. The battles to secure the rightful place for poets such as Hemans, after all, are real. Many scholars today imbibed the prejudices of Pound and Woolf, and first heard of Hemans, perhaps, in the "Clare and the Minor Poets" section of Ian Jack's volume in the Oxford History of English Literature, where she receives a paragraph topped off with: "She took the pulse of her time, and helped to prevent it from quickening."[39] Students today tend to gravitate toward narratives of unfair exclusion, and to side with underdogs, and it is tempted to tell them a story with that plot—and cast ourselves in the role of rescuers. However, while the previous generations of twentieth-century scholars got some things wrong, we should be careful of the tendency toward rhetorical hyperbole in cataloguing their sins; they were not as biased, blinkered, or clueless as we sometimes make out in our efforts to clear space for our own work.

It is space, in any case, that needs less clearing every year, which brings us to the issue of how we should present "popularity" in the teaching of Romantic women poets. Since this essay was conceived, the ground in Hemans studies has shifted away from the issue, and the excellence of much recent criticism is proof that we do not need to preface our introductions to Hemans with appeals to *vox populi*. Wu, in fact, has removed his first sentence from the second edition of *Romanticism: An Anthology* (1998), and his informative and accurate introduction to Hemans in *Romantic Women Poets: An Anthology* hardly discusses popularity.[40] Feldman's recent work in the publishers' archives and her careful estimations of Hemans's earnings is the sort of scholarship which is finally establishing a basis for answering questions about who was actually reading Romantic women poets, and how these acts of reading affected them. Sweet's work on Hemans and Reginald Heber also helps lay the groundwork for a study of Hemans's milieu and reception.[41] In 2004 it strikes me that the biggest decision teachers of Hemans face is whether to teach her with or against the grain of her popular image.

If we are going to teach Hemans against the grain, demonstrating how her poetry may be seen to be socially progressive, feminist, or more ironic than presumed, then raising the issue of popularity causes problems of intentionality because we must then assume that either Hemans's readers did not know how to read her, or that she was consciously pulling the wool over their eyes. In his review of Wolfson's edition of Hemans, Stephen C. Behrendt makes the case that to view Hemans's poetry as "a primer on domesticity and a comfortably imperialistic world-view" is a misreading, that in fact her readers did not know how to read her:

> Ironically, it was a "popular" audience of general readers that gave Hemans her greatest fame (and profit) during her lifetime and for much of the balance of her century. And if those readers misread much of what she wrote, it is fair to observe that they were often encouraged to do so by a professional reviewing press and a sociopolitical Establishment whose interests were better served—indeed preserved—by a public perception of "Mrs. Hemans" than they might be by the more troubling aspect of the author of culturally destabilizing works.[42]

Presenting this position in the classroom begs the question of how works that verifiably helped stabilize a culture can also be destabilizing. Reading against the grain, we assert that we now correctly understand poems that might have tended to destabilize Victorian culture, had they been properly read at the time. However, it is useful to remind students attracted by this proposition that perhaps these values are now perceived only because they reinforce our own dominant ideologies. Behrendt is somewhat aware of this irony, and makes the familiar case that Hemans brought the misreading on herself by choices she made out of economic necessity. If Hemans is, as Behrendt believes, "one of the greatest of British Romantic poets," students must negotiate these issues in order to find the specifically Romantic values (destabilizing the conservative world of patriarchy, aristocracy, and so on) that justify the claim, perceived perhaps as wheat within the chaff of the merely popular.[43] Hemans could perhaps be taught alongside Wordsworth, with his core of Arnoldian goodies weighed down by later (Tory) dross, though that raises the question of sincerity. For Wordsworth the narrative runs that he genuinely lost poetic power, and sincerely became more conservative. Teaching Hemans with Byron is a better strategy, and new resources such as the new online hypertext scholarly edition, *The Sceptic: A Hemans-Byron Dialogue (1820)* will make this classroom strategy all the easier.[44]

The opposite approach, reading with the grain, is the argument McGann makes for Hemans and many others in *The Poetics of Sensibility* (1996), where he asks us to respect Hemans's contemporary readers, and to try to understand and be moved ourselves by what they found moving.[45] In teaching Hemans from this angle, the trick is to avoid condescension—made trickier perhaps by the necessity of shifting gears in a Romantic literature class from an openly radical and heroically oppositional poet like Shelley on Tuesday to Hemans on Thursday. A way I have found to execute this shift is to focus on Hemans as a Christian poet, reminding the class that it is easier to be oppositional in a Christian world if you do not believe in God. To understand Hemans's audience, and the development (and rapid loss) of her position in the nineteenth-century poetry world, the issue of her religion is after all crucial. Hemans's work was perceived in her day as sanctifying the Romantic mode, and there was a large audience that appreciated getting its religion in verse. Wordsworth himself comments about *Paradise Lost*, that "when it is read by the multitude, it is almost exclusively not as a poem, but a religious book."[46] Many editions of poets, especially in America, seem to have been meant for the religious audience, or marketed as giftbooks safe for maidenly eyes. When Philadelphia pirate-publisher Griggs brought out omnibus volumes of English poets in the 1830s he put Coleridge, Shelley, and Keats in one volume, and Bishop Heber, the Rev. Pollok, and Mrs. Hemans in another. It is not surprising that even sharp contemporary critics emphasized how "one great and pervading excellence of Mrs. Hemans, as a writer, is her entire dedication of her genius and talents to the cause of healthy morality and sound religion."[47] For Hemans's reputation among the Victorian shapers of the Romantic canon, this was obviously detrimental, and helps account for the "increasingly condescending attitude towards Hemans" that Kelly finds in his survey of Hemans's reception.[48] How offputting was it for the *au courant* intellectuals of the Age of Darwin to encounter Hemans in this context? When Thackeray's Pendennis reads to his mother, the narrator comments: "as for Bishop Heber, and Mrs. Hemans above all, this lady used to melt right away, and be absorbed in her pocket-handkerchief."[49]

While critics have explored the packaging—self-induced or otherwise—of the "Poetess," I think we should also explore with our students the marketing of Hemans within a particular religious context. Does this explain the relative lack of reference to her by high-culture writers after 1850? After close comparisons of several poems by Hemans to comparable poems by Wordsworth and Scott, Francis Palgrave comes to an interesting conclusion:

> But women have, I think, been far less willing than men to accept that which necessarily flows from this first condition of poetry—that poetry, like all Fine Art, must not aim at doing us direct good. In this sense the often-abused phrase is true, that art—directly religious, of course, excepted—has no morality.... [I]t appears to me indisputable that the introduction of a definite, frequently indeed of a directly religious, moral, is not only a mark or note of poetry by women, but is one chief reason why they have not carried their poetry to greater excellence.[50]

If we begin to discuss Hemans in the classroom by stating, as Paula Feldman in her introduction to her splendid new edition of Hemans's poems, that "Felicia Hemans was one of the most influential and widely read poets of the nineteenth-century," we should go on to explore the nature of this audience, and how it differs from the audience for Romantics who were considered mad, bad, and dangerous to read, and then engage the issue of whether or not (and why if so) something as good as religion and morality should be bad for poetry.[51]

Another issue to present in the classroom is that of Hemans's prosody. In her own day Hemans was widely praised for the smooth and melodious quality of her verses. Our students, however, have somehow derived a melophobia when it comes to poetry; one of the few prosodic terms they are willing to use without prompting is the derogatory "sing-song." Hemans's natural inclination is towards regular verse. The critical expectations of her readers—issues of gender aside— overvalue the quality of smoothness. *The Royal Lady's Magazine*, for instance, explained how to judge meter in 1832: "every line must be dulcet and sweet to the ear; the slightest variation of the measure destroys the musical proportion of the period, and the reader of taste is offended. The effect on him is the same as a false note to an accomplished musician; it is revolting, and, in some instances, even painful."[52] Few lovers of poetry today would assent to this dictum; indeed, the poetry appreciation textbooks in our students' hands all assert the opposite. Modern scansion is the art of comprehending variation. A question for the classroom then might be to ask if Hemans's metrics are like Andrea del Sarto's paintings in Browning's poem—too perfect to be perfectly good—or whether we can tune our ears so that the music of Hemans that delighted the poet and her audience can give us pleasure too.

The combination of a religious-based popularity and an alien metrics is the chief challenge in teaching Hemans with the grain. It is true that our students (and ourselves, often) are comfortable with "popularity" in a way that the high Romantic tradition is not. Popularity and commercial success are measurements that make it easier to put poets on par with one another and free us from arguments based on taste, even if we believe such a thing should exist or is worth discussing. This point was anticipated as long ago as 1833 in James Montgomery's *Lectures on Poetry*, when, after naming a big five of Southey, Moore, Byron, Scott, and Wordsworth, he notes the "unprecedented" sales of Byron and Scott, and adds that there were fifty contemporary poets

> whose labours have proved profitable to themselves in a pecuniary way, and fame in proportion has followed the more substantial reward. This may appear a degrading standard by which to measure the genius of writers and the intelligence of readers, but, in a commercial country at least, it is an equitable one; for no man in his right mind can suppose such a rise in the market demand could have taken place, unless the commodity itself had become more precious.[53]

We too live in a commercial country in which the best-seller list is keenly followed and the weekly box office receipts of movies are featured on the evening news, and may agree with Montgomery more than we know. Nevertheless, our students, having outgrown for the most part teen idols, do understand that the most popular is not often the best. However we foreground Hemans's popularity, we know that our students are unlikely to warm to a poet under the banner of "healthy morality and sound religion." Even so, we must confront head on the "high and spiritualized tone of the generality of Mrs. Hemans' poetry"—perhaps by finding an entry into what the same critic in the *Metropolitan Magazine* notes is a strain of drollness found in her prose, where "when she chose [she] could quiz most cunningly."[54] Even without choosing an interpretive line that emphasizes savage irony, the poetry in the classroom can be made to unfold dissonances that please the modern ear.

Notes

1. The entry for "popular" in Raymond Williams's *Keywords* is instructive. He notes that it was not until the nineteenth century that the meaning of "well liked" comes into widespread usage. *Keywords: A Vocabulary of Culture and Society* (New York: Oxford UP, 1976).
2. Cited in the *Oxford English Dictioary* online edition; available at http://www.oed.com.
3. Sarah Austin, ed. and trans.,"Specimens of German Genius, No. 5," *New Monthly Magazine*, 29 (August, 1830): 183.
4. John Milton, *Paradise Lost*, book 7, line 31, in *The Norton Anthology of English Literature*, 7th ed., ed. M. H. Abrams and Stephen Greenblatt (New York: W. W. Norton, 2000).
5. Joseph Anthony Wittreich, ed. *The Romantics on Milton: Formal Essays and Critical Asides* (Cleveland: Case Western UP, 1970), 40.
6. See my *Browning's Sordello and the Aesthetics of Difficulty* (Victoria, B.C.: English Literary Studies, 1987).
7. William Wordsworth, "Essay, Supplementary," in *The Oxford Authors: William Wordsworth*, ed. Stephen Gill (Oxford: Oxford UP, 1984), 660.
8. William Hazlitt, "On the Living Poets" in *English Romantic Writers*, 2nd ed., ed. David Perkins (Fort Worth: Harcourt, 1995), 727.
9. Robert Pollok, *The Course of Time, a Poem, in Ten Books* 3rd ed., 1828 (Boston, 1828), 210. Pollok's poem appeared in 1827, the year before Blackwood also published Hemans's *Records of Women*. Blackwood's letters frequently mention the extraordinary success of *The Course of Time*, noting by October 1828 that 9,000 copies in five editions had been sold and that "the demand continues as great as ever" (qtd. in Margaret Oliphant, *Annals of a Publishing House: William Blackwood and His Sons: Their Magazine and Friends,* 2 vols. (New York: Charles Scribner's Sons, 1897), 2: 86. The sales for Hemans's poem were good enough for a second edition, but do not call for amazed comment in Blackwood's correspondence. Because the consumptive Pollok died en route to Italy in 1827, he missed the irony of his phenomenal success for a poem that scorned quick popularity.
10. John Wilson, *Noctes Ambrosianæ,* 4 vols. (Philadelphia, 1843), 1: 364–65.
11. William St. Clair, "The Impact of Byron's Writings: An Evaluative Approach," in *Byron: Augustan and Romantic*, ed. Andrew Rutherford (New York: St. Martin's Press, 1990), 3.
12. Paula Feldman, "The Poet and the Profits: Felicia Hemans and the Literary Marketplace," *Keats-Shelley Journal* 46 (1997): 176n.

13 "I think you do quite right in connecting yourself with these light things [annual gift books]. An Author has not fair play who has no share in their Profits—for the money given for them leaves so much less to spare for separate volumes. Look at my own—Gagliani [Galignani] has just published all my poems in one volume for 20 francs—here few will give £2 5/- for my five volumes when every body is going to and fro between London and Paris—as between town and country in their own island. Therefore let the Annuals pay—and with whomsoever you deal make hard bargains" (William Wordsworth, *The Letters of William and Dorothy Wordsworth*, 2nd ed. 8 vols., eds. Ernest de Selincourt, et alia (Oxford: Clarendon Press, 1967–93), 5: 28.

14 Stephen Gill, *William Wordsworth: A Life* (Oxford: Clarendon Press, 1989), 386.

15 See Stephen Gill, *Wordsworth and the Victorians* (Oxford: Clarendon Press, 1998), for a fine discussion of Wordsworth's deep influence on major Victorian figures.

16 Paula Feldman, "Introduction," *Records of Women with Other Poems, by Felicia Hemans*, ed. Paula Feldman (Lexington: UP of Kentucky, 1999), xi–xxxi; Susan J. Wolfson, ed. *Felicia Hemans: Selected Poems, Letters, Reception Materials* (Princeton: Princeton UP, 2000); Gary Kelly, ed., *Selected Poems, Prose, and Letters* (Peterborough, ON: Broadview Literary Texts, 2002). See also Susan J. Wolfson, "Editing Hemans for the Twenty-First Century," *Romanticism on the Net* 19 (August 2000); available from http://www-sul.stanford.edu/mirrors/romnet/19hemans.html. The first substantial collection of essays on Hemans appeared in 2001, in Nanora Sweet and Julie Melnyk, eds., *Felicia Hemans: Reimagining Poetry in the Nineteenth Century* (Hampshire: Palgrave, 2001).

17 Duncan Wu, *Romanticism: An Anthology*, 1st ed. (Oxford, UK, Cambridge, USA: Blackwell, 1994), 987.

18 Margaret Higgonet, ed., *British Women Poets of the Nineteenth Century* (New York: Meridian, 1996), 214; Susan Wolfson and Peter Manning, eds., "The Romantics and Their Contemporaries," in *The Longman Anthology of British Literature*, 2 vols., gen. ed. David Damrosch (New York: Longman, 1999), 706.

19 Anne Mellor and Richard Matlak, eds., *British Literature, 1780–1830* (Fort Worth: Harcourt, 1996), 1179. It is interesting to compare their introduction to Hemans with the treatment of Byron. Mellor and Matlak begin by noting that Byron "was the most famous poet of Europe" (881) and shortly after claim that "except for the Shelleys, very few, if any, of Byron's major literary contemporaries respected him as a man or artist" (881). The judgment of popularity is elided, and the qualitative judgment of the "major literary contemporaries" is foregrounded. The editors are presumably thinking of the opinions of the Lake poets, whom Byron satirized. Byron's artistry is certainly respected by literary figures considered major today—such as Scott, Hazlitt, Hemans, or for that matter Stendhal and Pushkin—as well as many considered major in the nineteenth century, such as Rogers, Moore, and Lockhart. Byron was published in many cheap editions around the world throughout the nineteenth century, in numerous languages, as much published scholarship records. I have been unable to locate a source for the claim that Hemans was the "most anthologized."

20 Daniel Albergotti, "Byron, Hemans, and the Reviewers, 1807–1835: Two Routes to Fame," *DAI* 56-08A (1995): 3133.

21 Nanora Sweet, "'Hitherto Closed to British Enterprise': Trading and Writing the Hispanic World circa 1815," *European Romantic Review* 8 (1997): 140; Stuart Curran, "Something Evermore About to Be: Teaching and Textbases," in *Approaches to Teaching British Women Poets of the Romantic Period*, ed. Stephen C. Behrendt and Harriet Kramer Linkin, eds. (New York: MLA, 1997), 25–31.

22 Peter Cochran, "Fatal Fluency: The Eminently Marketable Felicia Hemans," *TLS,* 21 July 1995, 13.
23 Jerome McGann, "Literary History, Romanticism, and Felicia Hemans," in *Re-Visioning Romanticism: British Women Writers, 1776–1837,* ed. Wilson, Carol Shiner and Joel Haefner (Philadelphia: Uof Pennsylvania P, 1994), 223. Of course we also have to take into account that, according to McGann, "No English writer of the 1820s and 1830s was more well known or more popular than L.E.L." See "Introduction," *Letitia Elizabeth Landon: Selected Writings,* ed. Jerome McGann and Daniel Reiss (Peterborough, ON: Broadview Press, 1997), 11.
24 Stephen C. Behrendt and Harriet Kramer Linken, eds., *Romanticism and Women Poets: Opening the Doors of Reception* (Lexington: UP of Kentucky, 1999): xi.
25 Marlon B. Ross, *The Contours of Masculine Desire: Romanticism and the Rise of Women's Poetry* (New York; Oxford UP, 1989), 13.
26 Scott Simkins, "Teaching Alien Aesthetics: The Difficulty of Difference in the Classroom," in Linken and Behrendt, 53.
27 Farringford cost Tennyson £6,900 in 1856. In 1867 when Tennyson finally left Moxon for another publisher, he was given £5,000 per annum for the right to republish older works for the first five years, and was given 90 percent of the profits of new works. See Robert Bernard Martin, *Tennyson: The Unquiet Heart* (New York: Oxford, 1980), 403, 477. Perhaps Cochran means, most successful for publishers who got to pay poets nothing—though that was almost certainly Byron.
28 Mellor and Matlak do not cite a source. My 28th edition of the massive *The Fireside Encyclopædia of Poetry, Comprising the Best Poems of the Most Famous Writers, English and American* (Philadelphia, 1888), where copyright was not an issue, includes eighteen poems by Byron and nine by Hemans—and thirty by Tennyson. Palgrave, who only included dead writers in the Golden Treasury, did not include Hemans at all. An admittedly unscientific troll through a number of such anthologies does not bear out Hemans's superiority.
29 See Simon Eliot's "Very Necessary but Not Quite Sufficient: A Personal View of Quantitative Analysis in Book History," *Book History* 5 (2002): 283–93, for an excellent discussion of the usefulness and the perils of book history statistics.
30 In Figure 2, Moore, Scott, and Campbell have been eliminated because of the frequency of allusion to others of the same names.
31 See my "'Presto, Engpo!' Reflections on the Chadwyck-Healey English Poetry Full-Text Database," *Victorians Institute Journal* 23 (1995): 1–9, for a fuller discussion of the limitations.
32 Anne Mellor, *Romanticism and Gender* (New York: Routledge, 1993), 1.
33 *Archives of the Royal Literary Fund, 1790–1918* (London: World Microfilms Publications, 1982).
34 "Corvey Collections at Nebraska," NASSR-L [discussion list]; accessible from http://www.rc.umd.edu/.
35 Nigel Cross, *The Common Writer: Life in Nineteenth-Century Grub Street* (Cambridge: Cambridge UP, 1985).
36 Ezra Pound, *Literary Essays of Ezra Pound,* ed. T. S. Eliot (1935; reprinted, Westport, CT: Greenwood, 1979), 279.
37 Virginia Woolf, *The Second Common Reader* (New York: Harvest Books, n.d.), 183. Woolf's point is perhaps a bit obscure. Her list, however, is interesting. All of the female poets in it have been raised above stairs into the drawing rooms of recent anthologies of Victorian literature, and the men have been left to their peas—though one of these books, the *Blackwell,* has over 150 Victorian poets. Robert "Satan" Montgomery—savaged by *Fraser's* in the 1830s—and Smith, who was one of the "Spasmodics" lampooned by Aytoun, were both decried for their

"popularity," though there is no evidence that, compared with figures like Byron or Moore, they ever had much of a following at all.

[38] Alan Grob, "William and Dorothy: A Case Study in the Hermenuetics of Disparagement" *ELH* 65.1 (1998): 191.

[39] Ian Jack, *English Literature, 1815–1832* (Oxford: Oxford UP, 1963), 168. While Jack's description of Hemans as a "female Campbell" is dismissive, it is perhaps less inaccurate than the statement that Hemans was at least as popular as Byron, and reminds us that Campbell's time for re-evaluation is also due.

[40] Duncan Wu, ed., *Romantic Women Poets: An Anthology* (Oxford: Blackwell, 1997). Conversely, Gary Kelly, in his recent Broadview edition of Hemans's selected poetry (2002), opens his introduction in the old way: "Felicia Hemans was the most widely read woman poet in the nineteenth-century English-speaking world" (15) and firmly places her in a state of accord with her reading public and their middle-class values.

[41] Nanora Sweet, "Hemans, Heber, and Superstition and Revelation" *Romantic Circles Praxis Series*. [Website]; available from http:www.rc.umd.edu/praxis/passions/sweet/sweet.html.

[42] Stephen C. Behrendt, "Review of *Felicia Hemans: Selected Poems, Letters, Reception Materials*, edited by Susan J. Wolfson," *Criticism* 44.2 (2002): 218.

[43] Behrendt, "Review," 220.

[44] Nanora Sweet and Barbara Taylor, eds., *The Sceptic: A Hemans-Byron Dialogue (1820)* [Website]; available from http://www.rc.umd.edu/editions/sceptic.

[45] Jerome McGann, *The Poetics of Sensibility: A Revolution in Literary Style* (Oxford: Clarendon Press, 1996), 72n. This does not mean one has to give up subversive readings. As McGann notes, "Hemans was a conservative poet and her works were appropriated for the most conservative ideological causes. Their force *as poetry* comes exactly from the extent of their own reactionary commitments, and the contradictions that emerge therefrom."

[46] Quoted in Wittreich, 142.

[47] William Henry Smith "Mrs. Hemans," *Blackwood's* 64 (1848): 656. William Henry Smith is a good example of a judicious, non-misogynistic critic who is seldom quoted. Smith thought Hemans was less than top rank because feeling dominated over intellect, and the blame for that could be found in a sexist education system: "a mind that could not be at rest was left to brood over sentiments, either the sad heritage of all mortality, or the peculiar offspring of afflictions of her own. We are not imputing, in this remark, any shadow of blame to her; we make the remark because we think that, eminent as she was, she still suffered from the unwise and arbitrary distinction which is made in the education of the two sexes" 611.

[48] Kelly, 78.

[49] William Makepeace Thackeray, *The History of Pendennis*, ed. John Sutherland (Oxford: Oxford UP, 1994), chapter three. Thackeray also satirizes the vogue of the annuals, most of which published Hemans, in three annual roundups in *Fraser's*, 1837–39.

[50] F. T. Palgrave, "Women and the Fine Arts," *Macmillan's Magazine* 12 (1865): 215.

[51] Feldman, ed., *Records of Woman*, xi.

[52] "S." "On the Power of Language in Poetry and Eloquence," *The Royal Lady's Magazine* 4 (1832): 69.

[53] James Montgomery, *Lectures on General Literature, Poetry &c. Delivered at the Royal Institution in 1830 and 1831* (New York: Harper & Brothers, 1838), 312.

[54] "Mr. Chorley's Memorials of Mrs. Hemans," *Metropolitan Magazine* 17 (1836): 61.

Table 1
Author and Subject Hits in WorldCat (OCLC) by Range of Dates

	1820–1835		1836–1850		1851–1865		1866–1880	
	Subject	Author	Subject	Author	Subject	Author	Subject	Author
Byron	538	544	229	282	190	238	275	225
Campbell	49	97	70	83	60	99	60	66
Hemans	53	175	88	134	65	108	33	49
Keats	27	22	32	33	49	41	69	43
Landon/L.E.L.		117		83		40		18
Moore	149	362	80	266	124	207	100	198
Rogers	10	47	21	54	46	62	24	20
Shelley	44	96	65	66	101	50	144	93
Wordsworth	41	72	88	78	126	111	108	116

Table 2
Poets Cited by Name by Other Poets

	1800–1835		1836–1870		1870–1900	
	entries	poets	entries	poets	entries	poets
Barbauld	9	7	2	1	0	0
Byron	304	64	213	45	120	40
Hemans	16	13	13	10	1	1
Keats	26	16	78	30	123	40
Landon/L.E.L.	9	6	23	12	0	0
Rogers	88	34	18	11	6	5
Shelley	44	14	88	38	195	44
Tighe	19	10	1	1	0	0
Wordsworth	232	54	173	55	139	35

Table 3
Separate Entries in Nineteenth-Century Short Title Catalog

	1816–1870
Barbauld/Aiken	39
Byron	848
Campbell	123
Hemans/Browne	82
Keats	25
Landon/L.E.L.	45
Moore	443
Rogers	52
Shelley	124
Tighe	3
Wordsworth	153

Figure 1. David Latané Jr., Tables 1–3

British Library Catalog:
Literary genre subtitle terms, specific years 1780–1830

All anon. and pseudonyms identified by BL catalog are under "Unknown."
Excludes non-UK writers and new editions of dead writers.

	MALE WRITERS			
	"Novel" "Romance"	"Tale" "Story"	"Drama" "Play"	"Poem" "Poems"
1825	9	31	13	96
1815	12	21	4	106
1805	7	14	7	72
1795	6	17	10	78
1790	0	7	0	32
	34	90	34	384

	FEMALE WRITERS			
	"Novel" "Romance"	"Tale" "Story"	"Drama" "Play"	"Poem" "Poems"
1825	5	26	0	20
1815	12	12	2	20
1805	5	10	0	13
1795	11	6	1	11
1790	11	1	0	5
	44	55	3	69

	UNKNOWN			
	"Novel" "Romance"	"Tale" "Story"	"Drama" "Play"	"Poem" "Poems"
1825	4	26	2	24
1815	10	16	0	13
1805	7	7	0	13
1795	7	9	0	8
1790	4	4	0	9
	32	62	2	67

TOTAL	876			Men		Women		Unknown	
			Novel/Romance (110)	34	31%	44	40%	32	29%
Men	542	62%	Tale/Story (207)	90	43%	55	27%	62	30%
Women	171	20%	Drama/Play (39)	34	87%	3	8%	2	5%
Unknown	163	19%	Poem/Poems (520)	284	74%	69	13%	67	13%

Figure 2. David Latané Jr.

CHAPTER TWENTY

Changing Course(s) At Mid- and Late Career: Teaching the Lives/Teaching the Works/Teaching the Teacher

William B. Thesing

As a full professor and senior scholar who has taught for the twenty-eight years of my career at a research, Ph.D.-granting institution in the South (the University of South Carolina), I am bemused by how my teaching interests on topics relating to gender have developed in the classroom. The various rituals of course reorganizations that I have witnessed over the years have been great opportunities for professional growth. I did my graduate work at a fairly liberal school, Indiana University, an institution that has been supportive of Susan Gubar's work for many years. Additionally, Indiana University's journal *Victorian Studies* was an early pioneer in publishing a special issue on women writers in the late 1970s. More recently, Indiana University has shown valuable leadership in establishing a Victorian Women Writers Project on the World Wide Web, maintained by Perry Willet,[1] that regularly adds recovered works by such Victorian women poets as Amy Levy, Mathilde Blind, Ada Cambridge, Dollie Radford, and Helen Taylor.

Nevertheless, when I completed my dissertation at Indiana University in 1977, it was already a dinosaur in a PC (Politically Correct) Jurassic Park. The dissertation topic seemed promising enough at first: an extensive survey of more than twenty Victorian poets' responses to writing poetry about urban life. The problem was that *not one* of the twenty poets covered in the five chapters was a woman. Looking back, I try to ask myself how this gender-biased selection process occurred. Was it the guidance that I received from the four male professors on my committee? Why was it that no one had ever suggested that I look at poems about city life by such poets as E. B. Browning or Amy Levy? Was I at fault in not searching out the rich treasures on the library shelves on that dark and windowless tenth floor of the white, limestone library in Bloomington, Indiana?

It was only when reviews appeared of the book version of my dissertation, *The London Muse: Victorian Poetic Responses to the City*,[2] that the arrows of attack started to pierce my flesh: Why were no women's voices included in the study? These same charges of gender bias and female text exclusion appeared again in book reviews of my editorial projects—two huge DLB (Dictionary of Literary Biography) volumes on Victorian Prose Writers—that were published by Gale Research Company in the mid-1980s.

By 1990 I think I got the message! The hostile criticism that appeared in various book reviews of my works penetrated my mind: it caused me to re-think my topics of study and interest. I repented. In private meditation, I realized that I *had* tended to overlook works written by Victorian women writers in graduate school and in my early untenured years. Although I may be deluded, I believe that I ignored texts by women writers not out of hostility but because of a pervasive climate of indifference. In both mid- and late career, I have radically altered my teaching style and even changed the focus of my research agenda.

In the mid-1990s, I began to see displayed at publishers' booths at various conventions some new Victorian anthologies. I was especially intrigued by the Blackwell anthology of *Victorian Women Poets*, edited by Angela Leighton and Margaret Reynolds.[3] Suddenly, there was a new and exciting range of women's texts available for teaching. At mid-career, I soon began to revamp my Victorian courses around such new textbook selections. I have tried teaching texts by and about women in an honors course for sophomores, a survey section for juniors and seniors, and a graduate course specifically designed as English 737, British Women Writers. In these various semesters, I have tried to include more and more texts written by Victorian women who were poets, novelists, and essayists. However, on each of these syllabi, I always mix these texts with a few male Victorian writers' works that substantially *represent* images of women. Thomas Hardy's *Tess of the d'Urbervilles* is a prime example.

Teaching newly discovered texts by and about women writers has been a very energizing experience for me. However, I have encountered a few obstacles in these classroom endeavors. Also, I have some lingering questions about my efforts. At the end of this chapter, I provide a list of general questions about teaching women writers that I distributed on the first day of class in the English 737, British Women Writers course. Here also are two of the final exam questions that most of the graduate students in the class chose to write about.

> [FINAL EXAM QUESTION 5]: Several women poets that we have studied ended their lives by an act of suicide. Using the tragedy of such an ending, discuss the larger question of the interrelations between biography and texts. Are the lives of the poets or the poems themselves more interesting? Why do we study several of the poets that we do? How is depression or unhappiness reflected in the works of several of the poets who committed suicide?

I feel that final exam question number five addresses some key issues in studying and teaching Victorian women writers. I may be mistaken—and I have not completely made up my mind—but I believe at this point in time that, on the whole, the lives of Victorian women writers are more interesting, more likely to capture our attentions, than many of their poems. Some of the poems are good and valuable; these works are as worthy of study as some poems written by Victorian male poets. Often, however the works themselves are overshadowed by the trials that Victorian women had to endure. It is in the lives of Victorian women poets that the true tragic drama is especially enacted. Students tended to agree. On their answers to exam question five, many noted the significance of biographical information to their personal experiences with the poems. Women writers' day-to-day struggles, especially those in a notoriously patriarchal society of the past, they claimed, gives women authors a unique voice and compelling subject matter. Learning about women writers within this historical and biographical context thus augmented students' appreciation of their poetry. Since poetry is often an expression of the self, as many students claimed, facts of the author's biography to some degree always heighten the experience of reading poetry, regardless of the poet's sex. The students who answered question five found this especially true with women writers.

At mid-career, I decided to devote a lot of my research time to edit the two companion volumes of the Dictionary of Literary Biography—*Victorian Women Poets* (1999) and *Late-Nineteenth and Early Twentieth-Century Women Poets* (2001) because I believe that both biography and works are essential elements to be studied in tandem.[4] We need to investigate further this relationship between an author's life and her texts as we teach and as our students understand. If, as my students asserted on their exams, an author's biography is key to interpreting his or her work, is this true with male and female poets equally? What is gained and what is lost by such a pedagogy? Is there a difference between the "self" as understood in women's poetry and men's? Do we not need to move beyond the old emotion/reason debate, the tired private/public dichotomy, to a new paradigm?

Clearly, "Teaching the Lives/Teaching the Works" is always a delicate balancing act: too much attention to the life of a poet without adequate analysis of the works is as unproductive as the opposite tendency. There is some wisdom, then, in an observation in the Introduction to the Leighton/Reynolds anthology: "This is the problem. If the woman is the poem, then you 'leave out' the work. Little wonder then that Victorian women's poetry has been neglected for so long. The purpose of this anthology is to provide the poems which are necessary 'to complete the poet.'"[5] We should study these women because of their lives, their careers, and their works. Each case is different: some of the women's lives are more interesting than their poetry and vice versa. The important point is that they all deserve the increasing amount of attention that is being paid to them.

[FINAL EXAM QUESTION 9]: Issues of Gender. In a rather unpleasant encounter on the elevator, a male English professor is attacked verbally by a hostile representative of a women's studies program in the Northeast. He is told candidly that he has no business teaching a course in British Women Writers. Furthermore, he is told that it is a travesty to even think of including any male-authored texts in the course. You are standing at the back of the elevator, which is now stuck between floors. You have one hour to offer your opinions on these controversial matters.

I will now offer some reflections on another arena of hostility: What is a male professor—"the Other"—doing in front of a women's studies classroom? I analyze as objectively as I can some of the reservations that I encountered on the final exam as many students chose to discuss the ramifications of a male professor teaching a course on women writers (one cross-listed under the Women's Studies Program course designator) and the decision to include some texts by male authors on the syllabus. In the interest of saving time, I will resort to categorizing and summarizing the various student responses rather than extended quotations from the exams themselves.

There was a spectrum of responses to exam question nine. An ardent feminist who had taken several courses in the Women's Studies Program in the past regretted the hostility in the elevator that was aimed at the male professor, but she agreed totally with the notion that male professors had no business teaching a women's literature course and male writers had no worthwhile place in any such course.

In another essay, a male student, who had been somewhat restrained in class discussions all semester, argued persuasively that some male authors in the past had actually worked hard to advance women's causes. He felt that it was worth examining both why some men held the traditional patriarchal perception of women and why others did not. Some of the male writers of the past obviously worked on behalf of their female peers, writing compelling treatises advocating the equal treatment of women. Another student (female and from that hotbed state of liberal causes, Wisconsin) took the position of a liberal humanist. After all, she claimed, we live in an age of increased tolerance, wherein literature should be approached from a perspective that views women's and men's work side by side, rather than one which capitalizes on women's differences and attempts to define a separate cultural history for women. By far the most intriguing essay was that written by an African-American female graduate student who linked issues of race and gender. She reported that she had faced the issues raised in the exam question in her previous educational experience. The day she walked into her African-American undergraduate English course and saw that the teacher was white, she was filled with rage and apprehensions. How could a teacher who was not black understand fully the writings of African-American writers? Because of her intense interest in the subject matter of the course, she did not fill out a drop slip. By the end of the semester she arrived at a more broadly tolerant or humanistic attitude: there was important political and cultural value in white and black readers studying African-American texts *together*. Due to this positive experience, she was willing to extend her feelings of grace and mercy in the gender camp as well. She was willing to allow me, a male professor, to teach women writers. Male students should also be encouraged to take the course. She expressed to me later how she had come to believe that allowing men to teach courses in a women's studies demonstrates progressive and positive thinking, "building bridges" of understanding between genders and cultures.

We need to think long and hard about the perplexing issue of men in feminism. The reports of a few years ago about Professor Mary Daly's deliberate exclusion of male students from her classes in feminism (whereby women students attend classes and male students receive individual tutorials) at Boston College are grounds for concern and discussion.[6]

The question of men teaching women's texts cuts to the core of gender being primarily a political construct. A number of fascinating theoretical questions that cannot be addressed here deserve to be at least posed: Does gender even exist in a classroom with a male teacher teaching male writers? With a female teacher teaching male writers? With a female teacher teaching female writers? At what point does gender begin to be an issue at all? Certainly, with women writers, the life—and therefore sex—of the author *is* an important issue in reading and teaching. We may very well ask as a final question: "Is the same true with men?"

Certainly the more controversial part of exam question nine involves the expansion of scope to include attention to representations of women in texts by male authors. Frankly, most of the graduate students had little sympathy with this idea. They pointed out that it was a long, hard struggle to get into the university catalogue courses that were designated with titles that "advertised" writings by women as their specific content. Who could be so perverse as to taint or water-down these courses with male texts under the Little Red Riding Hood Granny garb of an expansive definition of feminist criticism? The ardent feminist student continued to argue that juxtaposing female- and male-authored texts in a course nominally about Victorian Women Writers was inappropriate and even damaging to the integrity of the course. Only the student who argued for a more humanist approach to women's writings would yield any ground on this issue. She argued that men's texts, especially as they portray female characters, can interestingly texture the study of women's texts and thus enhance a course about women writers. Authors like Dickens, Tennyson, and Robert Browning, she explained, can provide examples of what women have historically struggled against, completing the historical and cultural background against which women's texts appear.

The title of my essay—"Changing Course(s) at Mid- and Late Career"—implies that I have changed *various* courses in various phases of my professional career. And so it is. In the area of Victorian nonfiction prose, my revisions have been assisted remarkably by the adoption of two fine textbooks. The one is *"Criminals, Idiots, Women, & Minors": Victorian Writing by Women on Women*.[7] Many prose selections written by Victorian women are conveniently available for the first time in this anthology. The other is a book by Phyllis Rose. In truth, my interest in completely reorganizing the graduate level course in Victorian nonfiction was first piqued by a book-of-the-month popular selection, Rose's *Parallel Lives: Five Victorian Marriages*.[8] The five cases involve men and women in power struggles and gender relationships. Except perhaps for the Dickens chapter, all of the other pairs included—Jane Welsh and Thomas Carlyle, Effie Gray and John Ruskin, Harriet Taylor and John Stuart Mill, George Eliot and George Henry Lewes—are writers who practiced in the genre of nonfiction prose. It is a short, but fascinating step from reading about the life story of John Ruskin to a study of his prose selections that focus on gender issues, such as *Of Kings' Treasures*, *Of Queen's Gardens*, and *The Queen of the Air*. Likewise, students can easily move from circumstances in the life stories of Harriet Taylor and John Stuart Mill to reflections in prose in such a text as *The Subjection of Women* (conveniently contained in the Oxford World's Classics paperback edition of 1991).

Since I plan to retire in about three years, I am now in the late phase of my teaching career. In a sense, anthologies have come around full circle. For example, in my sophomore survey class, I now use each semester the new Longman anthology of British Literature. It contains a superb mixture of texts by both Victorian male and female writers—from Florence Nightingale to Queen Victoria, from Thomas Carlyle to John Stuart Mill. In my upper-level Victorian course, I regularly use *The Broadview Anthology of Victorian Poetry and Poetic Theory* because it remarkably includes poetic works of 24 women and 47 men.[9] These two mixed-sexed anthologies are truly gifts from the editors and publishers for all teachers of Victorian writers who wish to cover both male and female authors of the period.

Also, in the final years of my teaching, I have moved away from lecturing the students to discussion and in-class and out-of-class written exercises that utilize the pedagogy of "engaged learning." This philosophy holds that students are ultimately responsible for their own learning so that they should be empowered to interact fully with texts and attempt to make sense of them on their own. Two practical examples can be briefly outlined. Before the class discusses Florence Nightingale's "Cassandra" essay, each student is required to list and analyze briefly five points of the argument in the essay as well as five rhetorical strategies used to convey these points. With William Morris's feminist poem "The Defense of Guenevere," I ask students to read the poem before class discussion and to list five points of her argument on her behalf and five examples of her body language that she uses to convey these points. Such class participation grade exercises lead to much fuller understanding of texts by students and to much richer class discussions than the old spoon-feeding lecture approach. It is an eye-opening experience to witness the students detecting the "oddity" of these two Victorian female voices amidst the other more conventional statements of the Victorian period.

In this chapter I have covered more professional biographical material than some readers may care to hear. But I have done this to show readers (as I do with both my undergraduate and graduate students each semester) how it sometimes takes years for a man to really understand the message, texture, and quality of various texts written by women. But I believe that it is not only possible, but exciting to do so. At the beginning of each semester I usually use part of a class session to review my own professional evolution as a way of authorizing my own teaching of women's texts. We cannot fully understand any literary period unless we examine fully its women writers' views of the city, of war, of poverty, of discrimination, of suffering, etc. It is my hope that students will understand this gender-based commitment to learning and also accept an authorization of a male professor teaching texts by women.

I trust that I have raised a number of controversial points in this essay. Reading literature from a previous period in terms of issues of gender and power is a guaranteed way to evoke interest and meaningful dialogue in any modern classroom. Such a commitment often requires the complete revamping of previously used textbook selections and syllabi. The rewards, however, are significant. The expanded opportunities to learn about the lives of previously ignored authors and the ideas that they record in previously unavailable texts are well worth the effort. At mid- and late career these changes in my courses have rejuvenated my teaching interests and expanded the range of texts, authors, and courses that I am allowed to teach. The horizons of my research as a senior scholar have also widened. Hopefully, all of this new energy and interest will serve as a rejuvenating pill to get me to the golden days of retirement!

Notes

[1] Perry Willet, ed. *Victorian Women Writers Project on the World-Wide Web* [Website] (Indiana University); available from http://www.indiana.edu/~letrs/vwwp/.

[2] William B. Thesing, *The London Muse: Victorian Poetic Responses to the City* (Athens, GA: University of Georgia Press, 1982); winner of the SAMLA Studies Award Prize in 1980.

[3] Angela Leighton and Margaret Reynolds, eds. *Victorian Women Poets: An Anthology* (Oxford: Blackwell, 1995).

[4] William B. Thesing, ed., *Late-Nineteenth and Early Twentieth-Century Women Poets*. Dictionary of Literary Biography, Vol. 240 (Detroit: Gale Group, 2001); William B. Thesing, ed., *Victorian Women Poets*, Dictionary of Literary Biography, Volume 199 (Detroit: Gale Research, 1999).

[5] Leighton & Reynolds, xxxiv.

[6] See *The Chronicle of Higher Education*, September 3, 1999, p. A-12.

[7] Susan Hamilton, ed., *"Criminals, Idiots, Women, & Minors": Victorian Writing by Women on Women*, (Peterborough, ON: Broadview Press, 1995).

[8] Phyllis Rose, *Parallel Lives: Five Victorian Marriages* (New York: Random/Vintage, 1984).

[9] Thomas J. Collins and Vivienne J. Rundle, eds., *The Broadview Anthology of Victorian Poetry and Poetic Theory* (Peterborough, ON: Broadview Press, 1999).

| **British Women Writers** ||
| Dr. Thesing ||

Reading Schedule:

Introduction. Brief history of women's studies and feminist criticism. General questions to ponder throughout the course	The place of Gilbert and Gubar in 20th century feminist criticism. Read intro and preface materials in *Madwoman*.
no class	Gilbert and Gubar on Jane Austen (report); J. Austen's *Mansfield Park* to p. 101
Dorothy Mermin's *Godiva's Ride* (report); *Mansfield Park*, 101–309	Gilbert and Gubar on *Jane Eyre* (report); C. Brontë's *Jane Eyre* to p. 211
Jane Eyre to p. 398	J. Rhys's *Wide Sargasso Sea* to p. 64
Wide Sargasso Sea to p. 112	Gilbert and Gubar on E. B. B. (report); E. B. Browning's *Aurora Leigh* to p. 107
Aurora Leigh to p. 215	Oral reports on criticism
Aurora Leigh to end	Selected poetry from Leighton & Reynolds, *Victorian Women Poets*
Zonana's "The Disembodied Muse" (report)	Midterm exam
Individual conferences	L.E.L. (L&R)
C. Rossetti, "Goblin Market"	C. Rossetti (L&R)
A. Brontë (L&R)	M. Howitt and A. A. Procter (L&R)
M. Field (L&R); O. Schreiner's "Woman and Labor"	A. Levy and C. Mew (L&R)
M. Ward's *Delia Blanchflower*, to p. 200	Ward's *Delia Blanchflower*, to end
Group project on *Delia* Hardy's *Tess of the D'Urbervilles*, phases 1–3	*Tess of the D'Urbervilles*, to end
Woolf's *To the Lighthouse*, to p. 100	*To the Lighthouse* to end

General Questions to Ponder:
1. Should a course like this study only texts written by women or should it also include texts written by men that offer pervasive, maybe typical images of women during the period?
2. How much is a course such as this dependent on the availability of textbook anthologies?
3. In our study and approach, what is the "proper" mixture of attention to text and biography, or the lives (often tragic) of these women writers?
4. Where did these poetic texts written by women go to during the past 100 years?
5. Will all of the texts "hold up" in another semester course or in a thesis, dissertation, etc.?
6. What types of critical theory should we be applying this semester to the study of these writers and their works?
7. What does a syllabus such as the one we have constructed do to your own "course of study" plans in graduate school? Will you need to sign up for a second half of the course to cover the traditional list of male writers?
8. Should we put more emphasis on studying the range and mixture of genres that women worked in, or should we organize our graduate courses according to strict genre divisions?
9. Do the evaluative terms apply? Can we very easily separate the Victorian women poets into "major" and "minor" categories?

Figure 1. William B. Thesing, Sample Syllabus

Contributors

Nicole Meller Beck is assistant to the Dean of the School of Business Administration at St. Edward's University in Austin, Texas. She completed her B.A. at Millikin University in 1998 and her M.A. at the University of Illinois at Urbana-Champaign in 2000.

Catherine B. Burroughs, professor of English and co-chair of the Women's Studies Program at Wells College, is also a visiting instructor at Cornell University. Her publications include *Closet Stages: Joanna Baillie and the Theater Theory of British Romantic Women Writers* (U of Pennsylvania P, 1997) and she is the editor of both *Reading the Social Body* (U of Iowa P, 1993) and *Women in British Romantic Theatre: Drama, Performance, and Society, 1790–1840* (Cambridge UP, 2000).

Diane Chambers is an associate professor of English and director of the Honors Program at Malone College in Canton, Ohio. Her previous research on the relationship of sisters in Victorian literature includes publication on the Deceased Wife's Sister Controversy. Her current projects include research on the Canadian writer Margaret Laurence and collaborative work on patterns of abuse in the diaries of exploited women.

E. J. Clery teaches at Sheffield Hallam University, UK. She is the author of *The Rise of Supernatural Fiction 1762–1800* (1995), *Women's Gothic from Clara Reeve to Mary Shelley* (2000) and *The Feminization Debate in Eighteenth-Century England: Literature, Commerce and Luxury* (2004) and co-editor of *Gothic Documents: A Sourcebook 1700–1820* (2000) and *Authorship, Commerce, and the Public: Scenes of Writing 1750–1850* (2002).

Elizabeth A. Dolan is the Frank Hook Assistant Professor of English at Lehigh University where she teaches British Romanticism and Medical Humanities. Her publications include essays on Mary Wollstonecraft, Mary Shelley, Charlotte Smith, and post-Napoleonic travel writers. Currently she is working on a book manuscript entitled *Seeing Suffering in Romantic-Era Women's Literature: Illness, Healing, and Social Justice*.

Kathryn T. Flannery is associate professor of English and women's studies at the University of Pittsburgh. In addition to *The Emperor's New Clothes: Literature, Literacy and the Ideology of Style*, and the forthcoming *Feminist Literacies 1968–1975*, Professor Flannery has contributed numerous articles and chapters in the field of literacy studies. She is currently working on a study of women's artists' books. She enjoys teaching a range of courses from early modern literature and culture to contemporary poetry.

Elisabeth Rose Gruner teaches English and women's studies at the University of Richmond, where she is an associate professor. Her articles on nineteenth-century literature have appeared in *Signs: Journal of Women in Culture and Society*, *Tulsa Studies in Women's Literature*, *The Lion and the Unicorn*, and elsewhere. She is currently working on a study of children's literature from the nineteenth and twentieth centuries.

Patricia L. Hamilton is an assistant professor at Union University in Jackson, TN, where her teaching specialties are eighteenth-century British literature and creative writing. She received her Ph.D. from the University of Georgia.

Peaches Henry is an assistant professor at Baylor University. A specialist in Victorian studies and comparative autobiography, she is the author of "A Revised Approach to Relationality in Women's Autobiography: The Case of Eliza Linton's *Christopher Kirkland*" and "*I, Rigoberta Menchu* and the Question of Truth-Value in Autobiography." She is completing *Frances Power Cobbe: Victorian Woman of Letters*, a book that assesses Cobbe's work in the context of Victorian prose studies.

Rick Incorvati is an assistant professor of English at Wittenberg University, where he teaches Romantic-period literature. He is the guest editor of "Women's Friendships and Lesbian Sexuality," a special issue of the journal *Nineteenth-Century Contexts*, and has published on eighteenth-century notions of sympathy. His current project considers the intersection between Romantic-period historicism and subsequent histories of sexuality.

David E. Latané Jr. is coeditor of *Victorians Institute Journal* and associate editor of *Stand Magazine*. He teaches nineteenth-century and contemporary British literature at Virginia Commonwealth University.

Jeanne Moskal is a professor of English at the University of North Carolina at Chapel Hill, the author of *Blake, Ethics, and Forgiveness* (1994) and the editor of Mary Shelley's travel writings, vol. 8 in *The Novels and Selected Works of Mary Shelley* (1996). She serves as the president of the International Society of Travel Writing.

Rebecca Shapiro is an assistant professor of English at St. Thomas Aquinas College. She has presented or published on Sterne, Edgeworth and sociolinguistics.

James R. Simmons Jr., associate professor of English at Louisiana Tech University, has had articles and reviews appear in *Brontë Studies*, *Victorian Studies*, *English Language Notes*, and *The Dickensian*, as well as in other journals and books. His book, *Factory Lives: Four Nineteenth-Century Working Class Autobiographies*, is in press.

Beth Sutton-Ramspeck is associate professor of English at the Ohio State University at Lima. She is coeditor, with Nicole Meller Beck, of *Marcella* by Mary Augusta Ward. She is the author of *Raising the Dust: The Literary Housekeeping of Mary Ward, Sarah Grand, and Charlotte Perkins Gilman*. Her work on Ward has also appeared in *South Atlantic Review*, *Victorian Studies*, and *Victorian Women Writers and the Woman Question*.

Kristine Swenson is an associate professor of English at the University of Missouri-Rolla. She has published articles on Victorian women and medicine, including, most recently, "The Menopausal Vampire: Arabella Kenealy and the Boundaries of True Womanhood" in *Women's Writing*. Her book, *Treating their Sex: Medical Women and Victorian Fiction*, is forthcoming from the University of Missouri Press.

William B. Thesing, professor of English, University of South Carolina, is the author of *The London Muse*, editor of five volumes in *Gale's Dictionary of Literary Biography* series, and co-editor of the *Blackwell Companion to the Victorian Novel*. He currently serves as editor of the *James Dickey Newsletter*. He has won several awards for teaching undergraduate and graduate courses in Victorian novel, poetry, and nonfiction prose.

Gina Luria Walker is chair of the Department of Social Sciences at The New School, where she teaches a sequence of courses on The Learned Lady. Her current projects include *Mary Hays (1759–1843): The Growth of a Woman's Mind* (forthcoming, Ashgate), *"The Idea of Being Free": A*

Mary Hays Reader (forthcoming, Broadview), and, with Felicia Gordon, *Intellectual Passions: Women and Scholarship in Britain 1709–1899, A Reader* (forthcoming, Broadview). She is a research associate in the Gender and Enlightenment Project directed by Barbara Taylor and Sarah Knott, and contributed the chapter on "Mary Hays (1759–1843): An Enlightened Quest," to *Women and Enlightenment 1650–1850: A Comparative History*, Volume 1, edited by Barbara Taylor (Palgrave, 2004). Her previous publications include the first modern scholarly edition of William Godwin's *Memoirs of the Author of a "Vindication of the Rights of Woman"* (Broadview, 2001) coedited with Pamela Clemit; *The Feminist Controversy in England 1788–1810* (Garland, 1974); and "Gender and Genre: Women in British Romantic Literature," with Irene Tayler, in *What Manner of Woman: Essays in British and American Literature*, Marlene Springer, ed., New York UP, 1978

Shannon R. Wooden is an assistant professor of English at the University of Southern Indiana, specializing in eighteenth- and nineteenth-century British literature. Her previous research has focused on the development of scientific racism as exemplified in the Victorian novel, and her publications and presentations include work on abolitionist poets of the Romantic period, George Eliot, H. G. Wells, Rider Haggard, and Mary Elizabeth Braddon. Her current research focuses on women and medicine in nineteenth-century literature.

Lawrence Zygmunt is a Ph.D. candidate in English at the University of Chicago. He has taught literature to undergraduates there and at Indiana University Northwest, and also to adult students through the University of Chicago's Graham School of General Studies.